PUBLICATIONS OF
THE COMPARATIVE CRIMINAL LAW PROJECT

Volume 15

Nations Not Obsessed
with Crime

The Fiftieth Volume
Published by

The Comparative Criminal Law Project

founded 1959

COMPARATIVE CRIMINAL LAW PROJECT
WAYNE STATE UNIVERSITY LAW SCHOOL

Edward M. Wise, *Director*

The Comparative Criminal Law Project was founded by Gerhard O. W. Mueller at New York University in 1959, and became in 1968 a division of the N.Y.U. Criminal Law Education & Research Center. In 1983 the Comparative Criminal Law Project was relocated at the Wayne State University Law School in Detroit. Wayne State University will continue to sponsor the translation and publication of material on foreign criminal law in the three ongoing series associated with this Project: The American Series of Foreign Penal Codes, Monographs, and Publications of the Comparative Criminal Law Project. Previous titles in these three series as well as of the occasional publications, are as follows.

I. THE AMERICAN SERIES OF FOREIGN PENAL CODES

1. The French Penal Code, transl. by Jean F. Moreau and Gerhard O. W. Mueller, intro. by Marc Ancel, 1960.
2. The Korean Criminal Code, trans. and with an intro. by Paul Ryu, 1960.
3. The Norwegian Penal Code, transl. by Harold Schjoldager and Finn Backer, intro. by Johs. Andenaes, 1961.
4. The German Penal Code, transl. by Gerhard O. W. Mueller and Thomas Buergenthal, intro. by Horst Schröder, 1961.
5. The Turkish Code of Criminal Procedure, transl. by the Legal Research Institute, the New York University Faculty Team, the Judge Advocate's Office of the Joint United States Military Mission for Aid to Turkey, William B elser, Yilmaz Altuğ and Tugrul Ansay, edit. by Charles Tenney and Mustafa T. Yücel, intro. by Feyyaz Gölzüklü, intro. transl. by Yilmaz Altuğ, 1962.
6. The Argentine Penal Code, intro. by Ricardo Levene, transl. by Emilio Gonzalez-Lopez, guest edited by Frederick W. Danforth, Jr., 1963.

7. The French Penal Code of Criminal Procedure, transl. and with an intro. by Gerald L. Kock, 1964.

8. The Japanese Draft Penal Code, 1961, transl. and with an intro. by Juhei Takeuchi, 1964.

9. The Turkish Criminal Code, orig. transl. by Orhan Sepiçi and Mustafa Ovaçik for the Judge Advocate's Office of the Joint United States Military Mission for Aid in Turkey, under the direction of William G. Belser, reviewed by Robert B. Levine, edit. by Tugrul Ansay, Mustafa T. Yücel, and Michael Friedman, intro. by Nevzat Gürelli, 1961.

10. The German Code of Criminal Procedure, intro. by Eberhard Schmidt, transl. by Horst Niebler, intro. transl. by Manfred A. Pfeiffer, 1965.

11. The German Draft Penal Code E 1962, transl. by Neville Ross, intro. by Eduard Dreher, 1966.

12. The Austrian Penal Act, transl. by Norbert D. West and Samuel I. Schuman, intro. by Roland Grassberger, and Helga Nowotny, 1966.

13. The Israeli Criminal Procedure Law, transl. and with an intro by U. Yadin, 1967.

14. The Colombian Penal Code, transl. and with an intro. by Phanor Eder, 1967.

15. The Swedish Code of Judicial Procedure, transl. and with an intro. by Anders Bruzelius and Ruth Bader Ginsburg, 1968.

16. The Greenland Criminal Code, transl. at the Center for Studies in Criminal Justice, University of Chicago Law School, intro. by Verner Goldschmidt, 1970.

17. The Swedish Penal Code, transl. by Thorsten Sellin, amendments transl. by Jerome L. Getz, intro. by Lennart Geijer, 1972.

18. The Greek Penal Code, transl. by Nicholas B. Lolis, intro. by Giorgios Mangakis, 1973.

19. The Penal Code of the Polish People's Republic, transl. by William S. Kenney and Tadeusz Sadowski, intro. by William S. Kenney, 1973.

20. The Penal Code of the Romanian Socialist Republic, transl. and with an intro. by Simone-Marie Vrăbiescu Kleckner, research associates were Bernard Stamler and Barbara Lacher, 1976.

21. Alternative Draft of a Penal Code for the Federal Republic of Germany, transl. and with an intro. by Joseph J. Darby, commentary by Jürgen Baumann, 1977.

22. The Social Protection Code: A New Model of Criminal Justice, by Tadeusz Grygier, 1977.

23. The Italian Penal Code, transl. by Edward M. Wise in collaboration with Allen Maitlin, intro. by Edward M. Wise, 1978.

24. The Swedish Code of Judicial Procedure, Revised Edition, edited by Anders Bruzelius and Krister Thelin, 1979.

25. The Criminal Code of the People's Republic of China, transl. and with an intro. by Chin Kim, 1982.

II. MONOGRAPH SERIES

1. The Legal Norms of Delinquency: A Comparative Study, by G.O.W. Mueller, Michael Gage, and Lenore R. Kupperstein, 1969.

2. Wiretapping and Electronic Eavesdropping: The Law and Its Implications. A Comparative Study, by Juris Cederbaums, 1969.
3. Horizons of Clinical Criminology, by Benigno Di Tullio, 1969.
4. Comparative Criminal Law in the United States, by G.O.W. Mueller, et al, 1970.
5. Delinquency and Puberty: Examination of a Juvenile Delinquency Fad, by G.O.W. Mueller, et al, 1971.
6. Responses to Crime: An Introduction to Swedish Criminal Law and Administration, by Alvar Nelson, 1972.
7. What Can a Police Officer Do? A Comparative Study: U.S.A.—German Federal Republic—Israel—Italy, 1974.
8. Perception of Police Power: A Study in Four Cities, by Anastassios D. Mylonas, 1973.

III. PUBLICATIONS SERIES

1. Essays in Criminal Science, G.O.W. Mueller, Ed., 1961.
2. International Criminal Law, G.O.W. Mueller and Edward M. Wise, Eds., 1965.
3. The General Part of the Criminal Law of Norway, by Johannes Andenaes, 1965.
4. Japanese Criminal Procedure, by Shigemitsu Dando, transl. B. J. George, Jr., 1965.
5. The Effectiveness of Punishment Especially in Relation to Traffic Offenses, by Wolf Middendorf, 1968.
6. Continental Police Practice, by Sheldon Glueck, 1973.
7. Legal Dimensions of Drug Abuse in the United States, by Harvey R. Levine, 1974.
8. Of Delinquency and Crime, by Sheldon and Eleanor Glueck, 1974.
9. Studies in Comparative Criminal Law, Edward M. Wise and G.O.W. Mueller, Eds., 1975.
10. Education for Crime Prevention and Control, Robert Joe McLean, Ed., 1975.
11. The Criminal Justice System of the Latin-American Nations: A Bibliography of the Primary and Secondary Literature, by Richard Rank, 1974.
12. Sentencing: Process and Purpose, by Gerhard O. W. Mueller, 1977.
13. Prostitution: Regulation and Control, by John F. Decker, 1979.
14. Law, Social Science and Criminal Theory, by Jerome Hall, 1982.
15. Nations Not Obsessed with Crime, by Freda Adler, 1983.

IV. OCCASIONAL PUBLICATIONS

1. Les infractions contre la famille et la moralite sexuelle, G.O.W. Mueller, et al., Eds. (published on behalf of the Comparative Criminal Law Project, as special issue 35/3-4, Revue Internationale de Droit Pénal. Paris: Recueil Sirey, 1964).
2. L'abus de drogues et sa prèvention, G.O.W. Mueller, et al., Eds. (published on behalf of the Comparative Criminal Law Project, as special issue 44/3-4, Revue Internationale de Droit Pénal. Rennes: Imprimeries Simon, 1974).

Nations Not Obsessed with Crime

FREDA ADLER

FRED B. ROTHMAN & CO.
Littleton, Colorado 80127

1983

Library of Congress Cataloging in Publication Data
ADLER, FREDA.
    Nations not obsessed with crime.
    (Publications of the Comparative Criminal Law Project ;
v. 15)
    Bibliography: p.
    Includes index.
    1. Criminal justice, Administration of—Cross-cultural
studies. I. Title. II. Series.
HV9443.A34 1983   364   83-11043
ISBN 0-8377-0216-X

© 1983 by Wayne State University
All rights reserved.

Printed in the United States of America

To my fellow criminologists and colleagues of the Crime Prevention and Criminal Justice Branch of the United Nations, who provided the intellectual and professional ambience which made the completion of this project possible.

Mohamed Abdul Aziz
Robin William Burnham
Irene Melup
Kurt Neudek
Slavomir Redo
M. Lamin Sesay
Eduardo Vetere
Antoinette Viccica
Emil Wandzilak

and to the then Chief,
Professor G.O.W. Mueller

Contents

Acknowledgments

A great many colleagues and friends have helped me with their advice and assistance, before, during and upon completion of the manuscript. I want to assure all of them that, without their help, I could not have completed this book. But I also want to absolve all of them of any responsibility for the way in which I may have interpreted their advice.

For the countries under study, the following persons deserve particular credit:

Switzerland:
    Professor Dr. Stefan Trechsel
    Hochschule St. Gallen für
    Wirtschafts - und Sozialwissenschaften
    St. Gallen, Switzerland

Ireland:
    Hon. John Olden
    Assistant Secretary
    Department of Justice
    Dublin, Ireland

Bulgaria:
    Excellency Svetla Daskalova
    Minister of Justice
    Sofia, Bulgaria

German Democratic Republic:
Professor Dr. sc. jur. Erich Buchholz
Sektion Rechtswissenschaft
Humboldt Universität
Berlin, D.D.R.

Costa Rica:
Dr. Jorge A. Montero
Director
Instituto Latino-Americana para la
Prevencion del Delito y Tratamiento
del Delinquente
San José, Costa Rica

Peru:
Dr. Francisco Morales Angeles
Lima, Peru

Algeria:
Dr. Chafika Sellami-Messlem
Director, Advancement of Women's Branch
CSDHA/DIESA/United Nations
Vienna, Austria

Saudi Arabia:
Dr. Farouk Mourad
Director General
Crime Prevention Department
Ministry of Interior
Riyadh, Saudi Arabia

Japan:
Miss Maneo Kubota
Director, (retired)
Advancement of Women's Branch
CSDHA/DIESA/United Nations
Tokyo, Japan

Nepal:
Excellency Ramanand P. Singh
Attorney General
Kathmandu, Nepal

For advice from the comparative perspective I owe particular gratitude to:

Dr. Inkeri Anttila
Professor Emeritus and former Minister of Justice
Helsinki, Finland

Professor Albert K. Cohen
University of Connecticut
Storrs, Connecticut, U.S.A.

Dr. Emilio de Olivares
Executive Assistant to the Secretary General
United Nations, New York

Professor Rosa del Olmo
Universidad Central de Venezuela
Facultad de Ciencias Juridicas y Politicas
Instituto de Ciencias Penales y Criminologicas
Caracas, Venezuela

Professor Dr. Albin Eser, M.C.J.
Universität Freiburg i.B.
Direktor des Max-Planck Instituts für
Ausländisches und Internationales Strafrecht
Freiburg i.B., G.F.R.

Dr. Matti Joutsen
Research Institute of Legal Policy
Helsinki, Finland

Dr. Ahmad M. Khalifa
Chairman of the Board
National Center for Social and Criminological Research
Cairo, Egypt

Professor Dr. Dr. Armand Mergen
Universität Mainz
Fachbereich Rechts- und Wirtschaftswissenschaften
Mainz, G.F.R.

Lt. Gen., A.F.P., Fidel Ramos
Chief of Constabulary
Directory General, I N P
Manilla, The Philippines

Professor Emeritus Thorsten Sellin
University of Pennsylvania
Philadelphia, Pa. U.S.A.

Dr. Patrick Törnudd
Director, Research Institute of Legal Policy
Helsinki, Finland

Professor A. Yakovlev
Institute of State and Law
Academy of Sciences of the USSR
Moscow, USSR

A particular note of thanks is due to Professor G.O.W. Mueller, of Rutgers University, for his much appreciated assistance in all matters of comparative criminal law and criminology, and to my teaching assistant, Miss Susan Okubo, for her faithful and constant staff support.

And above all, I want to thank the many friends on all continents covered in this volume, for so graciously receiving me in their homes, farms and tents, their offices, courts and prisons, their schools, kindergartens and places of assembly. They made it possible for me to gain first-hand knowledge of the ways in which, each society in its own way, strives toward synnomie.

FREDA ADLER
Newark, New Jersey
Christmas, 1982

Preface

The effect of the rise in criminality in recent decades on the public morale in the United States is as obvious as is the reaction of legislators and courts of justice. Although the rates of serious crimes of violence now appear to be declining, public fear and resentment are not likely to subside, and our retaliatory and harsh system of dealing with offenders will probably persist for years to come. The underlying causes of criminality are still neglected and largely ignored by those in power. Until they are recognized and understood and social action taken to deal with them, our complex society will continue to suffer the criminality it deserves.

There are nations in the world, however, which seem to have been able to maintain low crime rates, and Professor Adler has set out to discover the reason for it, selecting five pairs of countries in different regions of the globe. The basic data used for six of these countries are the arrest rates for a limited number of offenses reported to the United Nations in reply to a questionnaire distributed by that organization to its member countries in 1975-1976. Statistical data for three of the other countries became available after the offense rates were used. One of the countries included, Nepal, could supply no quantitative information. This deficiency was countered by the use of other sources of data.

All capable students of comparative criminal statistics are aware of the pitfalls on the road of an inquiry such as that undertaken by Professor Adler. So is she and she has dealt with them in a cautious manner. The results of her study are most interesting. The social control systems of the countries she has chosen for study are described and their effectiveness analyzed. She discovered that social solidarity, which Durkheim referred to in his great work on the division of labor, is the essential feature of the society of the countries with low crime rates. For this condition she coins the felicitous name synnomie.

THORSTEN SELLIN

Prologue

I am an American and I live in America. With my fellow citizens I share the pride in our national accomplishments. But I also share with them the national worries. As has been demonstrated in the research reports and books of many American colleagues, the prevalence of crime has become an American reality and the fear of crime an American preoccupation. Indeed, as studies have demonstrated, the fear of crime may even outstrip its reality. The point shall not be belabored in this book. It is a given. Nor shall it be argued that the cost of crime is the price for our liberty.

But as an American criminologist interested in the phenomenon of crime wherever it persists, it also occurred to me that in the far corners of the world which I visited, the preoccupation with crime is not a national past-time in more countries than one. Neither the design of doors and windows, nor the front page stories in the national press, nor the budgetary allocations of municipal and national governments, indicate any obsession with crime, the fear of crime, the fear of victimization, or indeed, the national destiny.

This book is about ten countries, two each from five quite divergent regions, where crime is not of any significant import. This is not to say that in these countries the protection from potential depredation through crime does not play a role. Per contra, as shall be demonstrated, protection of the citizenry in their rights to be free from crime—and to be free from the fear of crime—is a significant part of governmental policy in many of the countries that are, by comparison, relatively free of crime.

In America, crime has become our preeminent preoccupation. It has become an obsession. When I describe ten countries that are free of this obsession, I have the vision of an America that can shed its obsession with crime.

Nations Not Obsessed
with Crime

Introduction

The province and function of criminology has been thought to be the study of crime. For those criminologists who have interpreted their task in a fundamentalist manner, this has meant the study of the reason for the existence of crime. By emphasizing crime—the negative—the exploration of non-crime—the positive—has usually been excluded or neglected. The temptation for studying the prevalence of crime is particularly great for criminologists working in America with American data, where the abundance of crime is conspicuous. Yet the same reasons for studying the prevalence of crime—especially in America—should also prompt us to engage in a study of comparative criminology to ascertain the paucity of crime wherever such condition prevails.[1]

This study attempts to explain the low crime rates in ten identifiable countries for the purpose of ascertaining what it is that these countries may have in common, or what they have done differently in their crime prevention and criminal justice efforts, or their social control mechanisms. It is, of course, not easy to pinpoint, with exactitude, societies in which crime is rare. Until recently it was virtually impossible, since efforts to collect and analyze cross-national data, by and large, had been limited in scope, mostly restricted to the developed countries, to specific crimes,[2] or to partic-

1. One such study is that by Marshall B. Clinard, *Cities with Little Crime: The Case of Switzerland*, (London: Cambridge University Press, 1978).

2. Dane Archer and Rosemary Gartner, "Homicide in 110 Nations: the Development of the Comparative Crime Data File," *International Annals of Criminology*, 16, Nos. 1-2 (1977): pp. 109-139.

ular offender groups.[3,4] A few others have been more global in
perspective, some describing trends in criminality[5] and others relating various socio-economic indicators to the incidence of crime.[6] In
addition to the comparative projects, several working groups have
been assembled for the purpose of examining the complexities
inherent in the development of international crime statistics.[7] Not-
withstanding these efforts, there were relatively few advances until
1975/76 when the first major project was conducted to survey the
forms and dimensions of criminality on a world-wide basis. Ques-
tionnaires had been sent by the United Nations Secretariat to
Member States and to certain non-Member States, inviting them to
provide data on offenses, offenders, and measures of crime prevention and control in their respective countries. Sixty-four countries
responded to the request.[8] This first world crime survey provided a

3. Freda Adler, *The Incidence of Female Criminality in the Contemporary World.* (New York: New York University Press, 1981).

4. G.O.W. Mueller (with Lenore R. Kupperstein and Michael Gage), *The Legal Norms of Delinquency: A Comparative Study,* (New York University, Criminal Law Education and Research (CLEAR) Center Monograph Series No. 1, 1969), and volumes published pursuant to it.

5. Ted R. Gurr, "Crime Trends in Modern Democracies Since 1945," *International Annals of Criminology,* 16, Nos. 1-2 (1977): pp. 41-85.

6. Marvin Krohn and Charles F. Wellford, "A Static and Dynamic Analysis of Crime and the Primary Dimensions of Nations," *International Journal of Criminology and Penology,* 5 (1977): pp. 1-16. See also: H.R. Bloembergen, A.R. Hauber, C.W.G. Jasperse, L.G. Toornuliet and H.M. Willemse, "Criminality and Social Characteristics: a Report of Trial and Error," *Criminology: Between the Rule of Law and the Outlaws.* [Volume in honour of Willem H. Nagel, Kluwer-Deventer, The Netherlands], (1976): pp. 217-237.

7. Most recently the first major United Nations Interregional *Ad Hoc* Meeting of Experts on World Crime Trends and Crime Prevention Strategies, with experts representing all continents and all United Nations Institutes for the Prevention of Crime and the Treatment of Offenders, was convened at the School of Criminal Justice of Rutgers, the State University of New Jersey, at Newark, New Jersey, 5-9 October, 1981, in order to design the Second World Crime Survey, on the basis of the experience of the First World Crime Survey. For other comparative efforts see H. Campion, *International Statistics, Journal of the Royal Statistical Society,* Series A, Part II, 112 (1949): pp. 105-143: M. Ancel, "Observations on the International Comparisons of Criminal Statistics," *International Review of Criminal Policy,* 1 (1952): pp. 41-48; United Nations, *Criminal Statistics: Standard Classification of Offenses,* Report by the Secretariat, E/CN.5/337, 2 March 1959; *Id., Statistical Report on the State of Crime,* 1937-1946, E/CN.5/204, 23 February 1950. See also: *Suggestions for Development of Criminal Statistics,* Statistical Commission, ECOSOC, E/CN.3/102, 17 April 1950; M.E. Wolfgang, "International Comparative Statistics: a Proposal," *Journal of Criminal Law, Criminology and Police Science,* 58 (1967): pp. 65-69; Stanislaw Ziembinski, "Miezynarodowa statystyka kyrminalna (International crime statistics)," *Studia Kryminologiczne, Kryminalistyczne i Penitencjarne,* No. 1 (1974): pp. 111-122. See also: A.A. Tille and G.V. Schvekov, *Stravnitelnyj metod v Juriditscheskich disceplinach [Comparative Method in Juridicial Disciplines],* Moskva, 1973, Vyschaia Schkola.

8. United Nations, *Report of the Secretary General on Crime Prevention and Control,* A/32/199, of 22 September, 1977.

good base-line for the selection of countries which—within their culturally more or less homogeneous regions—have significantly lower rates of crime (as ascertained principally by arrest rates) than all countries of the same region, aggregated. Obviously, these figures are rendered imprecise by virtue of variations in legal terminology in both substantive and procedural law, by problems of honesty (or dishonesty) in the reporting of crime, and by sophistication (or lack thereof) in data collection and analysis as well as in the use of statistical method.

In the world crime survey the problems of variation in the use of legal terminology and classification had been largely overcome. Participating countries were asked to fit their crimes into very broadly defined categories which had been established for purposes of insuring comparability. The imprecision resulting from generalization, however, does not detract from the usefulness of the data in identifying countries with low (or high) crime rates; indeed, it makes such a task possible.

The problem of the honesty or dishonesty of crime-reporting officers, whether at the local, provincial or national level, is a more difficult one. Figures may be deflated or, perhaps less frequently, inflated, for a variety of reasons and the resulting differences in reported crime could destroy comparability. It became important, therefore, to "validate" the statistics by other quantified or unquantified information, such as rates of offenses reported to the police where available, or previous statistics, but, above all, by a process of informal peer-group evaluations within regions. In discussions with government leaders, administrators and scholars, region by region, there turned out to be surprisingly little disagreement as to which countries had the lowest crime rate and the greatest civil safety, within each region. Oddly enough, these views were, by and large, shared in countries with low and with high crime rates.

To some extent the remedies for overcoming the problems of honesty in reporting also helped in overcoming the problem of sophistication in data collection and analysis, but not entirely. Thus, it turned out to be impossible to identify countries with low crime rates for the region which is comprised of the countries of Africa south of the Sahara. These nations, which have emerged from colonial rule only recently, have been far too preoccupied with seemingly more important tasks of nation-building than the training of crime statisticians or the task of keeping crime statistics. When problems of famine, drought, industrialization and solvency

4

loom large, crime problems are given low priority—unfortunately, as some of these nations begin to realize. Consequently, the region of Africa south of the Sahara could not be included in this study.

For the remaining five regions of the world, the problem of national data analysis and reporting could be overcome to some extent, so that it became possible to select two countries per region in which the crime rate is the lowest—or among the lowest—for the region. For six of the ten countries included in this study, the low crime status could be ascertained by reference to the arrest rates reported by the respective countries for the purposes of the first world crime survey. These countries are Ireland and Switzerland, for the region of Western European countries; Costa Rica and Peru for the region of Latin American countries; Algeria for the region of Islamic countries; and Japan for the region of Asian and Pacific countries. In the case of countries for the region of European Socialist countries, some statistical reports became available only after the conclusion of the first world crime survey. They proved to be adequate for the selection of two countries with lowest crime rates. These countries are the German Democratic Republic[9] and Bulgaria.[10] For the region of Islamic countries, Saudi Arabia could be added as the second country with lowest crime rates on the basis of statistics which also became available after the world survey.[11] In case of the remaining country for the Asian and Pacific region, Nepal was added despite the absence of Nepalese statistics. Thus, the Nepalese low crime status rests on unquantified reports of national, regional and international specialists familiar with the social and crime conditions in the region in general, and in Nepal, in particular. All in all, then, the following ten countries were selected for this study:

Region	Country
Western European Countries	Switzerland
	Ireland
European Socialist Countries	Bulgaria
	German Democratic Republic
Latin American Countries	Costa Rica
	Peru
Islamic Countries (North Africa and Middle East)	Algeria
	Saudi Arabia
Asian and Pacific Countries	Japan
	Nepal

Following the selection of these countries, the effort was directed to a search for possible commonalities. Forty-seven socio-economic and demographic indicators (predictor variables), available through the statistical resources of various international agencies, were aggregated, and the ten countries under study were compared with the aggregate. This study, described in Chapter One, has had disappointingly insignificant results. Thereupon, a study of the criminal justice systems of all ten countries was undertaken, followed, for each country, by a study of less formal mechanisms of social control. The analysis of these qualitative data proved far more revealing than the evaluation of the quantitative data described in Chapter One.

While, for the purpose of this study, formal social controls, primarily composed of criminal justice mechanisms, were separated from informal social controls, this separation should not be regarded as a dichotomy. Informal social controls, e.g., the family structure, may receive such an amount of formal, i.e., governmental, support as to be virtually tantamount to a formal social control system. Moreover, in most instances the informal social controls are also reflected in the criminal justice control system, e.g., by popular participation. Informal social control systems and criminal justice social control systems are inextricably interwoven.

On the basis of the results of the country-by-country analysis of social control mechanisms, both through criminal justice and through other social controls, it was then possible to identify, albeit tentatively, theretofore elusive commonalities.

9. *Statistisches Jahrbuch 1980 der Deutschen Demokratischen Republik.* Staatliche Zentralverwaltung für Statistik, Staatsverlag der Deutschen Demokratischen Republic, (Berlin, 1980) pp. 379-381.

10. The statistics were obtained from the volume of the Bulgarian Academy of Sciences, Institute of Law, Vesselin Karakasher. *Certain Problems of Crime and Its Structure*, (Sofia, 1977) pp. 184-194.

11. *The Effect of Islamic Legislation on Crime Prevention in Saudi Arabia*, (Ministry of Justice, Kingdom of Saudi Arabia and UNSDRI, Rome, 1980) pp. 500-504. While in the case of all other national statistics the crime figures are offender-based, in the case of Saudi Arabia they are offense-based.

1

Quantified Socio-Economic Data: Can They Explain Low Crime Rates?

The world resource in statistics on the basis of which countries may be compared as to their social, economic and demographic conditions, insofar as these could conceivably relate to criminality, consists basically of forty-seven data banks.[1] The information contained in these banks had been collected by United Nations units, including the Department of International Economic and Social Affairs, and specialized agencies, including UNESCO, the World Health Organization and the International Labor Organization. In addition, information published in various demographic year-

1. (1) Population growth/annum V (computer variable) 6;
   (2) crude birth rate/1000 V8;
   (3) crude death rate/1000 V9;
   (4) male life expectancy V10;
   (5) female life expectancy V11;
   (6) proportion urban 1975 V14;
   (7) proportion urban 1960 V15;
   (8) total average persons/household V16;
   (9) urban average persons/household V17;
   (10) rural average persons/household V18;
   (11) population under 20 years old V21;
   (12) total population of major city V28;
   (13) world rank of major city V29;
   (14) total population as of 1975 V33;
   (15) population economically active V35;
   (16) population in agriculture 1960 V36;
   (17) population in agriculture 1975 V37;
   (18) population unemployed in 1975 V38;
   (19) growth gross domestic product 1970-76 V42;   *(continued)*

7

books, national and international,[2] has been utilized. Expense and time constraints precluded the preferable alternative of collecting new and original data. Furthermore, the massive volume of readily available figures which have been collected by international agencies for many countries, over a number of years, seemed an appropriate data source, given the fact that the study deals with exploration rather than hypothesis testing.

(20)	national income/person/annum 1976 V44;
(21)	number of radio receivers/1000 V46;
(22)	number of TV receivers/1000 V48;
(23)	number of telephones/1000 V50;
(24)	newspaper circulation world ranking V53;
(25)	population/physician 1976 V56;
(26)	illiterate males under 15 years 1966 V58;
(27)	illiterate females under 15 years 1966 V59;
(28)	population with no schooling 15-24 years 1966 V64;
(29)	population with no schooling over 25 years 1966 V68;
(30)	population with no schooling 15-24 years 1971 V67;
(31)	population with post-secondary education V70;
(32)	expenditures on education/pupil 1965 V75;
(33)	expenditures on education/pupil 1974 V77;
(34)	urban growth—proportion urban 1975 minus proportion urban 1960 V80;
(35)	population with no schooling 1966/15-24 minus population with no schooling 1974/15-24 V82;
(36)	population density per square kilometer V12;
(37)	divorce rate V20;
(38)	alien population V24;
(39)	city population in slums V31;
(40)	gross domestic product V40;
(41)	newspaper circulation/1000 V52;
(42)	population/hospital beds 1976 V54;
(43)	illiterate males under 15 years 1971 V61;
(44)	illiterate females under 15 years 1971 V62;
(45)	population with no schooling over 25 years 1971 V65;
(46)	expenditures on education as % of total public budget V72;
(47)	education expenditure change = expenditures on education/public, 1974 minus expenditures on education/pupil, 1965 V81.

2. *Demographic Yearbook 1977*, Department of International Economic and Social Affairs, Statistical Office, United Nations, (New York, 1978); *Compendium of Social Statistics 1977*, Department of International Economic and Social Affairs, Statistical Office, United Nations, (New York, 1980); *Statistical Yearbook 1978*, Department of International Economic and Social Affairs, Statistical Office, United Nations, (New York, 1979); *The World in Figures*, The Economist Newspaper Limited, (England, 1978); *Yearbook of Labour Statistics 1980*, International Labour Office, (Geneva, 1981); *World Statistics in Brief*, United Nations, (New York, 1979); *Statistisches Jahrbuch 1980 der Deutschen Demokratischen Republik*, Staatliche Zentralverwaltung für Statistik, Staatsverlag der Deutschen Demokratischen Republik, (Berlin, 1980); Banks, *Political Handbook of the World*, (New York: McGraw-Hill, 1979); *The Europa Yearbook 1981—A World Survey*, (Europa Publications Limited, 1981); *Encyclopedia Britannica—Macropedia*, (Encyclopedia Britannica, Inc., 1977); *Statistical Yearbook, 1980*, UNESCO, printed in England; *World Statistics in Brief*, Department of International Economic and Social Affiars, United Nations, (New York, 1979).

The first phase of the data analysis consisted of running correlations on each of the forty-seven independent variables with the dependent variable—arrest rates per 100,000 population. (For correlation coefficients, see Appendix I). Seven variables, chosen on the basis of correlation coefficients, plus a check on the multicollinearity among the independent variables, and on criminological theory, were then selected for a regression equation. Because of missing data, the N (number of countries) for the equation dropped down to two, yielding meaningless results. Consequently, an alternative approach had to be taken. *A priori* the variables were divided into seven categories intuitively clustered to reflect the following dimensions:

Population growth	(growth per annum)
Employment	(economically active population)
Rural to urban migration	(urban growth)
Social welfare	(expenditure on education)
Modernization	(telephones per 1000)
Urbanization	(urban population)
Industrialization	(gross domestic product)

Another regression equation was run using the one variable from each group which had data from at least 54 countries. The squared multiple correlation coefficient (R^2), i.e., the proportion of explained variance in crime rates, was 0.24. The highest predictor was population growth per annum,[3] (12.6%). The other variables contributed the following amounts (taken in the context of all variables considered):

Population growth per annum	12.60%
Number of telephones per thousand	10.00%
Gross domestic product	1.20%
Urban population 1975	0.19%
Expenditures on education/1974	0.14%
Urban growth, 1960-75	0
Population economically active	0

Given the fact that the regression equation provided so limited an explanation of total variation, little could be done in the way of further analysis except a check on whether the ten low crime rate countries fell above or below the means for the respective regions on the two best predictor variables, in order to ascertain whether there

---

3. Negative correlation.

are any discernible patterns. Results of the analysis show no uni-
formities with regard to the best variable, population growth. However, a similar analysis of the variable "number of telephones per
thousand"—the second best predictor—showed that seven of the ten
low crime rate countries had fewer telephones per 1000 population
than the mean number for their respective regions.

The remaining 45 variables were then similarly analyzed by
comparing each of the low crime rate countries with the mean of its
region (See Appendix II). Here, too, little was found in the way of
any uniform configurations. On only four of them (population
density, urban population/1960, population economically active,
number of radio receivers), seven of the ten subject countries fell
beneath the mean of their respective regions. On two other indicators (crude death rate, population in agriculture/1960), seven of the
countries fell above the mean.

This amounts to saying that most low crime countries have in
common lower than average population densities, lower than average urban population densities, lower than average urban populations (1960), lower than average population numbers which are
economically active, a lower than average number of radio receivers
and telephones, a higher than average population in agricul-
ture/1960, and a higher than average crude death rate. From this
constellation of variables, a theoretical profile of a low crime country emerges which appears to be primarily rural and underdevel-
oped. This profile might fit some of the ten low crime rate countries,
but certainly not others, e.g., German Democratic Republic, Japan
or Switzerland.

Even though, as noted, this study is concerned only with data
from ten countries with particularly low crime rates—and another
study, under way, will be concerned with comparable information
for countries with particularly high crime rates—it is useful to take a
look at the association between our 47 different statistical indicators
and the high crime rate countries so far identified[4] in an effort to
determine whether these indicators—by revealing the differences—
have a more meaningful indicator value for high crime rate countries than they have for low crime rate countries. Just as in the case of
the ten low crime rate countries, few solid patterns emerge, except
with respect to population growth. Nine of the eleven high crime

4. Inasmuch as the identification is purely tentative and the report on the countries with
highest crime rates is still in a formative stage, the list of countries is not yet available for
publication.

rate countries had a higher than average annual population increase. Oddly enough, with respect to the second best predictor, the number of telephones per 1000 population, eight of the eleven high crime rate countries had fewer telephones per 1000 than the mean number for their respective regions. Consequently, a low number of telephones per 1000 is consistent with both low and high crime rates, thus putting its predictor value in grave doubt.

As regards the remaining 45 variables, there was one, namely crude birth rate per 1000, on which eight of the eleven high crime rate countries fell above the mean. On six other variables (crude death rate per 1000, population density, percent urban in 1975, gross domestic product, national income per person and newspaper circulation per 1000), eight of the eleven countries fell below the mean. This amounts to saying that most high crime rate countries have a higher than average crude birth rate, and lower rates than average (for their region) for crude death rates per 1000 and for population density. Lower than average population density, thus, is consistent with both low crime rates and high crime rates. High crime rate countries also have in common lower than average urban populations in 1975, lower than average gross domestic products, lower than average national income per person and lower newspaper circulation. The theoretical profile of a high crime rate country is one which is less urbanized, less sophisticated (fewer newspapers and telephones), less productive, and less populous than an "average" country. Again, the theoretical profile probably does not describe many of the high crime rate countries realistically, nor does it meaningfully contrast them with the low crime rate countries. The two types do not appear to be all that different from one another.

It is clear from the statistical analysis presented here that the available "hard" data produced little in the way of meaningful information on the relationship between socio-economic and cultural indicators and crime rates. Perhaps the difficulty arose from the fortuity of the indicator types which are available, from the use of official data—with their own built-in biases—or from the statistical problems attributable to missing data. It became clear, then, that the search for explanations of low crime rates had to be conducted by different methods and on the basis of different data. Above all, the various systems of criminal justice prevalent in the countries under study had to be examined inasmuch as the populace and criminal justice administrators alike tend to attribute low crime rates to

effective criminal justice systems and high crime rates to the failure
of criminal justice.

It is not yet possible to conduct a comparative study of criminal
justice systems on the basis of quantified data. Apart from a few
relatively meaningless worldwide figures on the number of law
enforcement officers, judges and corrections officers in countries
which participated in the first world crime survey, no hard data are
available. A comparative study of ten distinct systems of crime
prevention and criminal justice including law enforcement, the
judiciary and corrections, therefore, had to be descriptive.

But the criminal justice system is simply one of society's several
social systems, although it perhaps is more formal than others.
Consequently, our country-by-country research had to extend to
other social controls extant in our ten countries. Just as criminal
justice systems are not comparable by quantified approaches, the
other social control systems are not comparable in any quantified
manner. In the following chapters, then, an attempt is made to relate
the phenomenon of crime to the as yet non-quantified, perhaps
non-quantifiable, variables of a socio-cultural nature. Profiles of
each of the ten countries are presented. These profiles are limited to
the criminal justice system and to those other social control organs
which are deemed most closely related to criminality. These include
the family and kinship groups, village and neighborhood communities, production communities, voluntary community organizations, political units, and religious organizations. In the following
chapters we shall deal with these informal social control systems as
encompassing all social controls other than criminal justice.

Western European Countries

2

Switzerland

INFORMAL SOCIAL CONTROLS

Switzerland is one of the world's leading industrialized nations, enjoying one of the highest standards of living in the world. It has a unique form of government without prime minister and head of state. Each year the President changes; while in office, he has no greater power than his peers on the council. The Swiss have an almost inflation-free society, with a high degree of affluence and virtually no unemployment (0.2% of workforce).[1] The transformation to an industrialized society began in the latter half of the nineteenth century and has progressed consistently through the years, with a sustained economic boom beginning in the 1950's. The economy is based on free enterprise and fair trade. Except for the post office, telegraph, telephone and main railroad, utilities are privately owned. The society remains basically egalitarian, with few class tensions. Conspicuous consumption is frowned upon and differences among the non-rich are minimal.[2]

The foundation of Swiss unity lies in its unique political structure which is based on direct democracy and federation. The Swiss confederation consists of 3,000 *Gemeinden* (communes), the basic unit of Swiss democracy, and twenty-six Cantons. Indeed, to be a

1. David Tinnin, "The Strange Ordeal of the Swiss," *Fortune Magazine*, 18 December, 1978.
   2. *Ibid.*

Swiss citizen, one first needs cantonal citizenship, which, in turn, is dependent on communal membership. The Swiss have historically resisted a strong central government (so common to the European countries) and have held firmly to local autonomy. Communes are of several types:[3] the *Einwohnergemeinde,* or political unit, which has jurisdiction over police, taxes, etc., the *Bürgergemeinde,* or citizens unit—to which one belongs by virtue of descent—which, *inter alias,* deals with relief funds; the *Schulgemeinde* or school unit, and the *Kirchgemeinde* or religious unit. While external affairs are handled by the Federal Government, by and large, domestic concerns belong to the local communities.

Almost sixty percent of the people live in the Cantons where they were born and grew up. Even if they work in neighboring cities, many reside in their places of birth (e.g., 180,000 daily commuters to work in Zurich)[4] and for those who do move, "home" is still the Canton. Generally, the cantonal flag is flown above the national flag. Cantons have fiscal autonomy and the right to manage their own internal affairs, including the criminal justice system, education and local legislation. Some of the Cantons submit all major financial decisions to a vote of their citizens. The Swiss treasure the autonomy and freedom of their local governments, where group loyalties transcend individual differences. Indeed, it often happens that, for the good of the order, they vote against their personal self-interest. For example, recent referenda have included decisions not to levy special taxes on the rich, not to lower the age for old-age pension coverage and not to decrease the work week, all arrived at for the good of the country. In addition, by referendum it was decided to raise taxes and to increase the price of bread. In their anti-inflation drive, labor was more interested in maintaining the competitiveness of their own companies than in receiving higher wages.[5]

Industrial harmony based on trust between management and labor (employees share information on financial status) has led to the signing of agreements to outlaw conflict in company disputes. In general, there appears to be a consistent accent on the acceptance of what adds up to the "common good" or what is known as "the Swiss way of doing things." Referendum instead of action groups, loyalty, non-violent settling of differences, citizens' participation

3. Marshall B. Clinard, *Cities with Little Crime: The Case of Switzerland,* (London: Cambridge University Press, 1978).

4. *Ibid.,* p. 106.

5. *Op. cit., supra.* n. 1.

and a commitment to local responsibility combine to achieve a remarkably stable country. It remains a highly conservative society with social change slowed down by the constant submission of legislation to the popular vote (e.g., the penal code proposal of 1918 was not adopted until 1937 and did not become effective until 1942).

Political decentralization plus a unique pattern of industrialization have resulted in yet another unusual dimension of the country—high modernization with slow urbanization. As industrialization took hold, factories were built in rural and semi-rural settings, near the rivers which were necessary as sources of power. Industry, then, did not foster the dislocation of massive numbers of laborers. No "industrial cities," or sub-cultures of city norms and values, sprang up overnight as they did in many other rapidly-changing nations. To the contrary, Swiss cities became trade, cultural and intellectual centers with none of them exceeding 500,000. The urban population went from 43.4% in 1940 to 58.3% in 1979, an increase of only 15% over a forty-year period.

There is no common ethnic heritage, religion or language among the Swiss. Within this heterogeneous population, four homogeneous language groups have existed as cohesive units, each maintaining a traditional value system. Throughout the country, strong social controls operate in the form of rigid family discipline, a less flexible life-style for teenagers than in most industrialized countries, a less permissive school system, dominated by strict school-masters, and good communication between generations. From early years, children are taught Swiss history, with particular accent on the Cantons and the fact that these Cantons predate the confederation. While working or at school, young people typically live at home in a patriarchal family system which still rejects working mothers. In fact, Switzerland has the smallest proportion of married working women among all Western countries.

The Swiss enjoy an almost unparalleled standard of living, even though there is no fully uniform, centralized social service system. The welfare state concept is totally unacceptable and assistance to the needy is generally thought of as the responsibility of individual families. Only since 1976 has there been mandatory unemployment insurance. Health insurance is still haphazard, by and large paid on an individual basis, with no compulsory contribution by employers. The number of guest laborers is carefully monitored and their stay is regulated by the needs of the marketplace. If there is a shortage of jobs for citizens, foreign workers are sent home.

In sum, full employment, high wages, low inflation, slow urbanization, decentralized industry, direct participatory government and strong allegiance to the local group, be it the family, the *Gemeinde,* or the Canton, are factors which have allowed the Swiss to enjoy a superior quality of life, relatively free from problems of poverty or gang subcultures[6] suffered by so many of their neighbors.[7]

THE CRIMINAL JUSTICE SYSTEM

In a Basel court room:

> The absence of mumbo jumbo, of professional side, goes further than the mere spurning of wig and gown, . . . it springs from the Swiss sense of the community of citizens, from their dislike of specialization, and from a humanistic inheritance, a still-living conviction that—outside of science at least—all branches of human activity are open to all men. . . . And so the law, too, is felt to be something that can be administered by any able-minded man of good repute. . . . The people do not only vote the laws and elect the judges, there is a cordial and adult relationship between bench and public in the courts.[8]

The most extraordinary aspect of Swiss criminal justice is its distribution along geographical lines: elections of judges, jurors and lay assessors are on the local level; criminal courts and the criminal process function on the cantonal level, yet the justice administered is national, under the Swiss Penal Code of 1973. This tripartition in justice follows the tripartition which appears to exist in every other aspect of Swiss life. It seems that the Swiss have a stake in the administration of criminal justice at every level. The crime rate has remained extraordinarily low, despite the fact that every male Swiss citizen keeps his government-issue firearms at home, firearms which rarely are used against another human being, though the suicide rate has been relatively high. Homicide offenses

6. Anne-Marie Conza and Danielle Siminet, *La Delinquance Juvenile. Enquete faite sur 100 Dossiers de garcons ayant passe devant la Chambre Penale de L'Enfance a Genève, 1965-1966.* (Geneve: Institute d'Etudes Sociales, 1971).

7. *Op. cit., supra.* n. 1.

8. Sybille Bedford, *The Faces of Justice,* (New York: Simon and Schuster, 1961), p. 257.

are largely a matter for scholarly discussion.[9] Petty delinquency[10] and prostitution[11] are taken a bit more serious, perhaps largely because of their aesthetic repercussions. But two problem ranges have recently aroused public concern: economic offenses which, perhaps, are fostered by Switzerland's unique economic position and legislation,[12] and the criminality associated with the youth counter-culture to which not even Switzerland was entirely immune.[13] The Swiss are prone to attribute the recent youth demonstrations to the emergence of the drug culture, although the question of cause and effect appears debatable to many.[14]

Yet, not even the "youth movement," with its drug culture, has made a serious dent into the Swiss crime figures, although, prominent Swiss intellectuals have warned of a possible conflict which may arise over the theretofore generally acclaimed Swiss attitude toward norm conformance, fostered in part by the moralistic attitude of the Swiss churches.[15]

The extraordinary popularity of the administration of criminal justice in the Swiss Cantons is owed not only to the fact that the procedural codes—and judicial systems—are cantonal, but that participation of the public at the local level is an entrenched institution.[16] While only the Canton Zurich still maintains the traditional jury of 12 in felony cases, all Cantons maintain various forms of lay participation, usually as assessors, quite apart from the popularly

9. Jean Graven, "La repression de l'homicide en droit Swisse," *Rev. Sci. Crim. et de Droit Penal Compare,* 21, No. 2 (1966): p. 233.

10. R. Hauser, "Die Behandlung der Bagatellkriminalität in der Schweiz," *Z ges. Strwsch.,* 30 (1980): p. 295.

11. W. Hubatka, "Probleme der Prostitution," *Kriminalistik,* 20 (1966): p. 503.

12. N. Schmid, "Der Wirtschaftsstraftäter," *Schweiz Z. f. Str.,* 92 (1976): p. 52.

13. The rebellion, or "youth movement," is sometimes associated with a cause, e.g., youth centers, nuclear power, women's rights, cheap housing. In other instances, it seems to be simply a demonstration against the traditional norms of school, family and society. Zurich police have reported 60 clashes in 1980, which included a Christmas Eve riot and an armed siege of the opera house with an attendant five million dollar damage, five hundred injuries and 1600 arrests. "A" for anarchy is the symbol, and slogans such as "Chaos is Beautiful" and "Fury Does Good" have been chanted in nude marches through the streets. (Christian Science Monitor, Monday, 13 April, 1981.)

14. D. Hall, "Sociale Devianz und Drogenkonsum," *Schweiz. Arch. Neurol., Neurochir., Psychiat.,* 120, No. 2 (1977): p. 217; Rolf Jenny, "Drogenkonsum und Drogenhandel im Blickpunkt des Kriminologen," *Zürcher Beiträge zur Rechtswissenschaft,* No. 425 (1973); D. Ladewig, "Entstehung und Auswirkung der Medikamentenabhängigkeit," *Med. Lab.,* 22 (1969): p. 171.

15. Eduard Naegeli, *Die Gesellschaft und die Kriminellen,* (Zurich: Flamberg Verlag, 1972).

16. See Robert Hauser, *Kurzlehrbuch des Schweizerischen Strafprozessrechts,* (1978).

elected judges who normally are not lawyers.[17] The popularity of the criminal process has not suffered by two aspects of criminal procedure which are requisite for effective and humane administration of justice, namely the questions of dealing expeditiously with scientific evidence and of applying basic human rights standards.[18] While the administration of justice has remained largely in the hands of laymen, the development of the system has always rested in the hands of outstanding jurists, many of whom have achieved world acclaim, from Carl Stoos, through Hafter, Pfenninger, Graven, Schultz and Clerc.

The Penal Code of 1937, effective January 1942, was the product of a long lasting scholarly reform effort, nine years of parliamentary debate, and a popular referendum which accepted the code by a narrow margin (358,438 yes, 312,030 no). Actually, if the vote had gone by Cantons, the code would not have been accepted, since only 9½ Cantons voted in favor, 12½ against the code. Carl Stoos who, around the turn of the century, had started the reform movement, had coined the phrase—"A penal code fulfills its purpose only if it proves effective in combatting crime."[19] Subsequent history proved Stoos to be prophetic, and the code to be effective. Only three revisions were necessary in the forty years since its promulgation, none of which required major structural changes.[20] Provisions on criminal responsibility and on the imposition and execution of sentences (with a view to resocialization on a more individualized basis) were amended; emphasis was placed on mentally abnormal offenders and drug addicts, and the treatment of juvenile offenders, as to whom the measures to be imposed are now highly individualized and where, in general, the trend set by the United Nations has been followed.[21] A high level of juridical culture has been maintained with respect to Swiss criminal law.[22]

17. Edgar Jacques Müller, *Die heutige Bedeutung der Schwurgerichte in der Schweiz*, (1957).

18. See R. Hauser, "Probleme and Tendenzen im Strafprozess," *Schweiz Z. f. Str.*, 88 (1972): p. 113; Peter Huber, "Die Stellung des Beschuldigten," *Zücher Beiträge zur Rechtswissenschaft*, No. 433 (1974).

19. Hans Felix Pfenninger, "Das schweizerische Strafrecht," in *Das ausländische Strafrecht der Gegenwart*, Vol. II, (eds.) Mezger-Schönke-Jescheck, (Berlin: Duncker and Humblot, 1957), p. 206.

20. Hans Schultz, "Dreissig Jahre Schweizerisches Strafgesetzbuch," *Schw. Z. Str.*, 88 (1972): p. 1.

21. Hans Schultz, "Schweizer Strafrecht," *Z. ges Strwsch.*, 84 (1971): p. 1045; Clerc, "Les recentes transformations du Code Penal Suisse," *Rev. de Sci. Crim. et de droit pen. comp.* (1972): p. 31; O.A. Germann, "Bestimmungen des Schweizerischen Strafgesetzbuches aufgrund der Revision von 1971," *Schw. Z. Str.*, 91 (1975): p. 255.

22. See the leading textbooks by O.A. Germann, *Schweizerisches Strafgesetzbuch*,

Swiss juvenile law is particularly interesting since it reveals best the Swiss approach to crime control. The provisions of the Swiss Penal Code devoted to juvenile and young adult offenders have been inspired by the sociological, psychological, educational and medical professions.[23] The Swiss educative approach, with its emphasis on character building for civic responsibility, goes back to Pestalozzi.[24] The various juvenile court systems were adapted from American models.[25] The structure of these courts and their procedures vary from Canton to Canton. While in some Cantons the ordinary criminal courts exercise juvenile jurisdiction, but with special youth counsellors, special juvenile courts exist in most French and Italian speaking Cantons.[26]

Everywhere juvenile courts exist side by side with a variety of public agencies whose jurisdiction extends to the concern over endangered children and youth.[27] Nevertheless, the wave of juvenile unrest did ultimately reach Switzerland, and it may be debatable whether it was due to the caring, paternalistic Swiss approach to endangered youth,[28] or whether, absent it, the wave would have hit much harder.

For youngsters in actual trouble with the law, the Code permits children below six years of age to be subjected only to the supervi-

---

(Zurich: Schulthess, 1972); Hans Schultz, *Einführung in den Allgemeinen Teil das Strafrechts*, (Bern: Stämpfli, 1977); Günter Stratenwerth, *Schweizerisches Strafrecht-Besonderer Teil*, 2 vols., (Bern: Stampfli, 1973). A large number of doctoral dissertations are devoted to criminal law and procedure, and several scholarly periodicals service the profession, especially the Schweizerische Zeitschrift für Strafrecht (Swiss Journal of Criminal Law) and the Revue Internationale de Criminologie et de Police Technique.

23. H. Veillard-Cybulska, *L'application des mesures psychosociales et educatives aux delinquantes mineurs*, (Lyons: Etabliss. Ed. Charix and S.A. Filanosa, 1971).

24. See G.O.W. Mueller, "Resocialization of the Young Adult Offender in Switzerland," *Journal of Criminal Law, Criminology, and Police Science*, 43 (1953): p. 578, discussing treatment measures for young adult offenders in the Canton of Zurich, under Art. 43.1 of the Swiss Penal Code.

25. Juvenile Courts were established in Geneva in 1912, in Neuchatel in 1971, in Basel in 1919, in Zürich in 1919, in Fribourg in 1924, in Bern in 1930. See Pfenninger, *op. cit. supra*, n. 19, p. 191.

26. H. Veillard-Cybulska, "Switzerland," in *Justice and Troubled Children Around the World*, Vol. 1, (ed.) V. Lorne Stewart (New York: New York University Press, 1980), p. 143; *Ibid.*, "Modern Juvenile Courts in Switzerland," *International Journal of Offender Therapy and Comparative Criminology*, 17, No. 2, (1973).

27. See, e.g., for the Canton of Geneva: R. Berger, "l'office de la jeunesse de Genève comme instrument de prévention," *Rev. Int. de Crim. et de Police Technique*, 26, No. 1 (1973): p. 71.

28. In general, see L. Burckhardt, E. Müller, H. Peter and R. Bang, *Verstehen, Helfen, Wege zum Verständniss der schwierigen Jugendlichen*. (Basel, 1965). T. Ceppi, "Ursachen der Jugendkriminalität und Möglichkeiten zu ihrer Verminderung," *Kriminalistik*, 23 (1969): p. 481. T. Ceppi, "Jugendkriminalität," *Kriminalistik*, 22 (1968): p. 378. "Die Minderjährigen im Strafrecht," *Fachbl. Schweiz. Heim. u. Anstalts W.*, 42, No. 1 (1971): p. 20.

sion of parents or guardians (Articles 82-88), while juveniles between 14 and 18 years of age are subject primarily to protective and welfare measures (Articles 89-99) and penal measures only in exceptional cases (Article 95). Minors between 18 and 20 years of age incur criminal liability, but are subject to lesser and now far more individualized sentences, to be served at special institutions. Normally educational measures are imposed, including admonition, educative assistance or placement in foster families or homes.[29] Juvenile punishment consists of reprimands, fines (for employed adolescents) or placement in detention centers. Measures are selected only after a careful and detailed investigation into the youngster's social conditions.[30]

The same concern for individual and communal welfare, with emphasis on individualized attention, is noticeable in the Swiss correctional system, which is cantonal, except that by inter-cantonal compact, three regional prison systems have been organized. Extramural sentences are widely used. Thus, in 1970, of 11,900 prison sentences imposed by cantonal courts, 7,992, or 67.1 percent, were suspended. This suspension can be imposed for any sentence up to 18 months.[31]

In case a suspension period has been successfully completed, the original judgment and sentence is extinguished for all public and private purposes, save only if the offender recidivates.[32] Suspension of sentence is regarded as part of a thorough system of social assistance to adult offenders.[33] Habitual offenders may be placed in a form of preventive detention,[34] but even here the emphasis is on efforts to instill orderly work habits.

The recent reforms are considered by some scholars as not going far enough. The creation of social therapeutic institutions has been recommended.[35] Overall, the Swiss correctional approach can be

29. See J. Rehberg, "Zum Verhältnis von Strafe und Massnahme im Schweizerischen Jugendstrafrecht," *Schw. Z. f. Str.*, 87 (1971): p. 225.

30. Veillard-Cybulska, *op. cit., supra.* n. 26, pp. 153 *et seq.*

31. Hans Schultz, "Der bedingte Strafvollzug nach dem Bundesgesetz von 18. März 1977," *Schw. Z. f. Str.* 89 (1977): p. 53, referring to procedures under amended Article 41.1.1 of the Penal Code.

32. O.A. Germann, "Zum bedingten Strafvollzug nach Schweizerischem Recht," in *Études en l'honneur de Jean Graven.* (Geneve: Librarie de l'Universite, 1969), p. 57.

33. "Die durchgehende Sozialhilfe bei Straffälligen," *Bewährungshilfe*, 20, No. 2 (1973): p. 126; W. Wiesendanger, "Aufgaben und Probleme der strafrechtlichen Schutzaufsicht," *Bewährungshilfe*, 13, No. 1 (1966): p. 50.

34. C. Bruckner, *Der Gewohnheitsverbrecher und die Verwahrung in der Schweiz gemäss Artikel 42 St. G.B.* (Basel: Helbing und Lichtenhahn, 1971).

35. Peter Noll, "Die Arbeitserziehung," *Schw. Z. f. Str.*, 89 (1973): p. 149.

regarded as relatively nonpunitive and aiming at re-integration of the offender into the community, under wide assistance of the community.[36]

The enforcement of criminal laws rests with well-trained and well-equipped cantonal police organizations.[37] The Swiss approach to police is basically a mixed one, including (and with emphasis on) the task of averting dangers threatening the public, but also (and perhaps based on tradition) the more social-welfare oriented approach of positive social intervention.[38] A federal police force exists only to maintain the external security of the Confederation, to supervise the flow of foreigners, and to provide inter-cantonal co-ordination.[39] Basic policing is the function of cantonal police forces and, in some urban areas, municipal police forces, subject to local citizens' control.[40]

36. *Op cit., supra,* n. 1.

37. "Les realisations et les projects de l'Institut Suisse de Police de Neuchâtel," *Rev. Int. de Crim. et de Police Techn.,* 24 (1970): p. 59; W. Loertscher, "Ideas on Crime Investigation," *Int. Crim. Police Rev.,* 21 (1966): p. 201; "Training Senior Police Officers and Police Laboratory Personnel," *Int. Crim. Police Rev.,* 24 (1969): p. 229.

38. Andreas Jost, *Die neuste Entwicklung des Polizeibegriffs im Schweizerischen Recht, Abhandlungen zum Schweizerischen Recht,* vol. 438.

39. Martin Müller, *Die Entwicklung der Bundespolizei und ihre heutige Organisation. Zürcher Beiträge zur Rechts-Wissenschaft,* (1949).

40. Harold Becker, *Police Systems of Europe,* (Springfield: Charles C. Thomas, 1973), pp. 156-157.

3

Ireland

INFORMAL SOCIAL CONTROLS

Officially called the Irish Free State between 1922 and 1937, the island nation off the northwestern edge of the European Continent became the Irish Republic on December 29, 1937. It had been colonized by Celts, Norsemen, Normans, English and Scots, but today few social or ethnic distinctions exist. Ninety-five percent of the families are Roman Catholic. "Judged by the standards of other Catholic cultures in Europe, the level of orthodoxy in belief, and commitment to religious practice, is extraordinarily high in Ireland."[1] Yet since the mid-1970s, younger, especially male, Irishmen have been less actively participating in church activities. Ireland is a parliamentary democracy with a mixed economy favoring private industry and commerce.

While agriculture is still the mainstay of the economy, accounting for 38 percent of the total exports, the rapid growth of industry, spawned in 1958 by the First Programme for Economic Expansion, has created major changes in the economy. The labor force, still predominantly male but with a rapidly-growing female component, has shifted recently from approximately half to one-fifth in agriculture.[2]

1. Damian F. Hanna, "Ireland's New Social and Moral Dilemmas," *New Society*, 18 November 1982, pp. 291-293.
2. David R. Rottman, *Crime in the Republic of Ireland: Statistical Trends and Their Interpretation*, (Dublin: The Economic and Social Research Institute, 1980) Hannan, *op. cit. supra.* n. 1.

24

Post-war economic growth in Ireland originally showed a slower pattern from that of other nations of Western Europe, averaging less than two percent annual increase in the gross national product between 1949 and 1960, four percent between 1961 and 1968, and below four percent between 1969 and 1974.[3] But in 1973, E.E.C. membership further favored free trade expansion and a successful alignment with the economy of the rest of Europe.

Another unique feature is Ireland's population configuration and change. While the populations of most Western European nations have experienced a doubling of their numbers over the past one hundred and fifty years, Ireland's population is little more than half of what it was then. To date, the number of Irish-born people residing outside of the country is approximately fifty percent of the present population. Until recently, then, emigration had drained off the majority of those who lost their means of survival when farms underwent mechanization. Basically, it was the young, the unattached, the rural poor and the less fortunate who made the move. The result has been a change in the age structure, with the proportion of the total population in the crime-prone age (15-29) having *declined* almost twelve percent between 1926 and 1971.[4] According to one study:

> An Irishman with criminal aspirations almost invariably leaves this country and goes to England, sometimes voluntarily, sometimes on the advice of the police or even a District Justice.[5]

It is clear, then, that emigration served the country as a safety valve with some 530,000 persons—half of the total labor force—leaving in the twenty-year period between 1951 and 1971.[6]

Due to this massive exodus the urban areas of Ireland never became a 'dumping ground' for "the usual offshoots of human misery." Whatever the social, cultural and emotional costs, emigration maintained a locally-centered system of social control in parts of rural Ireland and impeded the urban concentration of those with residual status and skills.[7] Between 1946 and 1961, only eight out of

3. High Level Conference on the Employment of Women, 16-17 April 1980, National Report, Organization for Economic Cooperation and Development, ER (8) 4/10.

4. *Op. cit., supra.* n. 1. but during the 1970s a reverse trend has set in, with large numbers of Irish emigres returning to Ireland.

5. Matthew Russel, "The Irish Delinquent in England," *Studies 53* (Summer, 1964): p. 146.

6. *Op. cit., supra.* n. 2, p. 31.

7. David B. Rottman, *Journal of Statistical Inquiry,* Society of Ireland, 23, pt. 5, (1977/78): pp. 163-216.

one hundred migrants from rural areas went to Dublin, with the number increasing to only twenty-one out of one hundred between 1961 and 1971. Furthermore, the Dublin Mobility Studies have shown that those who move to the city are in fact of higher social status and educational level than those born there.[8] This pattern differs markedly from that of most industrializing nations where a great number of village people descended into the subculture of poverty that awaited them in the cities which were not yet equipped to handle them.

Ireland, then, to the extent that it did become urbanized, did so in a planned manner. The slow city growth is largely the result of natural increase, not of mass migration from the countryside.[9,10] Rural counties, through Government initiative, were provided with employment opportunities. Thus, Galway was slowly expanded as an industrial center, thereby creating means of employment in an area of agricultural decline.[11]

Despite industrialization, and even considering that nearly one-third of all Irishmen live in Dublin, Ireland remains a land of traditional small, albeit growing, towns where property is passed on from generation to generation. For agricultural families, family farms are the rule, and there are only about ten percent hired laborers. The bulk of the duties falls to the kinship group. Most of the farms are small (almost half are under 12 hectares)[12] and family members tend to work closely together, bonded by a strong attachment to the land.

Fathers exercise considerable control over their family by determining testate succession. Farms are passed on to one son, while daughters may obtain a dowry. Even in the age of modernized farming, traditional behavior is expected and primary relationships serve as a strong control system.[13] Indeed, it is not uncommon for

8. Bertram Hutchinson, *Social Status and Intergenerational Social Mobility in Dublin.* (Dublin: The Economic and Social Research Institute, Paper No. 48, 1969).

9. Brenda Walsh, "Expectation, Information and Human Migration: Specifying an Econometric Model of Irish Migration to Britain," *Journal of Regional Science*, 14, No. 1, (1974): pp. 107-120.

10. *Op. cit., supra.* n. 2, p. 6.

11. Mary Cawley, "Rural Industrialization and Social Group Change in Western Ireland," *Sociologica Ruralis*, 19, No. 1, (1979): s. 43-57.

12. *World Conference on Agrarian Reform and Rural Development*, Country Review Paper of Ireland, No. 72, Rome, 11-20. July 1979.

13. Damian F. Hannan, *Displacement and Development, Class, Kinship and Social Change in Irish Rural Communities.* (Dublin: The Economic and Social Research Council, 1979).

members of farm families who work in city industries to remain living at home, commuting to jobs, thereby maintaining ties to parents, local church and neighbors.

Primary education is free and compulsory between the age of six and fifteen, with State grants available for secondary education. There is a network of 800 centers for vocational training, eight regional technical colleges, and the universities. Diagnostic service, child clinics, treatment of infectious diseases and some hospital services are free for all citizens. All health services are available to the poor without fee. Social welfare insurance is compulsory for manual and non-manual laborers. There are pension funds, various benefits (death, widow, maternity, etc.) and a children's allowance for all children under sixteen, regardless of means.[14] While class distinctions continue to exist, by virtue of tradition, tax structure and access to educational opportunities, these have not led to unrest of politically disturbing dimensions.[15]

Major attention has been given by both Government and private industry to the housing situation. Dwellings are provided by local authorities for various categories of persons (e.g., handicapped, disabled) who cannot provide their own. These dwellings are part of a comprehensive program which includes access to churches, schools and places of work. Good public utility services are available. There is also a national program for rural housing which includes both permanent dwellings and emergency prefabricated accommodations. The effort of raising the quality of the life of the nation includes programs for integrating itinerant families, and especially their children, into the life of the communities.

THE CRIMINAL JUSTICE SYSTEM

Article 45.1 of the Irish Constitution provides:

> The State shall strive to promote the welfare of the whole
> people by securing and protecting as effectively as it may a

---

14. World Conference of the United Nations Decade for Women, Copenhagen, Denmark, July 1980, National Paper submitted by Ireland.

15. See David B. Rottman, Damian F. Hannan, Niamh Hariman, Miriam M. Wiley, *The Distribution of Income in the Republic of Ireland: A Study in Social Class and Family Cycle Inequalities*, (Dublin: The Economic and Social Research Institute, 1982) Hannan, *op. cit.*, *supra.* n. 1.

social order in which justice and charity shall inform all the
institutions of the national life.[16]

This express social concern for the system as a whole is guaranteed, on the one hand, by the maintenance of the traditional and due
process oriented common law—in an application which is virtually
indistinguishable from its English counterpart[17]—and, on the other
hand, by the creation—albeit with a time lag compared with other
European countries—of social services, including those in the field
of criminal justice.

The judicial system of Ireland, pursuant to Article 34 of the
Constitution, is established by the Courts (Establishment and Constitution) Act, 1961, which, however, simply continues the previous
system.[18] Under the Prosecution of Offences Act, 1974, most of the
prosecutorial functions theretofore exercised by the Attorney General, were transferred to the newly created office of Director of Public
Prosecution, who is appointed by the Government but independent
vis-à-vis the courts.

Relatively minor (summary) offenses are tried at the Distict
Court level. Offenses scheduled to the Criminal Justice Act, 1951,
including perjury, forgery, certain types of assault and larceny of
values below £200, while indictable offenses, may also be tried
summarily provided the defendant does not object. Likewise triable
in District Court are indictable offenses other than murder, treason
or international crimes, where the defendant has pleaded guilty and
the judge is satisfied that the defendant understands the charges.
The district judge may deal summarily with the case, subject to the
consent of the Director of Public Prosecution. Otherwise, pursuant
to section 13 of the Criminal Procedure Act of 1967, the case is
transferred for trial to the Circuit Court or the Central Criminal
Court. If the District Court deals with the case, the maximum
punishment imposable is a £100 fine or a term of imprisonment up
to twelve months. District Court convictions are appealable to the
Circuit Court, where a rehearing of the whole case takes place.
(There is the possibility of an appeal by the prosecution as well, in
certain cases).

16. Paul C. Bartholomew, *The Irish Judiciary*, (Notre Dame: University of Notre Dame
Press, 1971), pp. 70-71.
17. See Robert L. Sandes, *Criminal Law and Procedure in the Republic of Ireland*, 3rd
ed., (1951). English standard works are in common usage and much of the older statutory law
of England is in force.
18. *Administration Yearbook*, (Dublin: Institute of Public Administration, 1974).

The District Court system has one president and 42 judges. "The actual trial procedure in the Republic of Ireland is identical with that in England save for some minor differences of form."[19] It is noteworthy that only ten percent of indictable offenses actually are tried; all others are dealt with summarily.

Indictable offenses not triable summarily are brought before the Circuit Court, after a preliminary hearing before the District Court—unless the defendant waives it—which results in the finding of sufficient cause. Under Section 25 of the Courts (Supplemental Provisions) Act, 1961, the Circuit Court may try any offense under indictment except treason, murder, attempt or conspiracy to murder, piracy and high state crimes. Here the judge sits with a jury. Traditionally, on application of either party the case is transferrable to the Central Criminal Court, but under Sec. 31 of the Courts Act, 1982, this right has been severely circumscribed. The Circuit Court has a president and eight judges. The Central Criminal Court is composed of a judge or judges of the High Court, nominated by the president of the High Court, and sits with a jury.

The High Court—successor to the Court of King's Bench— composed of a president, fourteen other judges and the President of the Circuit Court, *ex officio*, basically is an appellate tribunal, but it acts as a court of first instance in State-side applications (Prerogative Writs), e.g., certiorari and mandamus.

The Court of Criminal Appeal hears appeals by persons tried and convicted in the Central Criminal Court or the Circuit Court, where the trial judge certifies that the case is suitable for appeal or, where such a certificate is refused, when the Court of Criminal Appeal itself grants leave to appeal. This court is composed of three judges, one of whom is the chief justice or a justice of the Supreme Court nominated by him. The other two are judges of the High Court. To obtain an appeal, the appellant must obtain a certificate from the trial judge that the case is suitable for appeal, or else he must obtain leave to appeal. The Supreme Court hears appeals from the Court of Appeals, on certification. This court is composed of the chief justice and four other judges plus the president of the High Court.[20]

---

19. M. Russell, "The Preliminary Hearing in the Criminal Process of Ireland," in *The Accused—A Comparative Study*, (ed.) J.A. Coutts. One difference, however, is the existence of the American-style preliminary hearing, which offers the defendant a distinct advantage.

20. V.T.H. Delaney. *The Administration of Justice in Ireland*, (ed.) C. Lysaght, 4th rev. ed., (1975), pp. 45-55.

The juvenile justice system extends to youngsters below age seventeen. The district judge sits as Children's Court judge.[21]

> Where a juvenile has been detected in the commission of an offense there are three methods of disposing of the matter open to the police officer concerned: he may (i) recommend to his senior officer that the offender be prosecuted, (ii) recommend that the offender be formally cautioned, and (iii) finally, where he considers the offence of little consequence, simply, on his own initiative, give the juvenile an informal warning.[22]

If a youngster is charged, the parents or guardian are likewise charged and bound to appear at court with the young defendant. Proceedings are held in chambers. The court is aided by extensive background information from the court's welfare officer. There is wide judicial discretion to give the young defendant a chance to make it in open society, with the assistance of the social services. An interdepartmental committee recommended, in 1974, that, in order to integrate and improve the various services,

> There should be established, on a permanent basis, an inter-departmental committee to co-ordinate the activities of the Government Departments concerned in relation to children and young persons. Its aim should be to keep the changing needs of the situation under constant review, to advise on any further provisions—remedial, administrative, legislative or otherwise—which it considers, from time to time, to be neces-sary or desirable in relation to young persons who have come or are likely to come in conflict with the law or who may be in need of psychiatric treatment. It should also have the oppor-tunity of expressing its opinion on the provisions of any projected legislation likely to have an impact on the personal or social well-being of young people.[23]

21. *Ibid.*, p. 46.

22. Peter Shanley. "The Formal Cautioning of Juvenile Offenders," *The Irish Jurist, Vol. V* (n.s.) part 2, 1970, p. 262. The author describes the situation both as regards England (and Wales) and Ireland, and adds: "In Ireland the practice of formal cautioning takes place within the framework of the Juvenile Liaison Scheme."

23. *First Interim Report of the Interdepartmental Committee on Mentally Ill and Malad-justed Persons: Assessment Service for the Courts in Respect of Juvenile Offenders.* (Dublin: 1974), p. 4.

In its second interim report, the committee recommended:

> A close working relationship should be established between
> School Attendance Officers, the Welfare Service, the Special
> Education Section of the Department of Education and the
> Schools Health Services to ensure that special educational
> measures which are required for illiterate or semi-literate
> young people at risk are provided as soon as possible.

Further recommendations pertained to improved day attendance
centers, diagnostic and treatment services, the establishment of a
"secure centre" for young sociopaths, residential homes for boys and
"residential special schools."[24]

Ireland maintains a relatively small correctional system of nine
prisons and places of detention. Until well after World War II, the
orientation was punitive and disciplinarian. Since then, and due to
heightened interest on the part of the public, of professionals and of
pressure groups, considerable improvements have been made with
respect to training in prison, welfare, education, recreation, etc.,
necessitating vastly increased expenditures per prisoner. Parole was
extended, community service orders were created,[25] and improved
training of correctional officers was provided.[26] Nevertheless, the
most recent report on the Irish Penal System still finds the system to
be a closed one.

> The ideal of rehabilitation is more accepted by those respon-
> sible for running prisons. However, Irish prisons do not
> rehabilitate and at present they are punitive. . . . Prison work
> is menial and does not assist the prisoner's chances of
> employment on release.[27]

24. *Id.*, Second and Third Interim Reports, *passim.* The Task Force on Child Care
Services published its extensive "Final Report to the Minister of Health," presaging major
legislative recommendations by the Department of Health, which now has primary responsibility in this regard.

25. *Community Service Orders*, Laid by the Minister of Justice before each House of the
Oireachtas. June 1981.

26. For the present situation, see J.M. Moynahan, *Prison Officer Training*, an unpublished paper presented to the Annual Meeting of the Academy of Criminal Justice Sciences,
11-14 March, 1981, Philadelphia, Pa.

27. *The Prison Study Group, An Examination of the Irish Penal System.* (Dublin, 1973),
p. 88.

It is noteworthy that while only recently as many as 82 percent of Irish prisoners served sentences of less than six months,[28] as of 1981, forty percent of sentenced prisoners served sentences of three years or more, with a considerable overcrowding problem resulting.[29] Probation has been in existence for some time, originally only in Dublin, but now organized country-wide by regions.[30]

The Irish Police owes its origin to the very same Sir Robert Peel who became the father of English police. Indeed, Sir Robert commenced his Irish reform work long before his English reforms, namely in 1812, when he arrived in Ireland as Chief Secretary. The result was the Royal Irish Constabulary, which continued to exist until dissolved in 1922, to be replaced by the fledgling Irish Free State's own civil guards, now known as the Garda Siochana. For all practical purposes, the Guard is an organization which, in training, demeanor and operation appears indistinguishable from British police organizations. Despite recent criticisms of the Guard, it has been acknowleged that "it has been well integrated with the people among whom it works."[31]

In the 1950's police duty in the Republic of Ireland was viewed as idyllic, owing to extremely low crime rates. This situation has changed somewhat in recent years. While the police statistics of the Republic of Ireland show an increase of over 100 percent in offenses reported, as between 1970 and 1979,[32] the crime rate of the country continues to be one of the lowest in Europe. Indeed, criminologists in many countries are prone to attribute statistical increases in reported criminality for recent years largely to a more effective communications system, greater public awareness and a willingness, on the part of commercial establishments, to record and report their losses due to criminal activity. Indeed, the lion's share of increased reporting of crime for Ireland is in the category composed of larcenies, fraud, and crimes of forgery and uttering.[33] However, as elsewhere in Europe, drug-related criminality has increased, and, as

28. *Ibid.*

29. *Annual Report on Prisons,* (Dublin: Department of Justice, 1981), p. 8.

30. *Op. cit., supra.* n. 16, p. 13. See also, Department of Justice, *Report on the Probation and Welfare Service with Statistics for the Year 1980,* (Dublin, 1981).

31. Conor Brady, *Guardians of the Peace,* (Dublin: Gill and Macmillan, Ltd., 1974), p. 249. See also Seamus Breathnach, *The Irish Police from Early Times to the Present Day,* (Dublin: Anvil Books, Ltd., 1974).

32. Garda Siochana, *Report on Crime 1979,* (Dublin, 1980).

33. *Ibid.,* p. 1.

a spillover effect from the unrest in the Ulster counties, so have armed raids.[34] This led to the establishment of a new detective squad to deal specifically with the organized-crime-connected drug traffic.[35]

The recent increase in reported criminality has led to lively debate about the limitations on the functioning of the criminal justice system, with sides being taken by civil libertarians (e.g., Nobel-laureate Sean McBride) arguing for improving the civil rights aspects of the system, while law enforcement officials contend for a removal of some of the limitations.[36]

34. See "Crime Pays: says Garda (police) Body Chief," *Irish Echo*. New York, 20 March, 1982, p. 82.

35. See "New detective squad to take on Dublin crime," *Irish Echo*. New York, 17 April, 1982, p. 1.

36. See, The Address by Commissioner Patrick McLaughlin to Members of the Honourable Society of the King's Inns, *Garda Review*, 10, No. 1, (January, 1981): p. 6.

European Socialist Countries

4

Bulgaria

INFORMAL SOCIAL CONTROLS

Introduction

The People's Republic of Bulgaria has one of the fastest growing economies in Eastern Europe. Since 1969 the urban population has exceeded the rural population.[1] The per capita national income has increased over four times within the past 20 years. These rapid changes have occurred within the context of an overall planning process. The development or modernization of each town is accompanied by the establishment of housing projects, cultural and communal centers, public utilities, adequate transportation service and a vast array of social services.

The country has an ethnically homogeneous population with

1. Ministry of Information and Communication, Research Institute on Statistics, Population and Population Policy, People's Republic of Bulgaria, Sofia, 1974.

TABLE 1: DISTRIBUTION OF NATIONAL BUDGET
(percentages)

Branch	1952	1972
1. Industry	29	51
2. Construction	7	9
3. Agriculture and Forestry	40	24
4. Transport and Communication	2	7
5. Trade	19	6
6. Miscellaneous	3	3
Total:	100	100

Bulgarians making up over 88% of the total. The country is divided
into 28 districts and 1,161 communes. Members of the People's
Councils, which govern each unit, assist the national government in
implementing its social and economic goals.

The basic unit of society is the family. The institution is
revered, assisted and protected.[2] Even though society as a whole
takes over many of the functions of child-rearing, there is pressure
put on parents to be highly responsible in their social duties and to
maintain a healthly home environment.[3] There are legal sanctions
against parents who fail to take adequate care of their young. Families with children enjoy a number of privileges, including maternity
leaves from 120 to 180 days, lump sum grants to mothers after the
birth of each child and monthly family allowances for each child
under sixteen years of age. Unwed mothers who are not working are
entitled to the full amount of the national minimum pay until the
child reaches age two.[4]

Considerable significance is placed on education, both moral
and intellectual. The process begins early in the life cycle when the
children attend nurseries, kindergartens and other specialized children's establishments. Three quarters of the pre-schoolers attend
these schools. Education is compulsory for those between ages seven
and sixteen, thereby virtually eliminating illiteracy. Classes are free
for all types and degrees of learning. The social and moral education
of young people is given particular attention. At the various children's establishments, which function in close relationship with the
family, moral concepts are being inculcated. Groundwork for the
development of good social habits and a keen sense of responsibility,
organization and collective responsibility is laid. An important
feature of the education is its emphasis on psycho-physical growth,
aimed at teaching how to join together in collective action, to be
loyal to each other, to be aware of the consequences of one's own
actions and to obey instructions of elders. "The establishment of a
proper attitude towards the public life that surrounds them, towards
nature and the native town or village . . . is an important task of
moral education."[5] Toward these ends, twenty-three percent of the

2. Ivan Stefanov and Nicola Naumov, "Bulgaria," in *Population Policy in Developed Countries*, (1974), p. 161.

3. *Ibid*, p. 159.

4. Communication from Ministry of Justice, Sofia, 3 March 1982.

5. Elka Petrova, Tsonka Sheitanova and Radka Slavova, *Pre-School Education in Bulgaria*, (Sofia: Sofia Press, 1979), p. 24.

public consumption funds were channelled into the development of
education in 1977.[6]

Closely in line with the accent on family and scholastic life for
the child are the arrangements made for recreation. Holiday homes
of trade unions and factories, and tourist hotels are almost exclu-
sively made available to families with small children or to the
students themselves. These resorts are at the sea or in the mountains
and are either free of charge or half of stated rates. Recreation centers
are also operated by the Ministry of Education and the Committees
for Youth and Sport.[7]

In 1971 the National Assembly approved a new Constitution
which, among others, provided for the following economic, social
and cultural rights of citizens: equality of men and women, special
protection for the intellectual, moral and cultural development of
children, work, rest (paid leave, cultural clubs), education, pensions
and free medical treatment.[8] In addition, the Constitution assured
women the right to vote, to be elected and to be active in public and
political life.[9]

There is virtually no unemployment in the country. Eighty-
four percent of the women are either working or are being trained for
jobs.[10] Workers are entitled to compensation during sick leaves and
women receive full pay while on leave before and after childbirth.
Monthly child allowances and pensions add to the wage incomes.
Bulgaria was also one of the first countries in the world to provide
state-financed old-age pensions, unemployment compensation,
work hazard compensation and a network of establishments for
retired citizens.

Along with the industrialization of the country, plans were also
made to provide adequate housing. About fifteen percent of the total
capital investment in the early 1970s went into housing in order to
insure that urbanization would not destroy the quality of life. In
addition, Bulgaria has a highly sophisticated program of health
services which deals with both environmental factors involved in
community health and with individual patients.[11]

6. *Women in the People's Republic of Bulgaria, Demographic and Social Survey*,
Committee for the Unification System for Social Information at the Ministers and the
Committee of the Movement of Bulgarian Women [sic], (Sofia: Sofia Press, 1970), p. 46.

7. "Women of the Whole World," *Journal of the WJDI*, No. 3, 1973.

8. Committee on Human Rights, 31st Session, E/CN.4/1155/Add. 8 May 21, 1974.

9. *Ibid.*

10. Penka Duhteva, *Working Women*, (Sofia: Sofia Press, 1970).

11. D.K. Sokolov, J.E. Asvall and H. Zöllner. *The Gabrovo Health Services Model in the*

The rapid industrialization brought with it the expected migration. Unlike in most other countries, this movement was not directed solely to the large cities, but rather also toward neighboring towns and villages. Indeed, almost half of the migrations occur within the same small territorial unit, and one quarter occur between neighboring districts. These patterns, then, enable the migrant to maintain old loyalties, family ties and allegiance to communal authorities. A deliberate policy was pursued of agglomerating medium and small-sized towns so that, through cooperation among several such contiguous settlements, culturally, socially and economically viable population areas could be created which would, thus, combine the advantages normally to be found only in much larger population centers, without, however, partaking of the disadvantages of large metropolitan areas. The result was a system of urban areas with "human dimension, closer to nature, healthy and comfortable living. . . ."[12] Lately there appears to be a reversal of even these limited migrations. With the modernization of agriculture and the levelling of living standards between town and country, young people are returning to their places of birth where they enjoy the accustomed rural living conditions, a tension-free life, and particularly the familiar surroundings of home and family.[13]

THE CRIMINAL JUSTICE SYSTEM

The transformation of Bulgarian society into that of a people's republic required the creation of a criminal justice system which, while alert to the traditions of Bulgaria, had to incorporate the experiences previously made by the Soviet Union, which had traversed the same route one generation earlier and, thus, provided a certain model. This task appears to have been a difficult one since most jurists and criminal justice administrators, because of their unreliability to the new order, had to be removed from office.

The first post-war Penal Code, of 1951, thus, was largely inspired by the U.S.S.R. Penal Code of 1926 without, however,

People's Republic of Bulgaria, Regional Office for Europe, World Health Organization, Copenhagen, 1980.

12. G. Gusti, quoted in Jiri Musil, *Urbanization in Socialist Countries*, (White Plains, N.Y.: M.E. Sharpe, Inc., 1977), p. 137.

13. Nevena Abadjieva. *Tradition and Modernity in Bulgarian Village Life*. (Sofia: Sofia Press, 1980).

departing altogether from the conceptualizations and terminology of prior Bulgarian law.[14] Article 2 of that code defined crime as a socially dangerous act and permitted the use of analogy in interpreting the code. The special part of the code emphasized offenses against the public order, economic criminality and acts dangerous to the community. Interestingly enough, by article 98, offenses against other workers' governments were specially punished, indicating the solidarity of the Bulgarian people with other peoples' republics.[15]

The Penal Code of 1951 was in force until replaced by the more advanced Penal Code of 1968, which was stronger in its insistence on "socialist legality." The new code is premised on the idea that penal law is an important, but not decisive, means for crime control. The code seeks to restrict penal repression to a minimum, relegating many aspects of crime control to other juridical and extra-juridical means. The provisions of the code provide for individualized and differentiated responsibility, aiming at re-education of offenders.[16]

New procedural human rights guarantees are anchored in the Code of Criminal Procedure and include the presumption of innocence, the guarantee of independence of the courts, equality before the law, and the rights to public trial, to be judged on the basis of properly adduced evidence, to have counsel, to participate in all proceedings, to speak and to raise objections, to have the last word at trial, to be protected by law and to appeal.[17]

Bulgarian penal law regards criminal punishment as an exceptional resort in crime control and provides for a wide variety of other reactions to crime, upon conviction. Article 37.1 of the code recognizes eleven such non-institutional sanctions. The code is marked by what is called a system of inducements *(régles de stimulation).* These inducements include a variety of socialization efforts, mainly resti-

14. In general, see N. Mancév, *Offenses and Antisocial Manifestations* (Bulgarian). (Sofia: BAN, 1967); Vesselin Karakasher, *Certain Problems of Crime and its Structure* (Bulgarian), (Sofia, 1977).

15. "Code Pénal Bulgare," in *Les Codes Penaux Europeens, vol. 1,* (ed.) Marc Ancel and Yvonne Marx, (Paris, n.d.).

16. J. Nenov. "Le nouveau Code Pénal de la R.P. de Bulgarie," *Rev. Sci. Crim. et de Droit Pen. comparée,* 25, No. 1 (1970): p. 13. See also *The Review Int. Comm. of Jurists,* 2 (1969): p. 6: for a German translation of the new code, see *Das Bulgarische Strafgesetzbuch,* vol. 16, März 1968, (Berlin: Walter de Gruyter and Co., 1973).

17. Radka Radeva, "Protection des droits de l'homme dans la procedure penale de la republique populaire de Bulgarie," *Rev. Int. de Droit Penal,* 49, No. 3 (1978): p. 78. See also J. Nenov, "Le Droit Penal Bulgare et l'humanisme socialiste," in *Etudes en l'honneur de Jean Graven,* (Geneve: Libraire de l'Universite, 117, 1969).

tution.[18] Particularly effective appears to be the public reprimand, expressed before a social group to which the offender belongs.[19] Prison sentences, when applicable, are normally of short duration.[20]

The administration of criminal justice in Bulgaria is comparable to that in sister Socialist states, resting on the common base of continental criminal procedure, and including extensive participation of the public.[21] With regard to minor offense categories the comradeship courts play a strong role, adjudicating minor infractions in a manner deemed effective in socializing the offender back into conformity with social demands and laws. In addition to comradeship courts there exists a "system of committees for combatting anti-social manifestations of under-aged and minors" which, at the central, district and local levels, are responsible not only for delinquency preventive efforts but also for dealing with delinquents. At the preventive level there exist "voluntary detachments of the working people for the preservation of public order and peace," charged with the general preservation of internal peace and tranquility, as well as special social bodies for securing traffic safety. This system of massive involvement of the public in overall crime prevention is supplemented by an equal participation of the public at the correctional end of the criminal justice process, e.g., the commissions of observers, who are charged by law to supervise the resocialization of offenders sentenced to deprivation of liberty by assisting the correctional administrators in this task. This tightly-knit network of community-based agencies, integrated with a disciplined professional criminal justice system, makes it clear that there is very little opportunity to remain beyond the reach of crime control.[22] Criminal law is viewed as only one of the variety of legal and social measures dealing with the phenomenon of crime. Family law ranks

18. A. Stoinov. "Politique penale et regles de stimulation dans le droit penal de la republique populaire de Bulgarie," *Quaderni-Rassegna di Studi*, (Anno 1- Maggio 1978): p. 109.

19. "Public Reprimand." (Bulgarian), *Soc. Pravo*, 21, No. 1 (1972): p. 42.

20. K. Ljutow. "Zur Effektivität der Kurzfristigen Freiheitsstrafe und der Strafen ohne Freiheitsentzug im Kampf gegen die Rückfallkriminalität," *Staat und Recht*, 17, No. 5 (1968): p. 794; Zdravko Traikov, "Privation de liberte de courte duree et son execution." *Quaderni-Rassegna di Studie*, (Anno 1 - Maggio 1978): p. 285.

21. Like other continental procedures, Bulgarian law permits a variety of offenses to be prosecuted only on complaint of the injured party. See Changes in proceedings concerning offenses which will only be prosecuted if a complaint is lodged, 13, No. 5, *Pravna Misal* (1969): p. 51.

22. Memorandum 99-00-7 of the Ministry of Justice, People's Republic of Bulgaria (1982).

high on the list of means by which the stability of the family can be enhanced, in an effort, *inter alia,* to serve as a secondary means of delinquency prevention.[23]

While, unlike in several Northern European countries, alcohol-related criminality was never a major danger, Bulgaria, being located on the natural drug traffic route from the Near East to Central and Northern Europe, was exposed to drug traffic, even though the ecnomic and social conditions for drug abuse are minimal. Thus, in 1971, the total known addict population of Bulgaria was 119 men and 91 women, and the unregistered addict population was thought to be at most 30 percent higher.[24]

When the drug traffic danger was recognized, tight border control and customs inspection measures were instituted and Bulgaria rigorously enforced the Single Convention of 1961, which it had adopted by Decree No. 634 of 22 August, 1963, and supplementary laws adopted pursuant to the Convention. In 1971, 80 convictions for drug smuggling were obtained. All defendants were foreigners, mostly Turkish nationals. The national response to the drug danger, thus, consisted of:

1. Popular and media preventive measures;
2. Strict adherence to international conventions;
3. Strict control of production and sale for medicinal use;
4. Strict import and export control;
5. Treatment of addicts; and
6. Criminal liability of dealers and traffickers.[25]

Bulgaria has a well-developed system for dealing with juvenile delinquency, with the emphasis resting on intervention before the onset of delinquency.[26] Social-educational measures normally are imposed, and adjudication, with possible correctional sentences, are resorted to only in rare cases.[27] The Bulgarian Code of Criminal

23. See Liliana Nenova. "Le nouveau code Bulgare de la famille," in *Union des Juristes de Bulgarie,* Droit Bulgare, Nos. 2-3.

24. Baitcho Panev, Todor Stankoucher, Alexandrina Ketchkova and Joulia Miteva. "Abus et trafic de drogues—Rapport de la Bulgarie," *Rev. Int. de Droit Penal,* 44, No. 2-3 (1974): p. 123.

25. *Ibid.*

26. "Protection of children in the Bulgarian Criminal Code." in *The Criminal Legal Protection of Children.* Proceedings of the Second International Symposium of Young Jurists. Vol. 1. Der Schutz des Kindes im Strafrecht der Volksrepublik Bulgarien. Protokoll des 2. Internationalen Symposiums junger Rechtswissenschaftler der AIDP, (1980): 51-55.

27. P. Zdravkov. "Special Provisions in the new Bulgarian Penal Code relating to Juveniles," (Bulgarian). *Soc. Pravo,* 16, No. 5 (1967): p. 79. Regarding the age of imputability, see P. Rajcev, "Irresponsibility in minors," (Bulgarian), 9, No. 4 (1965): p. 56.

Procedure provides a set of special rules for proceedings in juvenile cases.[28] Even where a sentence of confinement is imposed, the code provides for exercise of judicial discretion as to whether a prison or reformatory sentence is indicated, as to the length of the sentence and as to whether, upon coming of age, the youth offender should be discharged.[29]

While Bulgarian crime prevention and criminal justice efforts had always tended to be systematized, the actual completion of the system was accomplished when the State Council of the People's Republic of Bulgaria adopted, in November 1975, a "unified program to combat crime and other law violations and anti-social manifestations," which envisages the implementation, on a nation-wide scale, of a number of measures, socio-economic, organizational, technical, ideological and legal, for improving preventive activities and enhancing their effectiveness, for perfecting the work of the courts, the prosecutor's offices and the investigating authorities, as well as for raising the level of training of personnel. Similar to action taken in some nonsocialist countries for the implementation of the unified program tasks in criminal justice, an interdepartmental office for coordination and management of criminal justice activities was created with the participation of several ministries.[30]

In order to keep the Bulgarian crime rate as low as it is,[31] this centralized criminal justice co-ordinating body emphasizes crime prevention efforts. The emphasis is on regional comprehensive programs, subject to central, national, co-ordination. While the vast amount of organized popular participation—also noted in the assessment of the situation in the German Democratic Republic—is shared by Socialist countries, the regionalization and localization in planning and programming crime prevention efforts is probably unique to Bulgaria and cannot be found to the same extent in other

28. "Special rules for investigation of juvenile offenses in the Bulgarian Code of Criminal Procedure," in *The Criminal Legal Protection of Children*. Proceedings of the Second International Symposium of Young Jurists. Vol. 1. Die besonderen Vorschriften für die gerichtliche Untersuchung von Straftaten Minderjähriger in der Strafprozessordnung der Volksrepublik Bulgarien, in *Der strafrechtliche Schutz des Kindes*. Protokoll des 2. Internationalen Symposiums junger Rechtwissenchaftler der AIDP, 1980.

29. I. Volkov. "Some Data on Trials involving Juvenile Delinquents and the Penalties Imposed on Them." (Bulgarian). *Soc. Pravo*, 17, no. 3 (1968): p. 46.

30. Cable of the People's Republic of Bulgaria to the Sixth United Nations Congress on the Prevention of Crime and the Treatment of Offenders, Caracas, Venzuela, 1981.

31. After twenty years under socialism, the Bulgarian conviction rate had dropped from 629 convictions per 100,000 population (in 1944) to 226 (in 1963). See M. Angelov, "Sur la criminalite an république populaire de Bulgarie et les perspectives de son deperissement," *Soc. Pravo*, 15, No. 1 (1966): p. 52.

Socialist countries. It is interesting to note, in this connection, that local courts and prosecutors' offices, in dealing with individual offenses, are not only investigating the facts necessary for adjudication of the case, but also the general circumstances and conditions which led to its commission so as to recommend steps for subsequent preventive efforts under involvement of the community, especially the popular mass organizations.

5

German Democratic Republic

Introduction

Following World War II, a Socialist system of government was established in the German Democratic Republic. Large-scale industry became state-owned and agricultural estates were divided up and distributed to peasants, who are organized in collectives. The USSR gradually transferred government control to German authorities and on March 27, 1954, granted sovereignty to the country. Industrial development has surged since 1961 and presently the GDR ranks tenth in industrial output and second next to the USSR among the Eastern European States. With this increased industrialization, the economic importance of agriculture has gradually decreased, leaving only ten percent of the working population in this sector.

From early childhood through university, education is a primary concern of the GDR. Eighty percent of all children between ages three and six are cared for by kindergartens.[1] A ten-year course at a comprehensive school is free and compulsory. Afterwards a student may stay on to take the Abitur (advanced level examination with a baccalaureat), or may take an apprenticeship to become qualified for admission to either a technical school or a university.

1. *Women in the GDR, Facts and Figures,* Verlag Zeit im Bild. (Dresden: 1975) p. 66.

46

All young people have both the right and the duty to learn a trade and everyone is guaranteed a job upon completion of requirements.[2]

Along with formal education, the populace has informal learning experiences by participation in various organizations. In the Free German Youth, for instance, 1.8 million members participate in conducting the affairs of the country at all levels. Here the young are provided political experiences, including managing their own parliamentary group, called the People's Chamber. The German-Soviet Friendship Society numbers 4.5 million. There is also a strong commitment in the GDR to athletics (as evidenced by Olympic successes) with 2.5 million young people being trained in the Gymnastics and Sports Federation.[3] In sum, between kindergarten, nurseries, after-school centers, formal school and intensive participation in various organizations and clubs, the life of the country's young is full, active and useful.

As evidenced by the dispersal of the GDR budget, the quality of life is a major concern. Out of a total civil budget (1979) of 140,633.4 million marks, 25% goes toward this end. The distribution is:[4] (in million marks)

Education	7,227.550
Culture, Radio and TV	1,451.343
Sports	161.087
Recreation	208.955
Youth	57.453
Health and Social	6,940.202
Social Security	19,838.344
Total:	35,931.934

There is no unemployment in the GDR. All employees, dependents and special groups of persons (e.g., students) have state social insurance which provides for medical and dental services, maternity leave, sick pay and various pensions. There are also family allowances and paid annual holidays of 18-24 days. Improvement of the quality of life is, in addition, a major component of the

2. Winifried Purgand, "The Experience of the GDR in the Situation of Women in Technical and Vocational Education," *A Report to the United Nations Educational, Scientific and Cultural Organization, International Congress on the Situation of Women in Technical and Vocational Education.* (Bonn, Federal Republic of Germany: 9-12 June, 1980).

3. *Op. cit., supra,* n. 1.

4. *Statistisches Jahrbuch 1978, der Deutchen Demokratischen Republik,* (Berlin: Staatsverlag der Deutchen Demokratischen Republik, 1980).

planning process. It is estimated that in the aggregate the social wage for a family of four will amount to about 900 marks per month by 1985.[5]

Having "inherited a well-developed and stabilized settlement system," the Government of the GDR has endeavoured to avoid the unbridled growth of urban and especially metropolitan areas and has, instead, stimulated urban growth only where industrial and employment prospects guaranteed the socio-economic development of a region in such a way that the population could be well serviced, both economically and culturally.[6] Consequently, despite the phenomenal economic growth, the population still is basically situated in manageable population centers with populations ranging between 10,000 and 50,000, whose social infra-structure is intact.

THE CRIMINAL JUSTICE SYSTEM[7]

During the first phase of the existence of the German Democratic Republic, the old German Penal Code of 1871, amended, had been in force. It was replaced on December 11, 1957 by a drastically changed version, resting on socialist principles.[8] This code was replaced by the new Penal Code of January 12, 1968[9] adopted after extensive debates and discussions by citizens groups. "Its norms emphasize, bindingly, for everybody, the uniform political will of the working class and of working people allied with it, [and define] which acts, within the jurisdiction of the socialist state, have been subjected to criminal liability because of their anti-social nature or social danger, either as felonies or as misdemeanors, which must be

5. Directives issued by the 10th Congress of the SED for Five-Year Plan for the GDR's National Economic Development 1981-85, 62.

6. Jiri Musil, *Urbanization in Socialist Countries,* (White Plains, N.Y.: M.E. Sharpe, Inc., 1980) p. 100, *et seq.*

7. In general see, John Lekschas and Walter Hennig, "On the Historic Conditionality and the Social Character of Crime in the Advanced Socialist Society of the G.D.R." In *Law and Legislation in the German Democratic Republic,* 1, No. 2 (1979): p. 5; and Ulrich Dahn, "The General Tendencies of the Struggle against Crime and the Socialist Penal Legislation in the G.D.R." *Ibid.,* p. 15. See also Erich Buchholz, Richard P. Hartmann, John Lekschas and Gerhard Skiller, *Socialist Criminology,* (Westmead: Saxon House, D.C. Heath, Ltd, 1974). As regards juvenile delinquency and juvenile justice, see Irmgard Buchholz, "Problems of Juvenile Delinquency and Juvenile Justice in the G.D.R.," *Int'l. J. Comp. and Appl. Crim.* 5, No. 1 (1981): p. 29. For an informed West German perspective see Friedrich Christian Schroeder, *Das Strafrecht des realen Sozialismus,* (Opladen: Westdeutscher Verlag, 1983).

8. *Strafgesetzbuch,* Textausgabe. Berlin: VEB Deutscher Zentralverlag, 6th ed., 1966.

9. This code, as amended to 1979, is now available in an English text. *Law and Legislation in the German Democratic Republic,* 1, No. 2 (1979): p. 37.

combatted by the organized force of workers, which must be prevented, and which, if committed, must be vindicated with the sanctions provided for them."[10] The principle *nullum crimen, nulla poena sine lege* is applicable, i.e., all prohibitions and sanctions are legislated.

Criminal procedure is governed by the Code of Criminal Procedure of October 2, 1952. It is noteworthy that, pursuant to its Article 2, "criminal procedure is intended to educate toward respect for socialist law, socialist property, work discipline and democratic watchfulness."[11] Generally, the approach of the Code of Criminal Procedure follows continental European practice and incorporates most of the typical procedural guarantees. The code recognizes the prohibition of double jeopardy, except that prosecutions may be instituted on felony charges after conviction for a misdemeanor in the same matter, and that trial may be instituted after imposition of a violations punishment;[12] however, previously imposed and served punishments are deducted from subsequently imposed punishments.

The structure of courts is governed by the Law on the Constitution of Courts of October 2, 1952, which "created the basis for the further development of the relations between the local organs of state power and the organs of state justice, whose significance is steadily increasing in the complex battle against criminality and other violations of law and, thus, for the strengthening of legality."[13]

All components of the criminal justice system, governmental and social, function in a highly efficient manner. From the commission of the act to the sentencing of offenders, cases are disposed of quickly and effectively and with strict regard for legal procedures. "Trials are conducted publicly, orally and directly."[14]

The people's police has a reputation not only for efficiency and effectiveness in clearing crimes, but also in their preventive activity. "Every member of People's Police must be in a position to explain law to ordinary people and to see that socialist law is observed in everyday life. In public relations, emphasis is laid on making obser-

10. *Ibid.*, p. 19.

11. *Strafprozessordnung*, Textausgabe. Berlin: VEB Deutscher Zentralverlag, 1966.

12. *Ibid.*, pp. 17-18.

13. *Strafrecht—Allgemeiner Teil, Lehrbuch.* Berlin: Staatsverlag der Deutschen Demokratischen Republik, (1976) p. 104.

14. Erich Buchholz. "The Role of Penal Law in Combatting Crime in the German Democratic Republic," *Int. Rev. Crim. Policy*, 35 (1979): p. 49.

vance of socialist law a customary habit of all."[15] There is a high
clearance rate of offenses, particularly due to the fact that people
provide the police active support in the uncovering and clearing of
offenses. Accordingly, the German Democratic Republic has succeeded in keeping the crime rate low, and reducing it further over the
years.[16] Even after an unexpected increase by 9 percent, in 1978, the
rate of criminality per 100,000 population was reported to be only
one-sixth of that of the Federal Republic of Germany.[17] Minor
transgressions and irregularities are not overlooked but, inasmuch
as they may be symptomatic of impending major problems, are
followed up and, where necessary, prosecuted.[18]

The success of the system in controlling crime is, indeed, attributed to the extraordinarily large role which the population in general plays in the administration of justice. With the removal of
nearly all functionaries of the national-socialist administration of
criminal justice in 1945, there had been a virtual vacuum of personnel to run the new system of criminal justice, posited both by the
occupying power, the USSR, and those socialists who had survived
the holocaust and returned to what was to become the German
Democratic Republic. Consequently, a strong emphasis was placed
on the election of "the best factory workers and peasants as lay
assessors," i.e., as quasi-jurors in criminal cases. In 1949, 4,495 lay
assessors and jurors were popularly elected for service at the criminal
courts. Subsequently, Article 130 of the Constitution of the German
Democratic Republic institutionalized the election of lay assessors
and jurors.[19]

Even after the creation of a new cadre of jurists, committed to
Marxist-Leninist principles of justice, the participation, if not
prominent role, of the citizenry has remained a hallmark of criminal
justice administration in the German Democratic Republic. Citizen
involvement is "no abstract principle but a living day to day real-

15. *The Importance Offered by the Socialist Society for the Activities of the People's
Police of the German Democratic Republic which are Aimed at Preventing and Combatting
Crime.* Material submitted by the Delegation of the German Democratic Republic to the Fifth
United Nations Congress on the Prevention of Crime and the Treatment of Offenders,
Geneva, 1975.

16. *Op. cit., supra,* n. 13, pp. 42-52.

17. *East Germany's Crime Rate is Up: Government Orders More Publicity.* Special to the
New York Times, East Berlin, 5 May 1980.

18. U. Dähn und H. Weber, "Probleme der differenzierten Anwendung des socialistischen Strafrechts," *Staat und Recht,* 25, No. 8 (1976): p. 836.

19. G.O.W. Mueller, *Laymen as Judges in Germany and Austria,* (Chicago: University
of Chicago, 1954).

ity.''[20] Hundreds of thousands take an active part in conflict commissions in factories and enterprises, arbitration commissions in the cooperatives, judicial service, investigation of crime, reformation of the offender and prevention strategies.

There is a provision in the Penal Code which opens the way for much of this involvement by allowing criminal cases to be dealt with by social courts if:

> . . . in view of the consequences of an offence and the guilt of the offender the offence is not too injurious to society and if, in consideration of the offence and the personality of the offender, an effective reformative influence can be expected to be brought about by a social court. Such cases are to be transferred by authorities concerned with the administration of justice, provided the factual circumstances have been completely clarified and the offender has admitted his guilt.[21]

The social courts are made up of locally elected persons who volunteer to take on extra duties after work and without pay. There are approximately 30,000 social courts with a membership of 270,000.[22] Decisions are made on the basis of public, informal discussion of the circumstances surrounding the offense, consideration of the crime, the condition of the offender, and the reform measures that would most benefit the offender and his community.

Another effective component of the crime control system is the national commitment to prevention strategies for counteracting criminogenic conditions in society, and for enhancing the social responsibility of the populace through positive reinforcements, such as the 1975 nation-wide competition for the best crime prevention proposal[23] or the 1974 competition among 20,000 collectives (3,400,000 people) for the title of "District with Model Order and Security."[24] Local communes also plan for an integrated program of crime prevention and control based on the commitment of all

20. *Op. cit. supra.* n. 14, p. 53.
21. Art. 28, para. 1 of the Penal Code as reprinted in Buchholz, *Ibid.*
22. Erich Buchholz. "The Social Courts in the German Democratic Republic—Bodies of Criminal Justice," *Int. J. Comp. and App. Crim. J.* 4, No. 1 (1980): p. 38.
23. See *op. cit. supra.*, n. 15.
24. H. Blüthner and U. Dähn. "Actual Problems and Results in the Battle Against the Prevention of Criminality in the German Democratic Republic," Nordiska Samarbetsradet, *First Seminar for Criminologists from Socialist and Scandinavian Countries* in Helsinki, Finland, August 26-29, 1974.

members, including children.[25] Of special significance is their
responsibility for the rehabilitation of the offender through the
provision of a meaningful job, social services and a solid support
system.[26] Above all, Marx's advice is revered and followed to the
effect that "the wise legislator will prevent crime in order not to have
to punish it, namely by establishing social living conditions that are
favorable to and worthy of man."[27]

25. Harri Harrland. "Zwanzig Jahre Kampf für die Zurückdrängung der Kriminalität in
der DDR." *Neue Justiz, Zeischrift fur Recht und Rechtswissenschaft*, (Juliheft 1960): p. 13. See
also Harri Harrland, "Trends and Control of Crime in the GDR." *Int. Rev. Crim. Policy*, 35
(1979): p. 49.

26. See, in general, Günter Lehmann, *Zum Entwicklungsstand der marxistisch-
leninistischen Theorie der Vorbeugung der Tat im Sozialismus, Postsdam-Babelsberg.*
Akademie für Staats- und Rechtswissenschaft der DDR, 1978.

27. *Op. cit. supra*, n. 14.

Latin American Countries

6

Costa Rica

INFORMAL SOCIAL CONTROLS

Central Americans frequently refer to Costa Rica as the Switzerland of the Americas. This comparison is justified, despite the fact that Switzerland has no oceans while Costa Rica has two, and Switzerland has snowcapped mountains while snow never falls in Costa Rica.

Costa Rica is one of the smallest of the Latin Ameican countries, with a basically homogeneous population, the majority of whom are of European descent, mostly Spanish. Blacks and Indians constitute small minorities. The country has a history which is rather different from that of its Latin neighbors. These had suffered the effects of the Iberian conquest, the importation of African slaves and the drafting of Indians.[1] Costa Rica experienced none of these. The small indigenous labor force diminished over the centuries. Absent an indigenous labor force, large estates could not be maintained. All farming was done on small farms, where family members had to work their own plots. A dispatch from the year 1718 reported that "everyone has to grow the food his own household needs, even the governor himself, for if he did not, he would die."[2] The settlers had a "natural right" to toil as much land as they needed for subsistence. Survival necessitated humility, mutual aid and a strong

1. "Costa Rica," *People*. London, 7, No. 2 (1980): pp. 14-20.
2. *Ibid.*, p. 14.

sense of social obligation, values which are still basic to the culture.[3] While social classes exist there is little class consciousness, with major emphasis being placed on human rights and social peace.

Because of its climate and fertile soil, the *Valle Central* has become the political, social and commercial center occupied by fifty-five percent of the total population and eighty percent of urbanites. Costa Rica is one of the least populated countries in Central America and has one of the highest gross domestic products. Political stability and the high educational level of the workers stimulated foreign investments which, in turn, expanded industry and opportunity. Although it still suffers some of the problems of developing countries, i.e., unemployment and underemployment, the job market is growing faster than the labor force, thereby easing the problem considerably. Unemployment went from 7% in 1963 to 4.5% in 1978.[4] The country is predominantly rural, mostly dependent on agriculture, especially coffee and bananas.[5] The government tries to discourage the concentration of the population in overcrowded areas, by allotting better services and resources to rural regions.

Families are tightly-knit groups in which male, female and child roles are exactly defined. Catholicism is the official religion of the country and is practiced by most of the population. The Church places a strong accent on the strength of the family unit and the maintenance of religious values in the home. By and large, basic tenets are strictly adhered to. While women are responsible for the functioning of the household and the care of children, there has been a steady increase of their number in the work force. In addition, women are attending the university, becoming politically active and, generally, taking part in all dimensions of social life. Family planning is handled by both public and private agencies. These have played an important role in both rural and urban areas. The birth rate has dropped from 48 per 100,000 in 1959 to 29.6 in 1975. All education is free, for children between six and thirteen it is compulsory. An investment of thirty percent of the budget in education has paid off with a return of ninety percent literacy and of ninety-seven percent school attendance for those between six and thirteen.

The Costa Rican Government places prime importance on

3. "Peripheral Capitalism and Rural-Urban Migration: A Study of Population Movements in Costa Rica," *Latin American Perspectives*, 7 (Spring/Summer 1980): pp. 75-90.

4. *Op. cit., supra.* n. 1.

5. *Profils demographiques.* (New York: Le Population Council, Juillet 1974).

meeting the basic needs of its citizens. This has historical roots in the eighteenth century, when the owners of the large estates then still in existence were expected to extend help to their poorer compatriots. This strong social consciousness constituted the basis for the country's social welfare system composed of workers' compensation, family assistance programs, and insurance benefits for sickness, maternity, disability, retirement and death. Costa Rica has no armed forces. Money saved on a defense budget goes to social welfare. Though poverty still exists, the quality of life is better than in Costa Rica's sister nations. Life expectancy is seventy-two, infant mortality has steadily decreased, and the malnutrition rate for children is 22 percent below the average for Central America.[6] The country has one of the most effective health systems in the world. The strength of the system lies in the fact that health care is decentralized in the form of local health posts. Each post consists of one man and one woman who keep files on each of the families within their district, make home visits for teaching prevention and aiding the sick, and gather the information used for making decisions on local health priorities.

In keeping with the strong accent on social welfare, there has been an affirmative action program for the fourteen thousand indigenous Indians. The National Commission for Indian Affairs was created in 1973 and since then has expanded reserves, made the land tax-free, and improved living and working conditions generally.[7]

Communal self-help groups have been active throughout the country. Villages have created associations for such efforts as building schools, health centers, sewage systems and fresh water supplies. Under one of the more ambitious programs neighbors band together to build homes and residential districts. Low mortgage rates are available for such projects.

"The character of present-day Costa Rica was set in 1943 in a letter written by Jose Figueres, who three times since then has been the country's leader. . . . In setting goals for the nation, Figueres listed (1) honesty in government; (2) liberty for the people; (3) professionalism in public administration; and (4) a distinct social orientation"[8] as the principle premises of the Costa Rican approach to communal life. The country has adhered to these premises.

6. *Op. cit., supra.*, n. 1.
7. *Social and Labour Bulletin*, International Labour Organization, Geneva, No. 1 (January 1980).
8. Encyclopedia Britannica, op. cit., supra, p. 213.

THE CRIMINAL JUSTICE SYSTEM

Costa Rica has managed to build a strong criminal justice system, anchored on a completely independent judiciary. Costa Rica's judges are elected—albeit by the legislature—pursuant to Articles 157 and 158 of the Constitution of 1949. Perhaps nowhere else is judicial independence as solidly founded as in Costa Rica: the Constitution (Article 177.2) provides that a sum of no less than six percent of the ordinary state income estimated for the year must be allocated to the judiciary.[9]

The organic law on the exercise of judicial power requires judicial control of corrections. Under Article 221, criminal court and municipal court judges are obligated to visit their local prisons and jails once a week, unannounced, to make sure that citizens imprisoned are properly lodged, fed and treated.[10]

The emphasis is on citizens for, indeed, few foreigners are in Costa Rican prisons, and relatively few Costa Ricans in prison have been sentenced: sixty percent of all inmates are pre-trial detainees, a figure which is high by world standards, yet low by Latin-American standards.[11]

The Penal Code and the Code of Criminal Procedure of Costa Rica are typical of those in force in the Americas. The Penal Code, Law No. 192 of 30 August 1941, covers the serious offenses, while the "Police Code," of the same vintage, covers minor offenses.[12] The Code of Criminal Procedure, in Latin-American fashion, is basically inquisitorial in orientation. A great number of procedural acts are required before a case can go to trial—which, in itself, may explain the large number of pre-trial detainees. There even was a reluctance to switch from the inquisitorial trial *in camera*, to a public trial, albeit the grounds of reluctance were said to be that the character of the defendant might be exposed to the public.[13]

9. Pan American Union, *Constitution of the Republic of Costa Rica*, 1949.

10. Atilio Vincenzi. *Ley Organica del poder judicial*. (San José, Libreria las Americas, 1957).

11. ILANUD (United Nations Latin American Institute for the Prevention of Crime and the Treatment of Offenders), *United Nations Training Course on Human Rights in the Administration of Criminal Justice*. (San Jose: Imprenta Nacional, 1975).

12. *Codigo Penal, Codigo de Policia,* (San Jose: Imprenta Nacional, 1950.) See also Atilio Vincenzi, *Codigo Penal y Codigo de Policia,* (San Jose: Imprenta Trejos Hermanos, 1965.) This edition also contains, *inter alia,* Ley de Reforma Social and Ley organica de la jurisdiction tutelar de menores, i.e., the juvenile justice code.

13. Manuel Lopez-Rey. "The Correction of the Criminal Offender in Latin America," in

Costa Rica has endeavored to introduce modern correctional practices. Suspended sentences may be granted for first offenders, where the offender has complied with social norms before the commission of the crime, where he/she is repentant, where the offender has tried to reduce the harm occasioned by the offense, and where the sentence which can be imposed is less than three years. Correctional establishments are operated humanely, and it has been reported that medical and psychological services are particularly favorable in the prison for women, which is administered by nuns, although not under religious regime.[14] Like other Latin-American countries, Costa Rica maintains an island prison, for serious offenders, at San Lucas Island. The writ of Habeas Corpus is available to test the legality of confinement.[15]

In the early 1950s Costa Rica, influenced by the world-wide social-defense movement, as particularly fostered by the United Nations, passed a Social Defense Law, of which it was expected that it would provide a pro-active solution to the crime problem. A national department of social defense was legislated to deal with all aspects of crime and delinquency, and a superior council of social defense was created to co-ordinate these activities. Article One of this law explained that the law was established:

> For the purpose of formulating and co-ordinating social action for the prevention of delinquency, crime control and the effective treatment of dangerous and anti-social elements with a view toward their useful readaptation into the community.[16]

The law also envisaged the establishment of a National Crime Prevention Institute. These plans did not materialize but, in lieu of establishing a national institute, Costa Rica invited the United Nations to establish, in San José, its regional Latin-American Institute for the Prevention of Crime and the Treatment of Offenders, which, since 1975, has played a leading role in research and training for the region. Costa Rican officialdom in the field has been a

International Corrections, (eds.) Robert J. Wicks and H.H.A. Cooper (Lexington: D.C. Heath and Co., 1979): p. 76.

14. *Ibid.*, p. 84.

15. Habeas Corpus Law, No. 35, of 24 November 1932. See Atilio Vincenzi (ed.), *op. cit.*, *supra*, n. 12.

16. *Ley de Defense Social*, with an introduction by Victor M.L. Obando Segura, Director de Defensa Social, 1953.

prominent beneficiary of the institute, so that, by now, it is safe to say Costa Rica has a forward-looking and effective criminal justice system, ranging from its non-conscript national (and district) police force, to the judiciary and to the correctional system.

Of particular significance within the general social defense orientation is Costa Rica's pro-active approach to juvenile justice, which exists side-by-side with the more traditional, but nevertheless progressive, system to deal with juvenile delinquency.

Pursuant to Article 25 of the Penal Code of 21 August 1941, juveniles below age 17 are exempt from criminal liability. They are, normally, assigned to their own families for treatment or, in lieu thereof, to an "honorable" foster family, for supervision, under the guidance of the National Committee for Children (Article 114). The National "Patronage" for children was created in 1930 (Law No. 39 of 15 August 1930), and the Children's Code was promulgated on 25 October 1932. The Juvenile Court was established by law of 17 August, 1937. The entire system emphasizes non-judicial, non-punitive procedures and interventions, aiming at the protection and upbringing of children. Special provision was made to assist mothers, to provide recreational facilities and services for children, and to care for children with special needs. Under Article 119 of the Penal Code, which pertains to children between 13 and 17 years of age, the emphasis is still heavy on parental control, with resort to institutional treatment restricted only to dangerous youngsters. Delinquents sent to such institutions may be transferred, upon reaching age 17, to special adolescent sections of adult prisons. The concern for endangered youngsters is also exemplified by the Children's Code, which defines ten categories of offenses *against* children, including parental neglect.[17]

Above all, the Costa Rican social defense attitude, aiming at prevention of crimes in the first place by reaching youngsters in the most endangered age range, is exemplified by a national

> program of instruction, designed for all students between 13 and 15 years of age, which is designed to promote feelings and attitudes of respect for the law, the family, civic institutions and the rights of others. It is a deliberate plan to show the place of the individual and the family in society. This focus

17. Jose Rafael Mendoza. "Les legislations de l'Amerique Latine relative a la delinquance juvenile; Systeme de Costa Rica." in *Societe Internationale de Defense Sociale*, Actes du Cinquieme Congres Internationl de Defense Sociale. (Stockholm, 1958): pp. 351, 422-426.

on the primary institutions of social control is regarded as a
potent strategy in the prevention and control of anti-social
conduct.[18]

18. *Incorporation of Crime Prevention Policies in Educational and Vocational Training
Programs. Report of the Secretary-General, E/A.C. 57/ - 1978.*

7

Peru

INFORMAL SOCIAL CONTROLS

Introduction

Peru, the third largest nation in South America, is a land of great economic, cultural, social and climatic diversity. In 1826, after three hundred years of Spanish rule, it became an independent nation. Throughout its history, from the time of the conquerors to the present, military governments have figured predominantly in internal affairs.

There are three major geographical regions: the coastal plain, the High Sierra of the Andes, and the inland wooded foothills and rain forests. Natural disasters have been an integral part of Peruvian life. For example, in 1959, most of Cuzco was destroyed by one earthquake, and, in 1970, another one took 70,000 lives, destroying six towns in the Sierra Valley. Quakes, avalanches, floods, volcanic activity and drought conditions have cost losses of up to eighty percent of crops, causing near starvation conditions. The population of the country in 1970 was probably not much greater than in Inca times.

Since the beginning of the republic there has been a small upper class made up primarily of descendants of Spanish colonists which, together with the military and the Roman Catholic hierarchy, has been the source of political power.[1] In 1968, General Juan Velasco Alvarada, commanding General of the Army and President of the Joint command, took over the Presidency, dissolved the Congress and challenged the old regime. Thus began a major transformation of the social structure toward that of a participatory model where either the workers or the state would own and operate the industrial and agricultural enterprises. By 1977, this plan was abandoned and a new policy was instituted which focussed on the restoration of private enterprise.

The ethnic structure is made up of whites, mostly descendants of Spanish colonialists, Indians, the indigenous population, and mestizos, a mixture of the two. The Spanish continue their heritage of European culture, the Spanish language and their Catholic religion. They still own most of the wealth. Although the mountain Indians, who make up half of the population, live in poverty, there is little conflict between the ethnic groups. The Indian population lives relatively isolated, some working as tenant farmers, some as day laborers at a minimal subsistence level. The prevailing pattern of living in Peru is the farm village where people live in small groups and cultivate the land. Due to the difficulty of travel in a country criss-crossed by ravines, on 30,000 miles of unpaved roads, settlements stay isolated, thus impeding the development of a sense of national unity.

Despite a changing society, most Peruvians, both of Indian and Spanish ancestry, continue to retain traditional ways of family life. The kinship group provides the mainstay of social stability. The majority of the Indian population lives in the hinterland, where many small groups lead a nomadic existence in search of simple subsistence. These units are basically extended families governed on the basis of custom and consensus rather than formalized law. They have little contact with the outside world. To survive they must depend on each other. This means that tribal values rather than individual interests remain dominant. The Hispanic population also leans heavily on traditional family units and group loyalty. Individuals seek their security and well-being from the mutual support of kin. Loyalty to one's family is an overriding obligation, carrying a moral priority which is greater than any other social

1. Thomas E. Weil, Jan Knippers Black, Howard I. Blutstein, David S. McMorris, Frederick P. Munson and Charles Townsend, *Area Handbook for Peru,* (Washington, D.C.: Government Printing Office, 1972.)

obligation. The patriarchal pattern stresses a reverence for the past and a duty to uphold the honor of the group. Beliefs based on the sanctity of interpersonal trust and personal worth *(personalismo)* are closely tied to the belief that men cause events to happen rather than impersonal social forces. No matter from which class a person comes, tradition dictates that everybody treat everybody and be treated in a dignified fashion.

Closely tied to the strength of the family are the traditional religious values. There is a wide diversity of indoctrinations, including various polytheistic, pantheistic and fetishistic religions. Complex ethnic and cultural mixtures include Spanish mysticism and African practices. In addition to Catholicism, there is a proliferation of Protestant sects. The power of religion in Peru is strong and pervasive, permeating daily life and providing a strong sense of group solidarity. There is no universal system of social security. By and large the indigenous population depends on the kinship group for assistance and support. While education is free and compulsory for ages six through fifteen, the average amount of schooling in 1970 was three years. Nearly all secondary schools are in urban districts.

Despite steady improvements,[2] massive problems remain. Infant and child mortality rates continue to be high. With a growing number of public health programs, there is a dramatic shortage of doctors and nurses. Within the indigenous tribes there remains a great distrust of modern medicine. The *curandero,* as traditional medical practioner, continues to use supernatural remedies, magic and varieties of herb mixtures. The country as a whole still suffers from poor conditions as to sanitation, water, sewage, electricity, refrigeration and housing. In addition, Peru has some of the worst poverty in Latin America, with a per capita income below the continental average.[3]

Commercial agriculture, subsistence agriculture and fishing employ forty-five percent of the labor force. There is a high unemployment rate of an estimated forty percent in the active labor market. One-half of the population exists on subsistence farming outside the cash economy. Nearly half a million depend for their livelihood on fishing.[4] Between 1973 and 1978 the standard of living

2. The 1980-83 health care plan calls for permanent service to 5.7 million people at 423 health centers and 1,153 first-aid stations.

3. Rosemary Thorp and Geoffrey Bertram, *Peru 1890-1977, Growth and Policy in an Open Economy.* London: MacMillan Press, 1978.)

4. Economic Report, *Peru.* (London: Lloyds Bank, Limited, March 1980.)

has gone down, with real wages dropping forty-seven percent while prices for goods and services increased. The protein and calorie intake is below the FAO established minima.[5]

An estimated one million persons migrated from the hinterland to the cities between 1940 and 1961 and the movement increased throughout the 1960s and 1970s. These migrations follow a distinct pattern. Initial moves are not directly to the cities. Rather, individuals go from subsistence farms to provincial towns where they can begin their preparations for a new life. The process of transition includes learning Spanish, giving up local Indian customs and preparing for non-agricultural jobs.

Peasants who successfully complete the assimilation process are the ones most likely to take the next step to the city, including Lima and Callao. For those who do migrate to these large cities, assistance is provided by regional clubs, consisting of people from the same area of origin, who function as both a security system and a socializing agent for the newcomer. They help the individuals not only with employment, education, etc., but also with the maintenance of group ties. It is not uncommon for a group living together in a tenement community *(callejon)* to gather at nightfall and move together to a selected suburban site. They bring with them prefabricated mats, poles, furnishings and belongings and by morning new communities called *pueblos jovenes* (young towns) have been created. Loyalty to one's group is a revered value.

THE CRIMINAL JUSTICE SYSTEM

Peru has a distinguished history of scholarship in law. Lima is the seat of the oldest university of the Americas, San Marcos University, founded in 1551. Education in law has been a tradition. Due to the large number of lawyers in the country, many are forced to practice marginally. Because of the devotion to legal scholarship, the system of codes and laws is regarded as at a par with the best in Latin America. The Penal Code was adopted on 24 July 1924. It is of the Continental-Latin-American model.[6] Subsequent code projects,

5. James Petras and A. Eugene Havens. "Peru: economic crises and class confrontation." *Monthly Review—New York*, 30 (February 1979): pp. 25-41.

6. See Julia D. Espino Perez, *Codigo penal, concordancias.* (Lima: Editorial Juridica, 4th ed., 1968.) An up-to-date version of the Penal Code is contained in Ricardo Levene (h.) and Eugene Zeffaroni, *Los Codigos Penales Latinoamericanos,* 3 (1978): p. 271.

and the participation of Peruvian scholars in the project of a Latin American Model Penal Code, have not yet led to a new codification of Peruvian substantive penal law. Criminal justice is administered pursuant to the Code of Criminal Procedure of 1940.[7]

Law enforcement, in typical Latin-American fashion, is entrusted principally to a *Guardia Civil.* The administration of justice rests principally with local courts, which have investigating and summary jurisdiction. Above these are the district courts (tribunal correctional), with general jurisdiction. These are normally composed of three judges. Appeals lie to the Supreme Court.

The preparation of a criminal prosecution commences with the investigation under the direction of the investigating magistrate *(juez instructor),* although much of the day-to-day work may be carried out by judges' clerks, including the taking of confessions and of the testimony of witnesses. All evidence is taken down in writing. These preliminary proceedings normally will take several months. It is only when the case has been fully investigated that the judge will summarize all evidence and provide his legal evaluation of the case. The file will then go to the prosecutor *(Ministerio publico*—a semi-autonomous branch of the judiciary) who, exercising considerable discretion, may present the case for trial. Unlike the preliminary proceedings, trial is public and constitutes a blend of written and oral proceedings, which begin with the reading of the prosecutor's report. Most of the evidence from the preliminary proceedings is read out in court. The same witnesses who testified in the preliminary proceedings may be heard again. Defense counsel may ask questions only through the court. After all the evidence is in, the prosecutor, or *fiscal,* makes his accusations and comments. While the defendant has the last word, this right is rarely exercised. The judges then deliberate briefly in chamber and return with a detailed written judgment and sentence. Both defense and prosecution have the right to appeal. The Supreme Court may increase sentences and frequently does so.[8]

Freedom of the press allows the mass media to exercise a consid-

7. F. Bonilla, *Codigo de procedimientos penales con todas sus modificaciones (anotado).* (Lima: Editorial Mercurio, 1968.)

8. H.H.A. Cooper. "A Short History of Peruvian Criminal Procedure and Institutions," *Revista de Derecho y Ciencias Politicas,* 32 (1968): pp. 215-267. *Idem, "Medico-Legal Problems in Peru," Int. J. Off. Therapy and Comp. Crim.* 19 (1975): p. 191. *Idem,* "The Administration of Justice in Peru," *Judicature,* 53, No. 8 (March 1972): pp. 338-340; *Idem,* "Peru's 'New Look' Judiciary," *Judicature,* 53, No. 8 (April 1972): pp. 334-337. *Idem,* "Law and Medicine in Peru," *Chitty's L.J.* 24, No. 1 (1976.)

erable public-opinion-making function in criminal cases. Many of
the due process guarantees exist in criminal procedure, including
the privilege against self-incrimination and the right to communicate with counsel. Bail exists, but is rarely granted.[9] Incommuni-
cado detention up to 10 days is permitted and the presumption of
innocence, as such, does not exist.[10]

When not suspended during times of military administration,
the writ of habeas corpus is available.[11] It has been said of the
Peruvian administration of criminal justice: "Peru has a copious
body of laws and lesser regulations, but much of this excellent
normative material remains dead letter. Delay, especially in criminal cases, is a notable feature of the judicial administration."[12]
Another noteworthy feature of criminal trial is its "adhesion" procedure, by which an injured party may stimulate, or participate in, the
criminal trial for purposes of recovering damages. Since criminal
trials are free, yet civil proceedings costly, many crime victims resort
to the criminal process for recovering damages. That temptation
may exist not only in homicide and general assault cases, but also
and especially, in sexual assault and statutory rape cases. It has been
reported that more than one third of all Lima defendants are charged
with sexual offenses, mostly committed on girls below age 16.
Unless financial satisfaction is offered in such cases, the inclination
is to prosecute all persons who have had sexual contact with the
victim. The penalties for statutory rape were increased from a maximum of three to one of five years. The remainder of Peru's relatively
small criminal population has been described as follows:

> The hard-core delinquency problem in Peru centers on
> Lima, whose criminal class is relatively homogeneous and
> well established with its own distinctive mores and folklore.
> Compared with other similar countries, the Peruvian crimi-
> nal case is decidedly backward; in attitude, it is parochial,
> almost clannish. Hence, the "new" population does not drift
> into crime, neither by invitation nor by contagion. Those of
> its members who are found in the prisons of the capital are

9. Bail, which is granted in accordance with the nature of the offense, is now governed by
Decree Law #18978.

10. Domingo Garcia Roda, "Proteccion de los Derechos Humanos en el proceso penal
Peruano," *Rev. Int. de Droit Penal,* 49 (1978): p. 233.

11. Domingo Garcia Delaunde. *El Habeas Corpus Interpretado,* (Lima: Industrial Grafica, 1971.)

12. H.H.A. Cooper, "Medico-Legal Problems in Peru," *Int. J. Off. Ther. and Comp.
Crim.* 19 (1975): p. 191.

there mainly because of innate propensities; a proclivity for
drunkenness and brawling common among those of the
highland stock, [or] economic necessity.[13]

Obviously, recidivism among the criminal class is relatively high,
and increased sentences are applicable.[14]

The administration of juvenile justice rests with juvenile
courts, the first of which was established in 1924, pursuant to the
provisions of the Penal Code adopted in that year, with jurisdiction
over youngsters between thirteen and eighteen years of age.[15] In
more recent years, police juvenile squads, specially trained for the
purpose, have begun dealing with the problem of urban juvenile
delinquency.[16]

Peru's correctional system has been governed by new legislation, passed on 16 April 1969 (Decree Law 19581). The law states as
its purpose the correction of criminal offenders, their classification,
the creation and expansion of the activities of the correctional
administration, introduction of the progressive system, the training
of personnel, the organization of prison labor and social and other
services, the classification of institutions, pre-release periods and
parole and post penitentiary assistance. Moreover, "the 1969 Peruvian law states that the personnel should be selected in accordance
with its social mission and shall possess academic or technical
knowledge."[17]

This legislation also incorporates the United Nations Standard
Minimum Rules for the Treatment of Prisoners.[18] The new legislation further envisages full compensation for prison labor.[19] Accord-

13. H.H.A. Cooper, "Crime, Criminals and Prisons in Peru," *Int. J. Off. Ther. and
Comp. Crim.* 15 (1971): p. 135.

14. J.L. Apaza Ramos, "La reincidencia en el Codingo Penal Peruano," *Rev. Policia
Tecn.* 36 (1969/70): p. 382.

15. See Helen L. Clagett, *The Administration of Justice in Latin America,* (New York:
Oceana Publications, 1952): pp. 133-114. Title XVII of the Penal Code is devoted to "Treatment of Juveniles." For a detailed discussion see Jose Rafael Mendoza, "Les Legislations de
l'Amerique Latine relative a la delinquance juvenile." Systeme Peruvien, in *Societe Internationale de Defense Sociale,* Actes du Cinquieme Congres International de Defense Sociale.
(Stockholm, 1958): pp. 351, 402-405.

16. J. Bernal Comez, "La policia y los problemas que causan los menores inadaptados,"
Rev. Policia Tecn., 38 (1971): p. 381.

17. Manuel Lopez-Rey y Arrojo, "The Correction of the Criminal Offender in Latin
America," in International Corrections, (eds.) Robert J. Wicks and H.H.A. Cooper (Lexington: D.C. Heath and Company, 1979): p. 71. See also H.H.A. Cooper, *Commentarios sobre la
nuova legislacion penitenciario en el Peru.* (Lima, 1972.)

18. *Ibid.*

19. Art. 42 of Decree Law 17581.

ing to knowledgeable observers, for a variety of reasons, these worthwhile provisions of advanced correctional legislation have not been put into effect, either for lack of funds, or for lack of training of personnel and, above all, because 75 percent of inmates in prisons are awaiting trial and, thus, are not subject to correction, as yet.[20] Lopez-Rey regards the entire correctional legislation as highly theoretical and not in tune with the real social conditions.[21]

Indeed, the detached criminological observer gets the impression that Peru is saddled with a formalistic system of criminal justice, advanced in some respects (correctional law), retrograde in others (the inquisitorial criminal procedure), but, above all, somewhat remote to both social conditions and advanced criminological thinking. The impression exists that, somehow, Peru's low crime rate is not explainable by reference to its unpopular criminal justice system.

20. H.H.A. Cooper, "Prison Problems in the U.S.A. and Peru," *Int. J. Off. Ther. and Comp. Crim.* 16, No. 1 (1972): p. 25. Also *Idem,* "Peru's Island Prison of El Fronton," *Int. J. Off. Ther. and Comp. Crim.* 13 (1969): p. 183.

21. Lopez-Rey, *op. cit., supra,* n. 17.

Islamic Countries

8

Algeria

INFORMAL SOCIAL CONTROLS

Introduction

Algeria, the second largest country in Africa, is an independent socialist republic, situated in the northwest of the continent. By virtue of history, language, custom and the Muslim religion, it is an integral part of the Arab world. The population is made up of indigenous Berbers and Arabs, who have intermingled to such an extent that it is difficult to distinguish pure ethnic types. In 1954, the Muslim majority began a war of independence against France, the colonial power. After seven years, the French succumbed and almost the entire European population of nearly one million left the country. With their departure, many businesses and farms closed, leaving an estimated seventeen percent of the active male population unemployed and twenty-eight percent underemployed.[1] The war was also responsible for over one million Algerian deaths, which left twenty-nine percent of married women widowed.

Since 1962 the Government has been laying the foundation for economic growth. The initial strategy involved heavy restrictions on the importation of "luxury" items and a strong commitment to building the capital-intensive sector (hydrocarbon, iron and steel,

1. "Land, Man and Development in Algeria." Part II: *Population, Employment and Emigration,* Field Staff Report, 1973, North African Series, Vol. VXII, No. 2.

chemical, engineering). This was followed by the 1974-77 four-year plan which turned attention to more labor-intensive projects, to small industry and to agricultural improvement.[2] The Government has either nationalized or taken a controlling interest in most foreign-owned companies.

Algeria is still primarily an agricultural country with ninety percent of the land consisting of area plateaux, desert and mountains. The economic development is financed ninety percent by oil and gas exports. Algeria is one of the most important oil-producing countries in the world and the largest exporter of liquified natural gas. In addition to local industry, the Algerian economy has relied on worker migration. Between 1930 and 1970, close to four million Algerians have migrated out of the country for extended periods of time. Presently, thirteen percent of the wage earners are in France, along with 230,000 of their children under eighteen. The annual earnings of those workers abroad support over one and a half million Algerians at home.[3]

According to Muslim tradition, the strength of the family is central. Group values are stressed, and individuals are thought of in terms of the families to which they belong and which provide strong social controls. Although there is a policy to modernize the female role, most women retain the traditional role of caring for the private life of the family. They are, however, increasingly represented in schools, training programs and the labor force. They participated actively in the liberation struggles and are entitled to vote and run for election.[4]

After independence, the Algerian Government encouraged the citizens to renew traditions and to become responsible for their futures. Development became focussed on education, health, recreation, social security and job training. Planners have designed their strategies based on the assumption that the move from rural to urban areas involves about 400,000 persons a year.[5] This planning process is responsible for the fact that, despite the extensive growth of Algiers (450,000 in 1954 to 1,953,000 in 1972), the city is still *"Alger la blanche"* and even though there is unemployment, there are few persons of marginal status (e.g., beggars) on the streets.

  2. Lloyds Bank Limited. *Economic Report.* (Algeria, February 1980).

  3. *Op. cit., supra.* n. 1.

  4. National Union of Algerian Women. *Report on the Role of the Algerian Women in the Economic Development of their Country.* Submitted by the Algerian Delegation to International Women's Year Regional Seminar for Africa, April 1975.

  5. *Op. cit., supra.* n. 1.

Shanty-towns have virtually disappeared.[6] All citizens have a right
to free medical services. Education is free and compulsory with
special aid programmes being established in the poorest regions
where education is considered as important as irrigation. The
Government allots more money to this area than to the military, and
high priority is placed on teacher training and adult literacy. Television plays a major role in national education programs. Youngsters
at school are urged to spend their vacations working and teaching in
the rural areas.

Since 1965 the Algerian Government has prompted the active
participation of citizens in affairs of state. Decentralization has
placed much of the primary responsibility for social, economic, and
cultural activities in the hands of the commune. All citizens are
grouped together in one of these units and members are expected to
handle their own affairs under the aegis of the national government.
Communal assemblies are elected by the local citizens. In addition to
planning and directing economic and social matters, particular
emphasis is placed on the educational and social activities of young
people.

THE CRIMINAL JUSTICE SYSTEM

French arms conquered Algeria in 1830; French law followed
soon thereafter and still continues its conquest, albeit in diminished
form. The French Penal Code and Code of Criminal Procedure
became the law of Algeria, although Islamic courts were permitted
to administer the Sharia for some time, and Berber courts administered tribal law; but efforts were made to subject the entire population to French law. This effort met with great difficulties. As
Maunier recalls, among the Khabylioun (Berber) population,
Rekba (homicide to revenge honor) is a duty, yet the French Code
calls it murder. Prosecution, however, is virtually impossible: no
witnesses can be found. Nobody knows anything about the event.[7]

The local justices of the peace and quadis having lost their
jurisdiction, French law being virtually ineffective via-à-vis the
native population, the French introduced the *indigénat* (native
code) system to the Algerians.

6. *Ibid.*, p. 12.
7. René Maunier, *Independence, Convergence, and Borrowing in Institutions, Thought
and Art,* (Cambridge: Harvard University Press, 1937): pp. 84-85.

This involved the addition to the penal code of special provisions permitting the French authorities to administer on-the-spot discretionary justice to their African subjects for minor infractions. These definitions defined certain acts when committed by native inhabitants and prescribed special procedures and punishments for those involved. The system also permitted colonial authorities to impose collective punishments, including fines, on whole villages or tribes. Its provisions did not apply to French or other European citizens.[8]

It has been said that this segregated criminal justice system contributed substantially to the revolutionary fervor of the Algerians, perhaps as much as the infamous guillotine which was kept busy at Barbarossa prison against the Algerian freedom fighters of the F.L.N.

It is perhaps extraordinary that, with the achievement of independence in 1962, Algerians continued the French legal system, perhaps in a purer form than before the revolution, certainly in the sense that inequalities were abolished. Fifty-eight prisons were closed, and the *indigénat* system fell by the wayside.[9] Subsequent efforts clearly show an earnest determination to apply the rule of law to all Algerians, under a well-established system of codes, albeit, with punishments that, over the years, were increased in order to curb abuses, especially of an economic and political nature.

With independence and the withdrawal of the French, combined with the revolutionary fervor to establish indigenous control and socialism, the country initially faced serious difficulties, mainly due to lacking expertise. One French writer refers to a paralysis of the judiciary, following the revolution. The myth of independence of the judiciary and of socialist justice, said he, had two victims: the judiciary and public power.[10] Algerian accounts were more optimistic,[11] and, indeed, it appears that Algeria has done rather well over the years in establishing an effective and humanitarian criminal justice system, but—and here is the paradox—largely with continued French assistance and expertise and by adherence to the

8. Harold D. Nelson, (ed.). *Algeria—A Country Study.* (Washington, D.C.: American University, 1976). Hereinafter referred to as *"Country Study."*

9. *Ibid.*, p. 309. And see, Alan Milner, *African Penal Systems,* (London: Routledge and Keegan Paul, 1969): p. 10.

10. Etienne-Jean Lapassat, *La Justice en Algerie, 1962-1968,* (Paris: Armand Colin, 1969.).

11. See Democratic and Popular Algerian Republic, Ministry of Information, Documents on Self-Management, 1964.

French legal system. At the same time, Algerians were looking to the Socialist countries for new models.

In 1966, Algeria adopted a new Penal Code and a new Code of Criminal Procedure.[12] The French parentage of both is undeniable, and only the Economic Offenses Ordinance is clearly in line with the type of statute which Socialist countries had adopted early on, in an effort to protect the state planning process.

> The most uniquely Algerian aspect of the [Penal] Code [itself] is the section designed to protect and advance the economy. The provisions of this section, which constitute the greatest departure from French legal traditions, reflect the ethos of the socialist evolution.[13]

At first an effort was made to create a "unity judge," who would provide for a uniform system of first instance justice. This system did not work out.[14] The new Code of Criminal Procedure of 1966 returned to more traditional concepts. The judicial organization consists of three organs: Prosecutors, responsible for prosecution; Investigating Magistrates, responsible for the "instruction," i.e., the preparation of the case for trial; and the Courts themselves, responsible for adjudication and sentencing. Jurisdiction is exercised at three levels. (1) *Le tribunal*—a single judge—*(section penale)* has jurisdiction over minor offenses *(contraventions)* and misdemeanors *(delits)*, while *le cour (chambre penal)*—three judges—hears appeals from *"le tribunal."* Felony cases *(crimes)* are adjudicated in the *"tribunal criminal,"* where three judges sit jointly with four jurors (lay assessors). In addition, special courts exist to deal with matters of juvenile delinquency, consisting of acts committed by persons under 18 years of age which, if committed by adults, would be violations of the penal code. Juvenile Courts are composed of one judge and two specially qualified lay assessors as consultants.[15] Special courts have been created, such as the Court of State Security and Courts for Economic Offenses, in which specialists in economic matters, including industrial workers, sit as magistrates and jurors.[16]

12. Codes of 18 June 1966, published in the *Journal Officielle de la Republique Algerienne*, Les 10 et 11 Juine, 1966. See Mahmoud M. Mostafa, *Principles de Droit Penal des Pays Arabes*, (Paris: 1973) p. 18.

13. *Country Study*, p. 295.

14. *Op. cit., supra*, n. 10.

15. M. Salah Bey Mohamed-Cherif, *La Justice en Algerie*, (1969) 3-6.

16. *Country Study*, p. 297.

The 1966 reforms have endeavored to bring Algerian-French justice in greater accord with socialist principles. It is noteworthy, however, that the *"action civile,"* under which injured parties may join the prosecution and recover damages, has been retained.[17] The Constitution of 1976 envisaged further innovations intended to bring the Algerian criminal justice system in line with socialist principles. Justice is no longer to be regarded as simply judicial power, but as an exercise of state power, political power. The debate about the new Constitution clearly indicates a searching for a congruence of the French-inspired system with socialist principles and, indeed, Islamic heritage. Unresolved remains the question whether, as is the custom in Socialist countries, the judiciary should be popularly elected. (The constitution is silent on this point.)[18] Heavy reliance, in these debates, on the experience of the Eastern European Socialist countries is noteworthy.

The Algerian legislation stresses the human rights aspects of criminal procedure. The presumption of innocence, demanded by the Universal Declaration of Human Rights (11 § 1), is anchored in Article 123 of the Code of Criminal Procedure. While preventive detention is recognized by the code—as it is in France—this procedural device is viewed very critically, and handled with restraint.[19]

A massive reform of the correctional system was accomplished by a new Code *(Code Algerien le l'organisation penitentiaire et de la reeducation),*[20] which switches the correctional approach to one which is consonant with the various promulgations of the United Nations in such matters (especially the United Nations Standard Minimum Rules for the Treatment of Prisoners). Reformation, re-adaptation, assistance to discharged prisoners and humane intramural conditions, have been legislated. The execution of a prison sentence is viewed as a measure of social defense, with the emphasis being placed on individualized treatment, aiming at reformation. An inter-ministerial committee supervises the implementation of the new approach; new national observation centers have been created. In particular, the "progressive system" has been established, which recognizes "semi-liberty" and conditional release. As in

17. M. Salah Bey Mohamed-Cherif, *op. cit., supra.* n. 10, p. 11.

18. Walid Laggoune, "La Justice dans la Constitution Algerienne, 22 Novembre 1976," *Rev. Alger. des sc. juridiques, econ. et polit.* XVIII, No. 2 (1981): p. 73.

19. M. Salah Bey Mohamed-Cherif, "La detention preventive dans la pratique judiciare," *Rev. Alger. des sc. juridiques, econ. et pol.* XIV, No. 1 (1977): p. 15.

20. *Journal Officiel.* 22 February and 3 March 1972.

France, a specially appointed judge, the "judge for the execution of sentences," supervises the proper execution of sentences.[21]

The law enforcement system is likewise built on the French model: the *Sûreté Nationale* is the primary policing authority in the cities and other urban centers, while the *Gendarmerie Nationale* polices the rural areas. Both forces are well trained and well-equipped, with considerable French assistance. Despite the successes of both forces, it appears that, in recent years, certain crimes, including drug trafficking and economic offenses, have been on the increase, while offenses of violence, thanks to an extremely strict system of gun control, have been kept in check.[22] There is no doubt that the suffering of the Algerian people under a harsh system of colonial criminal justice has resulted in a system which emphasizes a humanitarian approach.

21. Ahmed Lourdjane, "La reforme penitentiaire en Algerie," *Rev. Alger. des sc. juridiques, econ. et pol.* XV, No. 1 (1978): p. 75.
22. *Op. cit., supra*, n. 8, pp. 297-302.

9

Saudi Arabia

INFORMAL SOCIAL CONTROLS

Introduction

Saudi Arabia, the largest country in the Middle East, has a total area of 865,000 square miles and occupies about four-fifths of the Arabian Peninsula. Much of the country is desert, especially the southern part of the Kingdom, composed primarily of the Rub'al-Khali (or Empty Quarter), the world's largest continuous sand area, covering 250,000 square miles. The largest concentration of oases are located in the Eastern Province. The country has the largest known oil deposits in the world.

Saudi Arabia had been inhabited for centuries by self-governing and independent tribes. The national structure of present-day Saudi Arabia dates back to 1932, when Abd al-Aziz ibn Saud succeeded in defeating rivalling tribes to unite the three principal areas of Al Hasa, Najd and the Jejaz, to form the Kingdom of Saudi Arabia.[1] The success of Abd al-Aziz was highly dependent upon the Saudi family's support of, and commitment to, a puritanic Islamic outlook established in the 18th century by the Islamic revivalist Abd-al-Wahhab, who had preached a return to classical law and to the basic teaching of the Koran. Rejected by his family, Abd-al-Wahhab allied

1. T. McHale, "A Prospect of Saudi Arabia," *International Affairs.* (Oxford Univeristy Press, autumn 1980): pp. 624-626.

himself in the second half of the 18th century with Mohammed bin
Saud, an able and ambitious desert warrior, who then committed
himself to a jihad (holy war). The combination of religious zealotry
and military leadership led to the expansion of Islamic Puritanism
and Saudi political dominance, an alliance which remains the basis
of political power in the country today.

Saudi Arabia is a non-constitutional monarchy. Authority rests
ultimately with the king, who holds the positions of *"Sjeolj"* (tribal
leader), *"Imam"* (Commander of the Islamic faith) and *"Malik"*
(head of the secular state). The king is responsible for protecting the
institutions of Islam as well as the interests of the nation. There is a
central government consisting of a 25-member Council of Ministers,
appointed by the king. The Council advises him in matters of policy
and in the direction of the state bureaucracy. Legislation is administered by royal decree and justice is based on Islamic law *(Sharia)*.
The Government makes use of the Arab tradition of the *"majlis,"* by
which any citizen may petition the king or governing leader for a
sitting. This system allows for frequent and extensive contacts
between the ruled and the rulers. The *"ulema,"* who are religious
scholars and clergy are the administrators of *Sharia* and are the
authorities on questions of religion. They represent an independent
force in Saudi society, for they rule *with,* not *for,* the royal family. In
extreme cases, they can even censure the Government, as was the case
in 1964 when the king was judged unfit to rule.

The population of Saudi Arabia is estimated to be between
5,074,000 and 7,740,000.[2] Resident aliens account for more than one
million. Saudi Arabians are a relatively homogeneous ethnic group
with Sunni Moslems making up the overwhelming majority of the
indigenous population. All Saudi Arabians speak Arabic. There are
four traditional settlement areas; the Najd, Hijaz, Asir and Al-Hasa.
Najd is the political as well as the geographical heartland of the
country and includes the capital of Riyad. The Hijaz, in the West, is
the location of the holy cities of Mecca and Medina, as well as
Jiddah, the Kingdom's primary port and diplomatic centre. It is also
the home of the merchant class. Asir is the highland region South of
Hijaz where people live in mountain villages and are less conservative than other Saudi Arabians. Blacks who have mixed with Semites
inhabit the Red Sea Coast. Al-Hasa, more commonly known as the
Eastern Province, is located along the Persian Gulf. Saudi Arabia's
largest minority, the Shia Muslims, accounting for about 10 percent

2. Encyclopedia Britannica, *supra*, 1977, v. 16.

of the population, are concentrated in this area. As the region of principal petroleum production, it houses most of the resident aliens, i.e., Americans and Europeans, as well as non-Saudi Arabs (Palestinians, Yemenites, Jordanians, Lebanese, Egyptians, Syrians) and workers from Turkey, Pakistan, India, South Korea, Taiwan and the Philippines.

The family is the most important social structure in Saudi Arabia; family loyalty and influence pervade all aspects of social, economic and political life. The individual's loyalty to his family overrides most other obligations. "An individual's well-being is the responsibility of the whole family and the family's well-being is the individual's primary concern."[3] The role of the family is particularly important in marriage arrangements. Marriages are arranged by parents and the usual practice is to marry a first cousin. But the family's role also extends to political appointments, business arrangements and general access to the inner political elite. "Political power, business prowess and social influence all are derived from traditional family patterns and political alliances which date back generations and even centuries."[4]

Social activities are also usually restricted to family affairs and small gatherings among close friends. Saudis rarely seek public entertainment; drinking alcohol is forbidden; cinemas and dancing are prohibited. Division between men and women in Saudi Arabian society is very marked. Until very recently, the majority of Saudi women were illiterate (to 1966) although now educational opportunities are available in segregated schools and classrooms. The activities of women are still very restricted. They are not allowed to work in jobs or frequent areas where they could come into contact with men, to drive automobiles, or to travel independently. Most women appear fully veiled in public and are unveiled only in the company of male relatives within the confines of their own homes. They do, however, wield significant influence within the family. While they have not, in the past, supported aggressive feminism, nor directly challenged the existing order, the role of Saudi women is undergoing change. Since educational opportunities have opened up, many young males with secular educations have expressed preference for educated wives, and some have even married women of foreign countries instead of members of their families. In addition, the near exclusion of women in the work force is being taxed by

3. *Op. cit., supra*, n. 1.
4. *Ibid.*

the country's grave lack of manpower. As Planning Minister Nazar has stated, "The issue is not whether women will work, but where."[5] Thus, conditions are present which could lead to an important change in the family life of Saudi Arabian society.

"Unlike Egypt, Iraq, Syria and Yemen, with their historically important pre-Islamic civilizations, Saudi Arabia's contemporary ideology is based on a near total Islamic cultural heritage and historical experience. Islam permeates all aspects of Saudi life, not just as a state religion but as the very basis of the state.[6] The Islam of Saudi Arabia, dominated by the puritanical teachings of Mohammed ibn Abd-al-Wahhab, "is a belief in one God, a warm transcendent God to whom man must submit, or resign his fate. . . . Members of the Islamic community do not separate the spiritual from the temporal; everything in society is believed to partake of the religious essence, and all the elements of the society are part of the collectivity of Islam."[7] Faithful Moslems are obliged to perform five tasks, called the Five Pillars, consisting of repetitions of the testimony of faith (called the Shahadah: "There is no God but Allah; Mohammed is the prophet of Allah"), prayer (five times daily), fasting, almsgiving and pilgrimage. Islam requires the payment of a religious tax for charitable purposes. In Saudi Arabia, this alms tax, called "zakat," is the only tax collected by the Government from its citizens. Often referred to as the "land of the prophets," there is a deep sense of respect in Saudi Arabia for the protection of the holy cities of Mecca and Medina and for the well-being of all who make the Haj (pilgrimage). Ramadan, the ninth month of the Moslem year, is an important religious period.

The Koran, as Islam's holy book consisting of the words and teachings of God, is not only a religious document but also an all-encompassing social, political and economic code. The word for Moslem law, "Sharia," means the "path to follow."[8] "The idea of religious pluralism in the Kingdom has neither meaning nor support in any segment of the population."[9]

Obedience to the practices of Islam is enforced by the *Muttawa,* the religious police. Although some degree of liberalization has

5. T. Lippman, "Census Confirms Saudi Fears," *The Guardian,* June 12, 1977.

6. *Op. cit., supra,* n. 1.

7. R. Murop, *Area Handbook for Saudi Arabia,* 1977. Foreign Area Studies, American University.

8. "Moslem Justice—Islam's Revival Spreads Use of the Sharia Law." *Wall Street Journal,* May 11, 1979, pp. 1, 30.

9. *Op. cit., supra.* n. 1.

occurred (i.e., the ban on smoking is seldom enforced; there is a decline in the performance of daily prayer; some women are not wearing the full-length veil or covering their faces), the religious police still play an important role in regulating dress habits and public behavior.

Until 1954, organized education available at the village level was in the *"kuttabs,"* where the local *imam* (religious scholar) was the teacher. School curricula focussed on the memorization of the Koran and the few boys who did go to school usually did not attend for more than a few years. At major urban centers, schools were few. Due to Government policy, education has been greatly expanded in the 1970s. According to the 1975-80 (1935-1400 A.H.) Second Development Plan of the Kingdom, education has become one of the country's highest priorities, utilizing 25 percent of the Government's development budget.[10] Despite the opportunities for extended learning, most pupils do not continue beyond the primary school level. Although education is free, it is not compulsory and many Saudi Arabians do not consider formal education a valuable asset to their lives.[11]

There are now several programs which provide a basic minimum of education for the largest possible number of students. Grants are available for students and parents to ensure that school attendance does not cause financial difficulties for the family. Generous scholarships are available for those who wish to study abroad. "An extraordinarily high proportion of (these) Saudis return home. Neither the political system nor the constraint of the world's most conservative society seems to deter them."[12]

School curricula preserve many elements of traditional Islamic education, with secular subjects usually introduced in the secondary school level. "In the first grade, 75 percent of the school day is devoted to Arabic and writing and 14 percent to religion and Moslem law. In the second, third and fourth grades, the emphasis shifts to religious education. . . . Science is not taught and about 10 percent of class hours is given over to teaching of arithmetic."[13]

More than three-fourths of the population is rural with about

10. The Ministry of Planning, Kingdom of Saudi Arabia, *Second Development Plan, 1975-80*, p. 529.

11. R. Knauerhase, "Saudia Arabia's Foreign and Domestic Policy." *Current History*, (January 1981): pp. 18-22.

12. D. Hirst, "Saudi Arabia—A Sense of Fraternity," *The Guardian*. July 10, 1977, p. 8.

13. *Op. cit., supra.* n. 1.

54 percent of the active labor force involved in agriculture.[14] Many of
these are Bedouin, nomadic or semi-nomadic desert people, who are
estimated to make up between one-third and one-half of the total
Saudi Arabian population. In recent years, urbanization has
occurred at a rate of 6 percent per annum.[15] This growth is due to the
increased economic opportunities afforded by the oil industry, to
Government settlement policies and to the improved health care
available in the cities. By 1974, 24 percent of the total population
lived in the cities.[16] The major shift from rural to urban settlements
has caused severe overcrowding. Inadequate and insufficient housing remains today one of the most serious social problems facing the
country.[17]

The evolution of Saudi Arabia from a country dependent on
herding and date farming to a country that is the third largest oil
producer in the world has caused a change in the lives of the people.
One example is the emergence of a "new Saudi Arabian middle
class," consisting of managers, administrators, technicians, clerks,
teachers of modern subjects, etc. The first social group composed of
members brought together not by family ties but by personal skills
and qualifications is beginning to form.

One of the major problems facing the country is the lack of
available and educated manpower. The country is crucially dependent upon foreign workers to perform menial tasks as well as to fill
jobs requiring specialized training. There are approximately one
million foreign workers in the country, which means that there is
about one foreign worker for every Saudi in the work force. In some
cities, like Jeddah and Dammam, Saudis are a "minority in their
own land."[18] The Government is very concerned about the country's
dependency on such a large foreign labor force and, therefore,
encourages advanced education for its own citizens and strives for a
diversification of foreign labor in order to prevent any one group
from gaining a strong position.

The belief that it is incumbent upon the more fortunate
members of society to assist the less fortunate is deeply ingrained in
Moslem culture. Alms-giving and care of the poor is a religious
obligation enforceable by law. Familes are expected to take care of

14. *1977 Compendium of Social Statistics*, United Nations, New York, 1980.
15. *Op. cit., supra*, n. 1.
16. The 1977 *Compendium of Social Statistics* quotes 20.7% for 1975.
17. *Op. cit., supra*, n. 1.
18. *Ibid.*

the ill, aged, handicapped, widows, orphans, etc. In fact, generosity, especially from relatives, has been expected even to the extent of self-impoverishment.

A Ministry of Labour and Social Affairs, created in 1962, has developed an extensive pension and social security system, as well as a variety of social welfare programs including institutions for the rehabilitation of the handicapped, assistance to agricultural cooperatives and facilities for juvenile delinquents. Financial aid grants are available for children, for housing and for those affected by natural or social calamities. There is free medicine and medical care for all citizens and foreign residents. In 1980, there were sixty-seven hospitals, with yet others nearing completion. Despite the advancement of modern medicine, however, the belief in a supernatural origin of disease has not entirely disappeared.[19]

Communication ties have been extensively developed within the last twenty years. In the 1960's a road system connecting major population centers was completed and paved roads have been extended since then. Automobiles have become a common mode of transportation and even the Bedouin are driving trucks more often than camels. Air transportation also has been developed and in the 1970s Riyadh began accepting international flights. Air travel is one of the most common means of transportation for the Haj pilgrims. There is also a railway from Damman to Riyadh.

The introduction of television in 1967, constituted a logical step toward modernity. Until television appeared, no portrayal of the human form was permitted (for example, in painting). Television programs are censored to assure that foreign programs do not offend Saudi political and social values. About 30 percent of the programs are foreign broadcasts, about half of which are American in origin. Radio has also been expanded and there are now about 28 receivers per 1000 inhabitants.[20] The international radio services in Jiddah broadcast programs in seven different languages. Most newspapers and periodicals are published by privately-owned organizations, subject to the provisions of the Press Law. There are also popular periodicals published by the Government and by Aramco, which are distributed free of charge. Telephones and telegraph services were introduced in the country in 1926 but did not become widely available for general public use until the 1970s.

19. *Ibid.*, n. 1., pp. 18-22.
20. 1978 Statistical Yearbook, United Nations, New York, 1979.

THE CRIMINAL JUSTICE SYSTEM

King Abd al-Aziz Ibn Saud has been credited with the achievement of establishing internal security and organized justice in an
area which previously had little of either.

> Before his consolidation of the Saudi state, constant intertrib-
> al raiding for livestock and other loot and conflict over graz-
> ing areas or water rights characterized the life of the nomadic
> bulk of the population; crimes against persons and property
> were rampant and generally went unpunished even in cities.
> Settled agriculturists lived in terror of Bedouin raids, and
> each year hundreds of Moslem pilgrims to the holy cities of
> Hejaz were attacked and robbed.[21]

By bringing the tribes under the central government, King Abd
al-Aziz undertook to eliminate thievery and violent crimes. He
enforced justice based on Sharia and made the nomads, whose
traditional judicial practices were based on "urf" (tribal customary
law) subject to the laws of the new Kingdom. Sharia, as revealed in
the Koran, thus, is the basis of law, and particularly of criminal
justice, for Saudi Arabia. Its administration rests, ultimately, with
the King. It would be superficial, however, to regard Sharia as
simply the basis of the criminal justice system. It is, rather, the
proclaimed and ordained way of life, to be followed as a matter of
course and of duty and propriety if not piety. The need to resort to
the Sharia's penal provision is infrequent.[22] By the same token, the
King is not simply to be regarded as the chief law enforcement officer
in his capacity as Head of State and of Government, rather, he is the
custodian of the way of life, as unalterably proclaimed by the
Prophet.

21. Fahed al-Thakeb and J. Scott, "Islamic Law: An Examination of Its Revitalism,"
British Journal of Criminology, (January 1981): pp. 58-68. On Islamic Criminal Justice in
general, see (ed.) M. Cherif Bassiouni, *The Islamic Criminal Justice System*, (New York:
Oceana Publications, Inc., 1982.)
22. "The penalty system does not play a major role in Islamic legislation although in
others it is considered much more important." Taufeeg Ash-Shawy, Ministry of Interior,
Kingdom of Saudi Arabia, *The Effect of Islamic Legislation on Crime Prevention in Saudi
Arabia*, Proceedings of the Symposium held in Riyadh, 10-21 Shawa 1396, A.H. (9-13 October
1976). Translated, edited and printed in collaboration with the United Nations Social Defense
Research Institute (UNSDRI), Rome, 1980, p. 552; hereinafter referred to as "Proceedings."

A learned scholar of Islamic law has characterized this dual approach as follows:

> In order to protect the five important indispensables in Islam (religion, life, intellect, offspring and property) Islamic law had provided a worldly punishment in addition to that in the hereafter. Islam has in fact adopted two courses for the preservation of these five indispensables. The first is through cultivating religious consciousness in the human soil and the awakening of human awareness through moral education, and the second is by inflicting deterrent punishment which is the basis of the Islamic criminal system.[23]

Saudis credit the Sharia—in its multi-faceted function—with their low crime rate, which persists despite the enormously rapid economic development which the country has been experiencing. They do not necessarily attribute the low crime rate to the prescribed sanctions which, to Western observers appear harsh. For one thing these sanctions, capital or corporal, are relatively rarely utilized[24] for, while the provisions of the Sharia, with its sanctions, are immutable as the word of God, rules of evidence and procedure are largely deemed man-made and have been progressively changed so as to avoid the imposition of harsh sentences. (Some Western observers see herein the impact of the world-wide contemporary human rights movement on a system, the human rights aspects of which are of ancient vintage and appear formally immutable). Indeed, it has been recognized that

> When a certain crime is widespread the magistrate must choose the severest punishment; but when the particular crime decreases in the course of time, punishment should become lighter.[25]

As crimes have decreased, punishments have become lighter. The sources of Islamic criminal law are as follows:

The Holy Book (Quran—Koran)
Prophetic Reports (The Sunnah)

23. Mohammad Salam Madkour. "Defining Crime Responsibility according to Islamic Legislation," in *Proceedings*, pp. 91, 101.
24. It appears that between 1972 and 1976 one hand was amputated. Farouk Abdul Rahman Mourad, in *Proceedings*, p. 360.
25. Tawfug Al-Shawi, in *Proceedings*, p. 84.

The Consensus of Opionion of the Learned Scholars (Ijma)

Analogy (Kias)

Equity (Istihsan)

Textually Unspecified Interests of the Public (Muslaha Mursala)

Avoidance of Harm (Sad Al-Dharai)

Compatibility of Means and Ends (Istishab)

Checking What is Permissible and Prohibited

The fundamental principle is that everything is permissible (Halal) unless it is specifically prohibited, condemned, disproved or even frowned upon.[26] The Sharia recognizes two types of offenses: specified and unspecified. Of specified offenses, which are identified in the Koran or in the teachings of Mohammed (Alsunna), these are two types: Hadd (plural Alhuddoud) and Alkasas. Alhuddoud crimes are those which are committed against the rights of God. There are seven of these: (1) adultery or fornication; (2) accusing a person of adultery or fornication without proper evidence; (3) apostasy from the Islamic religion; (4) drinking alcohol in public; (5) theft; (6) highway robbery; (7) treason. For each of these crimes there is a specified punishment of either stoning, whipping, severing a limb, or capital execution. The punishments are to be imposed regardless of whether victims, judge or public demand leniency, but, the prosecution of Alhuddoud crimes requires such strict standards of proof, which cannot be compromised, as to make convictions extraordinarily difficult.

The second type of specified offenses are "Alkasas," offenses against the individual. These are premeditated assault and accidental injury. In these cases, penalties are imposed on the principle of "Aldia"—equal compensation or punishment for the harm or loss experienced. Penalties for unspecified crimes, known as "Altazeer" are given at the discretion of the "qadi" (judge) or by an "ijma" (the consensus of the majority) of local ulema.[27]

Islamic law is based on the principle of individual criminal liability of a person with capacity. Thus, children before coming of age, sleepers until they awaken and the insane until they become sensible, are not criminally liable. Nor are the concepts of corporate

26. See Sheikh Mohammad Ibn Ibrahim Ibn Jubeir. "Definition of Crime according to Islamic Law and Islamic Legislative Sources," in *Proceedings, passim.*

27. *Proceedings, passim.*

liability or liability for the acts of others (vicarious liability) recognized.[28]

The procedural system of Saudi Arabia rests on independent courts, with judges learned in the Sharia. Indeed, they must be graduates of Sharia colleges, and only scholars of high standing, long experience, capability and loyalty are selected and nominated by the Head of State. Judicial independence is underscored by the fact that judges cannot be removed from office or transferred. They enjoy immunity for any of their judicial actions. The requirement of integrity and impartiality prohibits them from exercising their judicial power in any cause in which they have the least interest or relation.

The court structure consists of courts of summary jurisdiction, a single judge presiding, as well as courts of general jurisdiction. The Supreme Religious Court, composed of seven judges, has jurisdiction over serious crimes. A series of courts of first instance, and appellate courts, located in Riyadh and Mecca, complete the structure, except for the Supreme Court of Saudi Arabia, which can revise a sentence imposed by any other court.

Complaints to initiate a criminal prosecution may be lodged by a private party, or, more frequently, by the police. After preparation of the case for trial, proceedings are open and public, in the presence of all parties, all of whom have the right to speak. The rules of evidence require proof through real evidence, documentary evidence or the testimony of witnesses.[29]

Saudi Arabia's juvenile justice system is particularly advanced and well-endowed. The system is designed primarily to ease the child into adulthood with its life commitment under Islam. Reforms were introduced in 1972 which created "social reformation centers" for endangered youngsters between 7 and 18 years of age. In 1974 a Supreme Council for Youth Welfare was established, and in 1979 a "Functional Committee on Childhood Welfare" was created, charged with the function of establishing national public policy on childhood welfare and the preparation of appropriate programs.

Children adjudicated as delinquents are lodged in any one of four social reformation houses. In 1977 these received 323 delinquents. Youngsters actually sentenced to youth punishments are being sent to a youth reformatory, at Riyadh or Jeddah.[30] Here, too,

28. Mohammad Salam Madkour, in *Proceedings*, pp. 91, 105-107.
29. Mohammad Sa'ad Rasheed, in *Proceedings*, pp. 563-566.
30. Abdullah Mohamed Al-Athl, "Saudia Arabia," Chapter in *Justice and Troubled*

the aim is re-educative, under employment of psychological and social services. Technical and academic training are provided, as well as cultural, artistic, athletic and recreation activities. Religious guidance plays a prominent role.

In 1951, a Ministry of Interior was created with the responsibility of maintaining law and order and the internal security of the state. The National Guard, consisting of members of noble tribes, responsible directly to the King, assists the police in the maintenance of internal order at times of emergencies.[31]

Criminological research is carried out by the Crime Prevention Research Bureau of the Kingdom of Saudi Arabia, which, through its staff of well-trained criminologists, *inter alia* keeps track of crime trends and the effectiveness of crime prevention policies.[32]

Children Around the World, III, (ed.) V. Lorne Stewart (New York: New York University Press, 1981) 117, *et seq.*

31. Fahad al Thakeb and J. Scott, *op. cit., supra.* n. 1.

32. See Farouk Abdul Rahman Mourad, Director General, Research Centre for Prevention of Crime, Ministry of Interior, "Effect of the Implementation of Islamic Legislation of Crime Prevention in the Kingdom of Saudi Arabia—A Field Research," in *Proceedings*, pp. 493-530.

Asian and Pacific Countries

10

Japan

INFORMAL SOCIAL CONTROLS

Introduction

From an obscure small island nation located in the Northwestern Pacific Ocean, Japan has grown so fast in one century that it has become one of the most highly industrialized countries in the world, with the second largest gross national product. Its postwar recovery has been termed an "economic miracle."[1] As the role of industries expanded, the number of Japanese employed in agriculture declined from 30% in 1960 to 19% in 1970 to 10% in 1980. The people are of one race, all Japanese-speaking, except for a small number of indigenous caucasoid people (ainu), 600,000 Koreans and an insignificant minority of other foreigners.

Over the past two thousand years of its recorded history, the Japanese have developed a unique culture, which combines old and new, East and West. While undergoing political upheavals, wars, social revolutions, urbanization and modernization, the Japanese have clung to their time-honored traditional codes of social behavior. Intricate, rigid and ancient norms and mores exist side by side with an open-minded and cosmopolitan life-style. Scientific sophistication has not interfered with the strengths of the ancient, simple

1. *National Paper for the United Nations Conference on Science and Technology for Development*, Japan, August 1978.

95

folk faiths and superstitions that have been passed down through the ages. For example, even in Tokyo, the third largest city in the world, before construction begins on a new building, ceremonies dedicated to the land god are performed. Without these rituals, workmen are not willing to begin. At completion, no matter how large or how many millions it cost, there is a shrine placed on the roof to house a protective deity.[2]

Since ancient times Japanese society has been hierarchical, with each individual occupying a given position which carries with it specific obligations.[3] Those higher in the pecking order are supposed to be respected, while those below are expected to show the respect. There is an intricate network of behavior norms which subjects the individual to the needs of the group.

In the 18th and 19th centuries, when many other nations were beginning to define human rights, Japanese society was still concerned with obligation and duty. Regulation and control characterized daily life, both public and private. Historically, citizens had few choices because status dictated one's dress, speech, eating, drinking, size of dwelling, quality of food and even gift-giving.[4] Under feudalism, each individual fit into a given place with its attendant rigid behavior mores. For example, the rules could be so draconian "that in the seventeenth century Shozun Leyasu authorized the samurai (warrior class) to kill on the spot any person of the three inferior classes guilty of rudeness."[5]

Although Japan is one of the most modern nations in the world, the historical traditions surrounding behavioral expectations have been preserved. Individuals tend to act within the confines of their familial and communal roles and are easily shamed if found deviating from them. There is a strong commitment to uphold the honor of one's family, community and nation. It is indicative of the values of Japanese society that the family name precedes the given name.

Since ancient times, rituals to mark various rites of passage have been celebrated in public ceremonies which announce the occasion to the whole community. These assemblies have served to maintain and strengthen group solidarity and social consciousness. Although some of these rites, like that held at the birth of a baby, have

    2. *Japan: Its Land, People and Culture.* Compiled by the Japanese Commission for UNESCO (Toyko: Printing Bureau, Ministry of Finance, 1958.)
    3. William Clifford, *Crime Control in Japan,* (Boston: Lexington Books, 1976.)
    4. *Ibid.,* p. 57.
    5. *Ibid.,* p. 59.

disappeared in the cities, there are still fishing villages where the inhabitants stop working for several days on such an occasion. Babies in these villages are inducted by a ceremony into both the family and the village.

As ties to families and rural areas began to break down with the advent of industry, company communities filled the vacuum by becoming, in essence, surrogate extended families.[6] The Japanese are accustomed from birth to a high degree of dependency and indulgence and, therefore, fit in very well with the security offered by a factory system which embraces all aspects of daily living. Corporation workers can find food, shelter, clothing, entertainment, education and leisure time activities within the confines of these closed societies which generally provide lifelong employment.

Low absenteeism, low "quit rates" and few labor disputes characterize Japanese industry, as compared with other industrialized nations. For example, a survey of absenteeism of firms in the United States, England, the Federal Republic of Germany, Sweden and Canada, carried out by the Japanese Productivity Center, shows a significant gap between Japan (less than 1.8%), and the other countries (over 11% on the average).[7] Worker satisfaction appears to be based on high salaries, high degrees of safety, excellent health and retirement benefits and job security. The strength of the worker/company bond remains strong even though the work week is more than five days and the annual average number of vacation days is 29. Wages are determined primarily by age, length of service and educational attainment, rather than by job classification, in keeping with the Japanese tradition of respect for elders.[8]

The society is based on a patriarchal family structure which is both highly restrictive and highly indulgent. Although the size of the average household is decreasing (from 5 members in 1920 to 3.44 members in 1975),[9] the strength of the family has been maintained. As regards the raising of children, sixty-nine percent of the women and seventy-six percent of men agreed that "boys should be brought up like boys and girls like girls."[10]

6. Hiroshi Hagama, "Changes in Lifestyle of Industrial Workers." *Japanese Industrialization and Its Social Consequences,* (ed.) Hugh Patrick (Berkeley: University of California Press, 1976.)

7. Naomi Maruo, "The Levels and Welfare in Japan Re-examined." *Japanese Economic Studies,* 8 (Fall 1979): p. 70.

8. Nabuko Takahashi, "Women's Employment in Japan in a Period of Rapid Technological Change," *International Labor Review,* 98 (December 1968): pp. 493-510.

9. *Women of Japan: Conditions and Policies.* Report on the National Plan of Action (2), Prime Minister's Office, 1980, p. 23.

10. *Ibid.,* p. 37.

Typical Japanese houses are small and built close to each other on very narrow streets. Social control systems operate well under such circumstances inasmuch as deviant behavior is hard to hide, and absences from home are noticed by many.[11] The needs of the household as a group supersede the needs of any one individual. Its members are well cared for emotionally and materially and, in return, are supposed to engage in conforming behavior. Although somewhat modified by modernization and urbanization, the strong family traditions have their roots in ancient times where a hierarchic system placed parents above children, older above younger, husband above wife, landlord above tenant and teacher above pupil. Confucion ethics dictated that father/son loyalty supersede all other relationships. The typical house (Ye) was made up of several generations, with property rights vested in the head.

While Shintoism is the predominant religion, there are many others existing side by side with it, Buddhism being prominent. Religious diversity appears to cause no conflict. Ancestral worship is central to the belief system, as is the preservation of the honor of one's house. Of the three main religions it is said that:

> Shotoko Taishi, who is the first distinguished founder of Japanese culture, compared Shinto, Confucianism and Buddhism to the root, trunk and fruit of a tree. Shinto is the root planted deeply in the soil of the personality of the Japanese and their national tradition; Confucianism is the trunk and branches as the Ritsuryo system of Moral Standards and Education Ideas; while Buddhism produced flowers of religious sentiment, which bore fruit in the lives of people. These three religions have successfully combined with each other up to the recent age, and have formed the spiritual traditions of the Japanese.[12]

Since World War II there has been a remarkable development of the social security system. Social welfare legislation passed since that time includes child welfare laws, the Physically Handicapped Persons Welfare Laws, and the Social Welfare Service Law. The progressive system guarantees basic assistance to every citizen in the areas of housing, material care, maternity, occupation and livelihood. In addition to public aid, there are many varied private

11. *Op. cit., supra,* n. 3.
12. *Op. cit., supra,* n. 1, p. 492.

insurances, workmen's compensation and unemployment insurance.[13] There is one welfare officer per 100,000 population with special attention given to the aged and the handicapped. Japan is one of the few countries in the world to provide a high calibre of education for almost all of its citizens. It has the third highest newspaper circulation system in the world, and one of the most effective communication systems. Sixty percent of the dwellings are owner-occupied and the quality of life, in general, is excellent.

THE CRIMINAL JUSTICE SYSTEM

Until the Meiji Restoration of 1868, Japanese Criminal Law was entirely traditional, with heavy Chinese antecedents. The drive for rapid modernization led to the importation of European models of criminal law and procedure. Japan's first modern penal code, drafted by Professor Boissonade of Paris, and resting on the Napoleonic model of 1810, was adopted in 1888. But, by that time, the French model was already 78 years old and, derived from pre-industrial social norms, was criticized from the outset. Nor did it successfully blend European and Japanese traditional thinking. This code was replaced by a new code of 1907, effective 1908, which heavily relied on the German code of 1871. This code was more suitable for a rapidly industrializing country, and the Japanese draftsmen succeeded in adjusting it to Japanese traditions. The successful blending of Japanese traditional mores with advanced foreign models was to remain a feature of Japanese criminal justice. The Penal Code of 1907 was constantly updated. Protective measures for juveniles were introduced by the Juvenile Law of 1922, including the establishment of juvenile training schools, along the lines of American practice.[14]

Following World War II, the American influence became pronounced. The Constitution of 1946, based on the so-called MacArthur draft, introduced democratic and due process notions which found their reflections in subsequent penal legislation, especially in criminal procedure. The Juvenile law of 1948 introduced American-style family court proceedings for youth below age 21; parole was introduced in 1949; an adult probation system was created in

---

13. *Op. cit., supra*, n. 1.
14. In general, see William Clifford, *Crime Control in Japan, op. cit. supra*, n. 3.

1953/54, although volunteers had worked as probation officers since 1950.[15]

Careful and constant reform efforts have marked the development of Japanese criminal law and procedure. Between 1926 and 1941, an advisory committee of eminent experts created a new draft penal code, which delimited criminal liability in strict conformity with the mens rea principle. These reform efforts were continued after World War II, culminating in the Preparatory Draft for the Revised Penal Code of Japan 1961,[16] which evoked much discussion and came close to adoption. However, subsequent efforts altered this draft, and the final version, of 1974, caused much criticism from bench, bar and citizen groups, and remains unadopted. Continuing reform efforts are guided by the 31-Member Legal System Council, headed by the Minister of Justice. Experts from all fields are involved in this standing criminal justice reform agency.[17]

The existing penal code has the typical continental bi-partition with a general part, covering the general doctrines, and a special part, covering the offenses. It rests on the principle of legality (nullum crimen sine lege) and adheres strictly to the guilt principle. Just as it was carefully drafted, it is being carefully administered by a highly skilled, not to say scholarly, judiciary.

The Japanese Code of Criminal Procedure is likewise the result of a blending of European and American thinking, engrafted upon Japanese culture. As stated by Mr. Justice Dando of the Supreme Court of Japan:

> The Japanese law of criminal procedure may be called a blending together of oriental, Continental European and Anglo-American law to form a unique system. Anglo-American law has had a strong influence after the close of World War II, and has offered a practical demonstration of the degree to which the Continental European and Anglo-American legal systems can be successfully combined.[18]

15. Kinsaku Saito, "Das Japanische Strafrecht," in Das ausländische Strafrecht der Gegenwart, (eds.) Mezger-Schönke-Jescheck (Berlin: Duncker and Humblot, 1955) 209, et seq.; Yoshio Suzuki. "Corrections in Japan." in International Corrections, (eds.) Robert J. Wicks and H.H.A. Cooper (Lexington: D.C. Heath and Co., 1979) 141.

16. B.J. George, Jr., (guest editor), A Preparatory Draft for the Revised Penal Code of Japan 1961, with an introduction by Juhei Takeuchi. (South Hackensack, New Jersey: Fred B. Rothman & Co.; London: Sweet and Maxwell, Ltd., American Series of Foreign Penal Codes, vol. 8 1964.)

17. Yoshio Suzuki, "Criminal Law Reform in Japan." UNAFEI, Resource Material Series, No. 13 (1977) p. 81.

18. Shigemitsu Dando. Japanese Criminal Procedure, B.J. George, transl. (South Hack-

The purpose of the Code of Criminal Procedure, according to its Article 1, is "to clarify the true facts of cases and to apply and realize criminal laws and ordinances fairly and speedily, while thoroughly accomplishing the maintenance of public welfare and security of fundamental human rights."[19]

The Japanese criminal justice system appears to have succeeded in this regard. The fairness and speed of the system begins at the police level, where highly trained and motivated officers, at the rate of one officer per 600 population, perform criminal investigation and other police functions. They are hierarchically organized, on a national basis.[20]

One of the major strengths of the police sector lies in the system of police boxes. These "boxes" are generally staffed by one officer who lives in the facility with his family and becomes a neighbor in the community. All residents are required to register with these local stations. It is typical for officers to visit homes, to counsel, to search for runaways, to initiate victim/offender transactions, to mediate family disputes, to refer to other organizations and to be of general assistance (e.g., renewing various licenses). These visits are, in fact, perceived as a social service provided by the Government.[21] In 1973, 13 percent of the telephone calls received were concerned with personal problems, 11.8 percent with non-payment of debts, and 9.7 percent with pollution.[22]

The adversary relationship between police and public that is so characteristic of many large Western cities does not exist in Tokyo. In fact, although police carry guns, in the last five years they have used them three times, each time to fire warning shots.[23] A unique officer/citizen rapport is believed by many to constitute the most important feature of the control strategy of the nation. Accordingly, there is an extremely high clearance rate for offenses. It rests, for

ensack, N.J.: Fred B. Rothman & Co., Publications of the Comparative Criminal Law Project, vol. 4, 1965). See also, Shigemitsu Dando, "Japanese Criminal Procedure," in *Essays in Criminal Science,* (ed.) G.O.W. Mueller (South Hackensack, N.J.: Fred B. Rothman & Co.; London: Sweet and Maxwell, Ltd., Publications of the Comparative Criminal Law Project, vol. 1, 1961.) pp. 447-460.

19. As quoted by G.O.W. Mueller in *Preface* to Shigemitsu Dando, Japanese Criminal Procedure, *op. cit. supra.,* n. 18 at XIX.

20. Ministry of Justice, Japan, *Criminal Justice in Japan* (1970) 2, *et. seq.*

21. Simon Dinitz. *Preventing Juvenile Crime and Delinquency,* International Union of Local Authorities. (Pre-Conference Draft), n.d.

22. *Op. cit. supra,* n. 3, at p. 80. On the Japanese police, in general, see David Bayley, *Forces of Order: Police Behaviour in Japan and the United States* (Berkeley: University of California Press, 1976).

23. International Herald Tribune, July 24, 1981.

penal code offenses reported to the public, at an astonishingly high 69 percent, (contrasted with 22 percent for the U.S.A.)

The Code of Criminal Procedure of 1948, and the Rules of Criminal Procedure of 1949, govern the process before the country's 570 Summary Courts, 49 District Courts, 8 High Courts (of Appeal) and the Supreme Court, all operating within a national, uniform structure. Cases are prepared for trial by the police and the prosecutor. Arrest normally requires a warrant. The arrested person must be brought before a prosecutor within 48 hours; the prosecutor has judicial standing. A judicial warrant is required for further detention. Defendants have constitutional rights to bail, counsel, confrontation and examination of witnesses, and enjoy the privilege against self-incrimination. Trial procedure is not unlike that in American courts. Public prosecutors have discretionary power to drop the prosecution, even where there is convincing evidence of guilt. Indeed, 50 percent of all cases are nolle-prossed.[24] The conviction rate has remained extraordinarily high, facilitated in part by the use of summary proceedings in the Summary Courts where 90 percent of all convictions resulted in fines. These decisions are rendered in camera; the judgement is mailed to the defendant who, in case of dissatisfaction, may demand a trial.[25] In 1973 only 43,000 convictions, out of 465,000, resulted in a sentence of imprisonment (and four death sentences), all others resulted in fines.[26] Yet prison sentences were suspended in 61 percent of all cases, including in 27 percent of murder cases,[27] and the length of sentences has been reduced over the years.[28]

The Japanese Constitution in Article 76, para. 3, has a unique "conscience clause": "All judges shall be independent in the exercise of their conscience and shall be bound only by this Constitution and the laws." According to Dando, this clause has been used by trial judges "to arouse the defendant's own conscience and to influence his mind and attitudes to putting him on the path towards resocialization."[29] In sentencing, the judge, within the framework of the

24. Only 13 percent of defendants nolle-prossed committed subsequent offenses. Yoshio Suzuki, Corrections in Japan, *op. cit., supra*, n. 15, p. 145.

25. *Ibid.*, at 146.

26. *Op. cit., supra*, n. 17, p. 89.

27. Yoshio Suzuki, "Corrections in Japan," *op. cit., supra*, n. 15, p. 146.

28. Tadahiro Tanizawa, "Sentencing Standards in Japan," UNAFEI, *Resource Material Series*, No. 16 (1979): p. 197.

29. Shigemitsu Dando, "The Conscience of the Judge: His Role in the Administration of Criminal Justice," in *Studies in Comparative Criminal Law*, (eds.) Edward M. Wise and G.O.W. Mueller (Springfield, Ill.: Charles C. Thomas, publisher, Publications of the Criminal Law Education and Research Center, vol. II, 1975) 13-24.

code provision, considers the gravity of the offense, the degree of the blameworthiness of the offender and the prospects of rehabilitation (or, perhaps, the opposite, i.e., the degree of the defendant's dangerousness to society). While general deterrence is a consideration, it can be viewed only within the limits of "blameworthiness." Sentencing guidelines exist, but only in the minds of the judges, collectively, very much aided by their common bond through the Judicial Training and Research Institute.[30]

The Japanese correctional system works with the same degree of effectiveness and efficiency as the other components of the criminal justice system.[31] Due to the large amount of diversions, incarceration rates are low.[32] There are 67 prisons in the country, (including nine for young adults, four for females and three for prisoners with special medical needs), plus 9 branch prisons and 69 juvenile training schools. Prison labor is required and compensated. Classification is according to vocational and training needs. The United Nations Standard Minimum Rules for the Treatment of Prisoners are applied. According to Suzuki, the system is humane and effective, for the following reasons: (1) there is a reasonably uniform and nationwide administration of corrections, (2) there is an extensive and organized use of volunteers, (3) there is emphasis on close personal contact between correctional workers and their charges, inside and outside the institution, (4) there is a high level of staff training and (5) research and evaluation of programs are standard practice.[33]

The juvenile justice system in its present form was created by the Juvenile Law of 1948, covering all defendants below age 21. These are initially referred to the Family Court, where a social inquiry report is prepared by the probation department, and a diagnosis report by the Juvenile Classification House. Proceedings before the Family Court, if initiated at all, are relatively informal. Ultimately, less than 1 percent of all juveniles proceeded against by the Family Court are referred to training schools.[34]

The most extraordinary aspect of the Japanese criminal justice system is the amount and intensity of popular participation, at

30. Yoshio Suzuki, "Corrections in Japan," *op. cit., supra*, n. 15, p. 149.

31. Tadahiro Tanizawa. *Op. cit., supra*, n. 28, p. 117.

32. In 1974, 43 prisoners per 100,000 population, i.e., half the rate of, e.g., Canada and the German Federal Republic. See *The Treatment of Offenders, in Custody or in the Community, with special reference to the Implementation of the Standard Minimum Rules for the Treatment of Prisoners adopted by the United Nations.* Working Paper prepared by the Secretariat. A/CONF. 56/6, 1975.

33. Yoshio Suzuki. "Corrections in Japan," *op. cit., supra*, n. 15, p. 159.

34. *Ibid.*, pp. 142, 148/9.

virtually every level of the process. Community involvement in crime prevention stems from historical obligations: "In feudal times the gonin-kumi, groupings of five families under a leader, kept law and order among themselves and were held responsible to deliver up an offender."[35] Presently there are Crime Prevention Associations in 3,405 cities and towns, with 540,000 liaison units and 10,725 Vocational Unions for Crime Prevention. In addition, there are 380,000 Traffic Safety Volunteer Workers (mainly for school children), a local and national Juvenile Problem Council (concerned with guiding and protecting youth), a yearly "Brighter Society Campaign" (to mobilize delinquency prevention), 38,000 volunteer cooperators for Juvenile Guidance (doing street work with juveniles), 8,000 members of Big Brothers and Sisters (working with delinquents) and 320,000 women volunteers in the Women's Association for Rehabilitation. In addition, there are an active voluntary Probation Officers Association, with 80,000 members, Voluntary Guidance Hostels, and voluntary associations for prison visiting.[36]

35. *Op. cit., supra,* n. 3, pp. 98-99.

36. The extent of community involvement can best be illustrated by reference to the articles on the topic published in volumes 1 to 10 of the UNAFEI Series, published by the United Nations Asia and Far East Institute for the Prevention of Crime and the Treatment of Offenders, at Fuchu, Tokyo, Japan, (Reference is to the volume and page number):

How to Ensure Co-operation in the Field of Police, Prosecution and Court Operations (Art.) by Kiyoshi Hara (1) 63

Public Participation in the Decision to Prosecute (Art.) by Jiri Otobe (1) 70

How to Utilize Volunteers in the Field of Probation (Art.) by Shozo Tomita (1) 96

The Participation of Private Citizens in Crime Prevention—The Case of the Naikan-Ho in Japan (Art.) by Ryoji Takeda (2) 145

The Necessity of Public Participation for Individualized Treatment (Art.) by Yutaka Ono (2) 189

Anatomy of Volunteer Probation Officer System (Art.) (2) 192

Private Guard and Security Business (G.W.), by Hiroyoshi Murayama (3) 49

Public Role in Crime Prevention: The Recovery of Family Function (G.W.) by Kenzo Fujiwara (3) 68

Participation of Laymen in Trial (Art.) by Takeo Takahashi (3) 70

Use of Professional Volunteers (G.W.) by Masaru Matsumoto (3) 86

The Establishment of the Allocation Center and the Public Participation (G.W.) by Sakae Ono (3) 86

Regarding the Necessity to Organize Volunteers System for Delinquent Children Admitted (G.W.) by Yasuyuki Tsuji (3) 86

Public Participation in Short Term Treatment for Juvenile Traffic Offenders (G.W.) by Yoshitsugu Kori (3) 92

Recruitment of Volunteer Probation Officers (G.W.) by Mitsuru Saito (3) 92

Public Participation in Police Activities (G.W.) by Toshinori Kanemoto (3) 105

Role of the Public in the Administration of Regional Parole Board System (Art.) by Takashi Nagasaki (3) 121

The System of Special Defense Counsel as Public Participation in Criminal Trial Proceedings in Japan (Art.) by Sukeaki Tatsuoka (3) 125

In sum, the Japanese criminal justice system has succeeded in successfully blending:

morals with law,

social interests with individual interests,

the professional criminal justice system with popular participation,

the tradition of Japan with the models of the Western world, and

efficiency with humanity.

As Saito put it, "man can live and be creative only in society. Where there is a social living, norms will make their appearance in order to regulate the activities of men: in religion, morals and law. Criminal law is part of the law."[37]

Public Participation and the Crime Prevention Activities of the Probation Office (G.W.) by Noriaki Kawamoto (3) 131

Relations between the Local Community and Children in the Children Education and Training Home—The Future Prospect of "The Cooperation Association," a Supportive Body for the Children in Fukushima Gakuen (G.W.) by Mitsuo Kitagawa (3) 131

Public Role in the Treatment of Offenders Suspended from Prosecution (G.W.) by Kazuo Kusuhara (3) 131

Public Participation in Open Institutions (G.W.) by Kohmei Yoshimura (3) 131

Public Participation in Prison—A Study Related to the Revision of the Prison Law (Art.) by Masahiro Inagawa (3) 143

Prevention of Crimes through Public Cooperation (G.W.) by S. Kitano (5) 130

Some Considerations of the Volunteer Probation Officer System (G.W.) by M. Yamada (5) 170

Practical Use of the Social Resources in Community Treatment (G.W.) by (Miss) Takako Naomoto (6) 172

Collaborative Attitudes between Probation Officers and Volunteer Probation Officers (G.W.) by Shigemi Sato (9) 100

More Effective Utilization of Volunteer Probation Officers (G.W.) by (Miss) Hiroko Sogabe (10) 113

37. Kinsaku Saito. *Op. cit., supra*, n. 15, p. 233.

11

Nepal

Introduction

Nepal is a remote country in the Himalayan Mountains, relatively untouched by industrialization. Its history has been marked by tribalism and factionalism. To cope with these endemic problems, in 1960 King Mahendra suspended the constitution, banned political parties, and assumed full governmental powers. A new constitution was proclaimed in 1962, and amended in 1967. This constitution established the "panchayat" system, a pyramidal structure of assemblies and councils, rising from the village to the national level. It presents the country's first uniform system of local administration, meant to hasten the integration of the nation under the leadership of the king. The panchayat is established at four different levels: the village and town, district, zone and nation. The village panchayats, the country's most basic unit of government, are elected directly by the villagers, the other panchayats are indirectly elected by the lower bodies. Zonal and national panchayats include members from class and professional groups. The National Panchayat resembles a Parliament. The king also rules with the help of a Council of Ministers whose members are appointed by him from the National Panchayat. In December 1975, the King announced some

106

changes in Nepalese law, including a broadened franchise, more frequent elections and a provision for the recall of legislators.

As a result of lack of adequate resources for economic development, the mountainous terrain, inadequate transportation facilities and years of self-imposed isolation, Nepal is one of the lesser developed nations in the world. The economy is principally agrarian, with agriculture employing 90 percent of the population, whose food and livelihood depend largely upon subsistence farming. Food shortage is a severe problem in the mid-mountain region, due to limited arable land, insufficient farming techniques, natural calamities, and lack of suitable communication ties with the rich Tarai region.

Industrial establishments, primarily orientated toward nondurable consumer goods, are few in number and small in scale, although this segment of economic activity is growing. Natural resources include timber, copper and iron ore, which have not yet been exploited, as well as an immense hydroelectric power potential. Nepal receives economic assistance from both Eastern and Western countries, as well as from various international organizations, such as the United Nations.

Almost all Nepalese (90%) live in agricultural villages or small market centers, many of which lie in remote mountain valleys accessible only by foot-path. The typical village has less than 600 residents, consisting of a few family groups or clans. Apart from the capital, Katmandu, there are no major cities. Most of the migration caused by growing population pressure has been towards the less densely settled areas of the Tarai (a vertical migration, therefore, from the mountains to the lowlands) rather than to the towns. The total urban population in 1975 was still less than 5 percent.[1]

The ethnic, linguistic and religious diversity of the Nepalese people results from a process of long interaction among numerous ethnic groups who penetrated into Nepal from India on one side and from Tibet on the other. There are more than thirty languages and a multitude of local dialects in the country. The Nepalese can be roughly divided into two basic ethnic groups: the Indo-European, broadly characterized by Indian linguistic origins, Hindu religious and social organization and North Indian physical traits, and the Tibetan-Burman, characterized by Tibetan linguistic and cultural

---

1. *1977 Compendium of Social Statistics*, United Nations, New York, 1980.

traditions, Lamaist Buddhism, and Mongoloid physical traits. The Hindu population has been the dominant force (90% of the population is considered Hindu, 9% Buddhist). European ancestry, traditionally a source of prestige, accounts for as much as 80 percent of the population. Because of the high degree of isolation and separation between the various communities, a unified sense of nationality is limited. "Except for a small educated elite with a more assertive national consciousness, citizens of the Kingdom usually still identify themselves in regional terms, e.g., Pahari (hill man), Madheshi (plains man)—or by their ethnic community. . . ."[2]

Although ethnic groups and village communities differ greatly in cultural traditions, social values and religious practices, there is a similarity of family and community life throughout the country. Villages vary in size and composition but, for the most part, the extended family forms the basis of the social structure. Not only is the family the most important social institution, but it is also the basic economic and political unit. Village political authority is likely to reside with the heads of the senior kinship lineages. Marriage, the place of residence, and one's occupation are restricted by customary rules and are subject to family decision. The average rural household consists of a man and wife, unmarried children and married sons with their wives and children. The men traditionally do the agricultural work while the women raise the children and manage the household. However, women often help the men in the fields during the planting and harvest seasons. Although monogamy is generally practiced, polygamy is frequent among Hindus. Polyandry is practiced among the Bhote.

In addition to the immediate family, clan and lineage also play an important role in Nepalese society. Families with common lineage are united into a clan with a remote common male ancestor. Clans represent the largest unit organized by kinship in the country. Clan leadership, as well as household leadership, rests with the senior male member. Functions range from ceremonial to regulation of marriage and to management of communal land. Although clans play an important role in determining social power and prestige, social status is mainly determined by the caste system. Traditionally there has been a prohibition of marriage between certain clans, due to caste traditions.

Of the limited sense of nationality it has been said: "Little,

2. L. Rose, *Profile of a Himalayan Kingdom,* (Boulder, Colorado: Westview Press, 1980) 1-2.

except the frequently remote authority of the royal government and limited trade relationships, exists to relate the various areas of the country and the numerous ethnic groups to each other."[3] As for economic goals, there is no sense of common interest which would have to cross ethnic or caste lines.

Although Hinduism is considered the predominant religion of Nepal, it has been deeply influenced by Buddhism and vice versa. There seem to be no overt conflicts between the two. Many elements of Shamanism, a folk religion based on a belief in supernatural beings as personifications of natural phenomena, have been assimilated into both Hinduism and Buddhism. Bon, a type of Shamanism with a strong Buddhist influence, exists in some northern areas of Nepal. Almost all villages have Shaman, a person believed to be able to communicate with supernatural beings and to be able to assist with illness and misfortune.

In Hinduism, the "absolute" is considered to be too vast to be contained within a single set of beliefs. The religion involves a wide variety of metaphysical systems, and religious practices differ widely from group to group. Most Hindus do not need any formal creed to practice their religion. Common to all Hindus is the concept of "dharma"—a concept of natural law and the social and religious obligations it imposes. "It holds that every person should play his property role in society as determined by his dharma."[4] Each person is born into a particular caste whose traditional occupation is graded according to the degree of religious purity or impurity inherent in it. The four castes are Brahmans, Ksha triya, Vaisha and Shudra. Those without castes are the "untouchables." The souls of men are regarded as being separate portions of an all-embracing world soul and man's ultimate goal is reunion with this absolute. Like Buddhists, Hindus believe in rebirth, which is required by "dharma"—the belief that the consequences of every good or bad action must be fully realized. Thus, the role an individual must play throughout his life is fixed by his good and evil actions in his previous existence. Important religious activities include public worship and pilgrimage. Philosophical doctrines play a very limited role in village religious life. More importance is given the village Shaman, and each village tends to have its own set of deities. The majority of these gods are perceived as bringing difficulty and

3. L. Harris, *Area Handbook for Nepal, Bhutan and Sikhim.* (Washington, D.C.: United States Government Printing Office, 1973) 69.
   4. *Ibid.*, p. 110.

misfortune and are, therefore, worshipped out of fear of their power and wrath rather than out of love.

Buddhism finds its origins in the teachings of Siddhartha Gautama, who was born around 563 A.D. Buddhist religious doctrine is based upon "Four Nobel Truths" which are briefly: (1) life is a process of unceasing change, is inherently imperfect and sorrowful, and misery is a quality that permeates all experience; (2) the cause of sorrow is desire, the emotional involvement with existence which leads to the continuing process of rebirth through Karma; (3) sorrow can be ended by eliminating desire; (4) a prescribed "Eightfold Path" leading to the elimination of desire, rebirth and sorrow and to the attainment of "Nirvana." Nirvana is the extinction of desire, hate and the illusion of selfhood, and culminates with the unification with the universal soul.

There is a significant difference in individual and group relations between Hindu and Buddhist cultures. Among the Hindus, concern lies with the social rather than the personal effects of conduct. Such values as charity, honesty, moderation and abstention from taking life are among the most cherished. Because the Hindu caste system blocks upward movement in the community, Hindus may tend to be indifferent to the affairs of others outside their own circles, be defensive about status and be more pessimistic about their surroundings. The only real escape from the caste system is to renunciate the world and its mundane pleasures for the life of a holy mendicant.

While Hindu social values originate from India, the Buddhist values come largely from Tibet. The Buddhists are more ethnically varied than the Hindus and the communities are not subject to a caste system. Important Buddhist social values include a universal belief in the brotherhood of man, hospitality, respect for others and a sense of right or wrong independent of social status or prestige. Unlike in Hinduism, there is no concept in Buddhism of "racial pollution." Moral worth is attributed to the individual rather than to the group and social responsibility is a personal rather than collective concern.

There are six different types of schools in operation in Nepal: English schools, which offer a traditional British education at both the primary and secondary levels, national schools, taught in the Nepali language and offering at least 3-5 years of primary school education, community schools providing secular education and some limited vocational training, Buddhist and Sanskrit schools devoted to religious training, leading to either the priesthood or Government posts, and Ghandian schools, of which about one-third are supported and controlled by the Government, offering training in a variety of handicrafts.

Education has traditionally been a prerogative of only the higher castes. From 1946-1960, under the rule of the Ranas, who opposed all forms of public schooling, formal instruction was available for the elite only. The remainder of the population was largely illiterate. The training of most Nepalese children consisted of informal apprenticeships in work performed by adult family members. Most children were able to perform adult tasks by the age of ten or eleven. Since 1961, there has been a rapid expansion program supported by the Government, by private initiative and by financial aid from foreign countries and various international agencies. Although respect for education is growing, many villagers still do not consider it a universal right.

In 1975, the King decreed that primary education should be free, though not compulsory. By 1978, about 60 percent of eligible primary school children were receiving instruction. The long-standing prejudice against the education of women is breaking down.[5] Principal hindrances to education are the burdens imposed on families whose children attend school and are, to that extent, not available as workers. The distance between village homes and schools exacerbate these burdens.

The standard of living is quite low for most of the population. Families suffer from inadequate diet, sub-standard housing and from the general unavailability of modern medical care and other social services. Although there is plenty of water in Nepal, the difficult terrain, lack of available manpower, pollution and difficulty in the maintenance of water distribution facilities create a lack of an adequate and pure water supply. Transportation and communication ties remain a big problem for the country. The overwhelming majority of the population are peasant cultivators who produce just enough food to feed themselves. They usually live in simple and sparsely furnished dwellings and many farmers are in debt to Brahman moneylenders or to the large landowners of the village. There are few radio receivers, no television service and a paucity of newspapers.

5. P. Kharas, *Profile of Women in Rural Development—Nepal.* Home Economics and Social Programmes Service, Human Resources Institution and Agragarian Reform Division, FAO. (Rome, March 1978) p. 8.

Although there are more than fifty hospitals and ninety-three health clinics in the country, facilities are generally overcrowded, understaffed and frustrated by undependable electric current sources. The majority of the villagers still treat illnesses with roots, herbs, plants and the supernatural. There is a very high infant mortality rate, short life expectancy, and a prevalence of a variety of virulent diseases, in particular malaria and tuberculosis. There are also a large number of handicapped persons. Nutritional deficiencies are manifested in all parts of the country and in 1976 about 70 percent of Nepalese children were estimated to suffer from malnutrition. Shortages of food develop often, due to natural calamities or marketing and transportation difficulties. Drug (cannabis) misuse has been reported among some middle class persons.[6] In addition, alcoholism is a problem among Gurkha veterans "who drink heavily out of boredom in their retirement."[7]

THE CRIMINAL JUSTICE SYSTEM

Until 1853 Nepal had relied entirely on the "Muluki Ain," uncodified law based on religious usage and custom. In 1853 the Muluki Ain was codified. It still obtains, though with considerable amendments. Above all, after the democratization of 1951, the caste system, according to which persons belonging to higher classes would be subject to more severe punishment since they were supposed to live a purer life, was abolished. All discriminatory practices, e.g., lesser penalities for women, were removed, and Panchayat democracy, consisting of village and regional governing councils, was established. The present constitution, which governs the criminal justice system, was adopted in 1962.

The orientation of Nepalese criminal law is deterrent, retributive as well as rehabilitative. Children below age 8, as well as mentally ill persons, cannot be punished. Children between ages 8 and 12 violating criminal law can be punished by imprisonment of up to 2 months for very serious offenses, otherwise they can be warned or fined. Juveniles between the ages of 12 and 15 can be punished by up to one half of the sentences for adults, while persons above age 15 are treated fully as adults.

6. In a comparison of chronic users of cannabis in Nepal, it was found that cannabis had no apparent influence on the incidence of crime. See B.P. Sharma, "Cannabis and Its Users in Nepal," *British Journal of Psychiatry.* 27 (1975): pp. 550-552.

7. *Op. cit., supra,* n. 2.

Trials are heard in District Courts, of which there are 75 in the country. District courts can pronounce any sentence, except that death sentences require the confirmation of the next higher court, the Zonal Court, of which there are 14, acting as courts of appeal. To speed up the criminal process, a system of summary proceedings in District Courts was recently instituted, and the procedure in all courts was streamlined. District Court decisions with sentences above 3 months may now be appealed to a new layer of Regional Courts, above the Zonal Court level, while decisions with sentences below 3 months continue to be appealable to Zonal Courts. The Supreme Court exercises jurisdiction in constitutional matters or on questions of law of great significance, and hears appeals in murder convictions.[8]

Under the Special Courts Act of 1958, the King may institute special courts, e.g., in corruption cases, and has indeed done so. Under the Government Cases Act of 1961, prosecutors have been appointed for each District and Zonal Court. They are responsible to the Attorney General.

To retain the aspect of popularity which normally is lacking in a fairly sophisticated bureaucratic system, the "on-the-spot," inquiry procedure has been instituted. Under this practice the police and the public prosecutor conduct the investigation of a case in the vicinity where the crime has been committed with the Chairman or Vice-Chairman of the village panchayat in attendance. All of the villagers are also required to be present at such an inquiry and every individual must give a statement of his knowledge, if any, of the facts relating to the crime.[9]

Despite these efforts at popularization of the criminal justice process, the geography of the country, with its enormous distances, isolation of communities and inhospitable mountain climate, conspire with ancient tradition to maintain a certain reluctance on the part of Nepalese villagers to collaborate with the official criminal justice system, and villagers prefer to resolve matters by private settlement or revenge.[10] Until the problem of communication between the agencies of criminal justice and the populace serviced by it can be overcome, so that distant police posts can be properly

8. Abhay Kant Tha, "Speedy Trial," UNAFEI *Resource Material Series*, No. 11 (1976): p. 83; Ved V. Kishatri, "Criminal Justice System in Nepal," UNAFEI *Resource Material Series*, No. 2 (1971): p. 99.

9. Indra Rai Pandy, quoted in "Public Role in Crime Prevention, Police, Prosecution and Courts," UNAFEI *Resource Material Series*, 13 (1972): p. 49.

10. B.K. Bantawa, "On Juvenile Delinquency in Nepal," UNAFEI *Resource Material Series*, No. 10 (1975): p. 116. See also p. 114.

notified and respond swiftly, and villagers can more easily travel to courts, there will likely be little change, and perhaps this is all to the good.[11]

For the time being, this somewhat uneasy relationship between crime control by the extended family and by the official system still provides an effective control mechanism. The below 21 population, amounting to a total of 20 percent, is accountable for only 14 percent of criminality.[12] The "headman" of the extended family is still "duly respected and observed, since it is his duty and obligation to maintain prestige and decorum within his clan. He has the full right to impose necessary punishment on the wrong-doing members as well as to protect their rights."[13]

But the signs of change are making their appearance. There is a slight increase of delinquency rates, especially in urban areas, where peer group pressure tends to be more negative than positive, while in rural areas youngsters are still economically dependent on their families and therefore more tractable.[14] The urban problems are not very severe yet, since only 4 percent of the population live in urban areas, principally Katmandu, the capital. But there, gang fights, prostitution and drug abuse have made their appearance.[15] Traditionally, hemp has been permitted to grow, and indeed was cultivated, for use in Nepal. An addiction problem had never existed.[16] But the availability of hemp attracted a very large group of foreign tourists, principally hippies who commercialized its production, sale and illegal export. Earlier efforts to control the smuggle in hemp and its derivatives under the "Essential Commodities Act" having failed, the government in 1973 banned the production and sale of hemp and its derivatives altogether; but a certain amount of damage had been reported to have been done to the youth of Nepal through the unwholesome influence of the hippie culture and its smuggling operations.[17]

11. Sudarshan S. Thapa, "Special Problems Related to Criminal Justice Process," UNAFEI *Resource Material Series*, No. 12 (1976): p. 147.

12. *Op. cit., supra*, n. 10.

13. Bahuan Thakur, "Role of Environment on Juvenile Delinquency," UNAFEI *Resource Material Series*, No. 17 (1980): pp. 176-177.

14. *Ibid.*

15. UNAFEI, "Crime Trends and Crime Prevention Strategies in Asian Countries," *Int. Rev. Crim. Policy*, 24 (1979): p. 34.

16. Moreover, a 1975 study showed that cannabis use appeared to have no significant impact on the incidence of crime. See B.P. Sharma, "Cannabis and Its Users in Nepal," *British Journal of Psychiatry*, 27 (1975): pp. 550-552.

17. Dhenu Shisjere Rana, "Drug Abuse and Other Problems," UNAFEI *Resource Material Series*, No. 9 (1975): p. 129.

Other social problems have arisen. To some extent the ancient social customs are beginning to have a negative effect. Thus, custom requires elaborate festivities on many occasions, which families no longer can afford. The temptation to obtain illegal earnings arises. Similarly, the dowry system imposes burdens in the contemporary economic system which were not in existence, to this extent, in earlier times. Migration to India for economic reasons imports not only cash, but also undesirable habits; drinking and gambling are on the increase. These problems, together with the effort of youth to break with the conservatism of the clan system, have prompted governmental reforms. Under the new Marriage Act, small families are being encouraged. This could, of course, prove counterproductive as long as clans have social control strength. Child marriage and polygamy have been forbidden, a return-to-the-village movement has been instituted, and the government aids socio-economic development by financial and technical assistance.[18] Unhappily, as one noted Nepalese judge pointed out, "as a developing country, my country has given its planning priority to the development of industrialization, education, transportation, communication, etc., rather than to the field of crime prevention."[19]

While, as noted, certain criminal justice reforms have been instituted, and hope is placed on the positive role which public education and the mass media can play in crime prevention,[20] no master plan has yet been created to deal with the change in the crime situation which economic development is likely to bring about, not by itself, but by undermining the strength of the indigenous social control system. Only the prison system, as a reactive control, has been strengthened and improved by the Prison Act of 1962 and the Prison Rules of 1963, while the use of capital punishment has been severely restricted to high treason and offenses under the Army Act. Banishment, imprisonment to hard labor and whipping have been abolished. Parole and probation do not yet exist, the burden on prisons being occasionally eased by remission of sentences on the King's birthday and other festive occasions.[21]

There are no special laws, courts or institutions to deal with delinquent or pre-delinquent youth, apart from a few provisions in the Muluku Ain. Reformers have called not only for these, but also

18. Sudarshan S. Thapa, *op. cit., supra*, no. 11; B.I. Bantawa, *op. cit., supra*, n. 10.
19. Balram Singh Malla. "How to Change Negative Public Attitudes toward Criminals." UNAFEI *Resource Material Series*, 1 (1970).
20. *Ibid.;* Bahuan Thakur, *op. cit., supra*, n. 13.
21. *Ibid.*

for broadening public school education to include civic education and the transmission of values of virtue which under urban conditions can no longer be transmitted as easily. More recreational and social programs have been called for but, above all, public efforts are said to be needed to resolve the dangerously escalating conflict between conservative old-timers and liberal youth.[22] With the changes that are now in progress, the crucial question is: How long can Nepal's social control system, of which the criminal justice system appears to be just an appendix, keep the crime rate as low as it has been?

22. *Op. cit., supra,* n. 10.

12

Summary of Qualitative Data

... what we call necessary institutions are often no more than institutions to which we have grown accustomed

... in matters of social constitution the field of possibilities is much more extensive than men living in their various societies are ready to imagine.

Alexis de Tocqueville

In Chapter One, it was demonstrated that available "hard" data produced little information on any meaningful associations between socio-economic and cultural indicators and crime rates. It became, then, necessary to search for cultural indicators which have not yet been quantified, or, perhaps, even defy quantification. The quest for these elusive "soft" factors led to an in-depth study of the formal (criminal justice) and informal social control mechanisms of our ten low crime rate countries. In Chapters Two through Eleven the resulting country profiles were presented. A brief *precis* of those findings follows:

Switzerland

As one of the world's leading industrialized nations, this country enjoys one of the highest standards of living in the world. There is virtually no unemployment. Swiss society is characterized by diversity of ethnic heritage, religion and language. Swiss unity lies in the direct popular democracy in which three thousand communes and their citizens participate. "Home" for most Swiss remains the Canton of birth where group loyalties transcend individual interests. Industrialization took on a unique form of slow urbanization, thereby avoiding massive dislocations of persons and the formation of "industrial cities." Family and school discipline are rigid, the life-styles of Swiss teenagers are more restrained than those of their peers in most other modern societies. There is no uniform, centralized social service system, yet one of the highest standards of living prevails.

The Swiss criminal justice system is completely reflective of its social system, i.e., law enforcement and the administration of justice rest predominantly in the cantonal and local levels, where direct citizens' influence is most pronounced. All judges and jurors are elected; all laws are adopted by popular referendum. A greater degree of direct popular participation in the administration of justice is hardly imaginable. Yet, juridical culture rests at the highest level of scholarship, and the detail of social attention accorded to offenders reflects an extraordinary degree of participation of university trained personnel, including psychiatrists and social workers.

Ireland

Agriculture is still the mainstay of the nation's economy, although industrialization is in progress. The population is homogenous. A unique emigration pattern exists whereby those from rural areas who are in search of urban jobs tend to leave the country rather than go to its cities. Urban areas grew slowly and without the typical problems of subcultures of poverty. Communities maintain traditional mores and family members retain a close attachment to their land. Social services are good and include a national program for housing. In planning the construction of dwellings the availability and proximity of schools, churches, jobs and utilities is considered.

The criminal justice system of Ireland is adopted and adapted from the English criminal justice system. There is a due process orientation. Population participation in the system is at a relatively low level, being restricted to the jury and a few aftercare services for prisoners. Law enforcement, too, while highly effective and efficient, is virtually a carbon copy of the English model. Ireland was slow among European countries in introducing a social service oriented, preventive, and rehabilitative approach, as mandated by her constitution.

Bulgaria

With one of the fastest-growing economies in Eastern Europe, this nation places major importance on the planning process. The population is homogeneous with, by now, less than one-quarter engaged in agricultural work. Nevertheless, a deliberate effort was made to keep urban areas from becoming unmanageable. Instead, smaller communities were consolidated for administrative and cultural purposes (group settlement system). The basic unit of society is the family, which is well supported by other establishments to ensure the care and training of children. Social and moral education are given the same significance as academic learning. Citizens have the right to education, to free health services, to family vacations and to a network of welfare benefits. There is no unemployment. One of the unique features of the country is its migration pattern, half of which occurs within territorial units. Young people stay close to home and family, some even returning to rural areas after a period of urban living. There is total integration of the generations.

The Bulgarian criminal justice system exhibits an extraordinary amount of popular participation in the formulation of laws and policies regarding crime control, in an effort to achieve a state of national and community conformity. The system appears to have succeeded in combining Bulgarian heritage with the traditional culture of continental legal doctrine and the aspirations of Socialist society. The emphasis of the State and the people is heavy on crime prevention efforts through education and involvement of the populace in general.

German Democratic Republic

The tenth-ranking country in world industrial output spends one-quarter of its annual civil budget on the social sector. Through planning, a swelling of existing metropolitan centers was avoided. The population is homogenous. Young people have the right and the duty to learn, and they are guaranteed jobs. Active participation in group activities is expected (e.g., 2.5 million youths are enrolled in the sports federation). Families are assisted with respect to the care of the young by various children's centers. There is no unemployment, and all basic needs are covered by governmental and communal services.

Since the beginning of the German Democratic Republic, emphasis was placed on involving citizens, i.e., workers and peasants, in the administration of criminal justice at all levels, with an emphasis on the prevention of crime before its occurrence through broad-based mass efforts aimed at instilling a spirit of community solidarity and conformity. The legislation on which this approach is based itself was popularly debated at all levels and the implementation of the legislation was entrusted to specialists or citizens who are directly responsible to local, regional, or national bodies. This system achieves its high grade of effectiveness by an integrated structure of highly trained and well-equipped specialists in the area of crime control.

Costa Rica

Unique in its region, the absence of a large indigenous population to work the land led to citizens' owning and caring for their own small farms. The country is characterized by political stability, high education levels, increasing industrial opportunity, and one of the highest gross domestic products in Central America. Costa Rica is predominantly rural. Families are tightly-knit, and religious values are strictly upheld. Thirty percent of the annual budget goes to education. There is a strong social welfare system and a constant effort to maintain a high quality of life. Central to its welfare strategy are the local health posts which keep track of the needs of citizens in their local communities.

Costa Rica, equipped with a penal code resting on traditional Latin American scholarly conceptions, and a code of criminal procedure which, in Latin American fashion, is inquisitorial in approach, has nevertheless managed to create and maintain a criminal justice system which has put the emphasis on the prevention of crime by reaching out into the community, especially to the young. Thus, the country exhibits a dichotomy between a classic and disciplinarian approach to crime and corrections, and a social defense oriented effort to prevent crime in the first place, or at least its repetition.

Peru

This land of economic, cultural and social diversity (Whites, Indians and Mestizos) has suffered natural disasters and intense poverty. Half of the population lives in isolated villages at subsistence level, with little outside contact. Communication is generally difficult. Traditional family life has rested on the kinship group's providing the mainstay of stability. Among both the Indians (where tribal values outrank individual values) and the Hispanics (who espouse strong family loyalty), group bonds are an overriding force of social control. The influence of religion is strong and pervasive, permeating daily life. There is no universal system of social security, and there are massive health and welfare problems. Unemployment is extremely high. Over half of the population exists outside of the cash economy. For those who do seek urban employment, the migration pattern involves an initial move to a nearby town or village. If migrants are successful in the transition, they go on to the cities where they are assisted by regional clubs, groups of persons from the same origin, who combine to offer group support and controls. Loyalty is revered.

The criminal justice system of Peru appears to be rather typical of those in vogue in South America. Both the substantive and the procedural codes are the product of a traditional and highly developed juridical culture and the correctional approach is of a disciplinarian and rigid nature. Popular participation in the system of criminal justice is minimal. There is virtually no official or popular outreach aiming at prevention. The criminal justice system appears to exist for a fairly well-defined subculture of criminal perpetrators, with little applicability to the rest of the population.

Algeria

One of the most important natural gas-producing nations in the world, Algeria is still basically an agricultural country. Thirteen percent of the wage earners and 230,000 of their children (i.e., a substantial portion of the crime-prone population group) have left the country and are migrant laborers in France. Following Muslim tradition, the strength of the family depends on the honor of each member. Social controls at this level are rigid. Urbanization has been planned to such a degree that there are very few shanty towns.

Education is free and compulsory. Citizens are urged to uphold old traditions, and the commune is central to social, economic and cultural life.

Algeria, in a manner which is not atypical of formerly colonial countries, has retained, yet adapted for its own purposes, the criminal justice system of the former colonial power. This was accomplished not without difficulties due to the exodus of those formerly in charge of the system. This process was further complicated by the desire of the new government to combine the French-based system with modern Socialist principles and Islamic heritage. The effort appears to have succeeded to a certain extent. The resulting system, however, still largely has the imprint of the French system of criminal justice, yet with more citizen participation than in France. There is little evidence that pro-active crime prevention efforts have been put into effect.

Saudi Arabia

This country has gone from dependence on herding and date farming to being the third largest oil producer in the world. Three-quarters of the population is rural, made up of a homogenous ethnic group, plus over one million foreigners. An individual's loyalty to his family overrides most other obligations. There are strong religious controls which dominate the socio-political and economic life. The Government devotes twenty-five percent of its budget to education, which is free but not compulsory. Moslem law is one of the most important components of the curriculum. There is a rapid shift from rural to urban settlements, causing overcrowding problems in the cities. The deeply rooted Moslem culture dictates that the more fortunate members of society must assist the less fortunate. Social services are good.

The Saudi Arabian criminal justice system, unlike any of the others reviewed in this work, is totally integrated with the socio-religious structure of the country. Inasmuch as this structure is shared by the entire population, the criminal justice system is the most uniquely integrated system imaginable. Nevertheless, the Saudi Arabian system was faced with a considerable challenge, namely to provide for the administration of a system developed by a highly trained religious-scholarly caste under circumstances requiring the deployment of highly trained agents of law enforcement versed in the use of modern systems and technologies. The development of the nation, moreover, needed an expertise in research and planning which had to meet high standards of sophistication. The wealth of the country permitted a reconciliation of these divergent perquisites.

Japan

This nation has grown so fast in one century that it has become one of the most highly industrialized countries in the world. The population is homogenous. Despite rapid development, it has remained one of the most traditional societies, clinging to ancient faiths and time-honored codes of behavior. Regulation and control characterize daily life, where the indivdiual is strongly committed to the group. A unique factory system has become a surrogate family in urbanized areas. The company offers security in return for loyalty. Families are patriarchal in structure and are both highly indulgent and highly restrictive. Social services are excellent, and the calibre of education extremely high. The criminal justice system operates in an orderly, speedy fashion. A unique police/citizen rapport is believed by many to constitute the most important feature of the nation's crime control strategy, at all levels of the criminal justice system.

Few countries investigated in this study evidence as large a degree of citizens' involvement in all aspects of criminal justice as Japan. Yet this citizen participation is engrafted on a structure of codes and laws which are derived from the highest degree of scholarly effort and which are grounded in both the doctrinal pursuits of continental criminal law and the due process orientation of Anglo-American procedure. Only the unique nature of Japanese culture can possibly explain the extraordinary congruity of morals and law, social interest and individual interest, and professional administration of criminal justice and popular participation.

Nepal

Nepal remains one of the lesser developed countries of the world with 90 percent of the Nepalese living in agricultural villages of less than 600 residents. There is ethnic, linguistic and religious diversity. Citizens are directly involved in government through the local panchayat system. Most of the people depend on subsistence farming for their livelihood. The extended family forms not only the basis of the social structure, but also serves as the most important social institution and as the economic and political unit. Education is free but not compulsory. About sixty percent of eligible primary school-age children receive instruction. Families depend on the manpower of their members. Transportation is a major problem. Medical care is poor and there are few social services.

There is no doubt that the low crime rate of Nepal exists despite the absence of a developed criminal justice system. The commendable efforts of the royal government to establish modern policing, a structured court system, and a correctional service, and to combine these with the traditional administration of justice in the communes (now established as panchayats) have not yet led to the development of an integrated system. The available evidence indicates that in the rural areas, which harbor the vast majority of the population, it is still the indigenous system which succeeds in keeping the crime rate low while in urban areas, particularly Katmandu, the capital, the challenges of an evolving youth counter-culture must yet be met. An incipient effort in this regard could be noted.

Discussion

Can it be concluded that the profiles of our ten low crime countries reveal certain common characteristics in their formal (criminal justice) or informal social control mechanisms which might explain their low crime status? Or are we dealing with country-specific phenomena that do not readily lend themselves to comparison? To begin with, can it be said that our ten countries should credit their criminal justice systems for their low crime status?

At first glance the diversity of approaches to crime prevention and control among our ten countries appears baffling. Our ten countries belong to diverse legal systems, including the civil law system, whether Capitalist (Costa Rica, Japan, Peru, Switzerland), or Socialist (Bulgaria, German Democratic Republic and, to a certain extent, Algeria), the common law system (Ireland), indigenous system (Saudi Arabia) or mixed (Nepal, i.e., common law and indigenous). Largely derived from these systems are totally varying approaches to the criminal process, including, inquisitorial (e.g., Peru and Costa Rica), adversary (e.g., Ireland) and accusatory (e.g., Japan and Switzerland). Nor can it be the political orientation of the criminal justice system for here, too, we encounter great diversity.

Is there a detectable difference in the success rate of our ten countries in solving reported crime? Unfortunately, available data, crude and incomplete as they are, permit us to say little more than that we are probably dealing with a success spectrum ranging from high (Japan, Saudi Arabia) to low—probably among some of the countries whose figures are not available. On the other hand, somewhat more reliable data are available on the punitiveness of the criminal justice systems in question, namely as measured by their resort to capital punishment. Data for our ten countries are available through the report "United Nations Norms and Guidelines in Criminal Justice: From Standard-setting to Implementation—Capital Punishment."[1] One-half of the subject countries no longer resort to capital punishment, for all practical purposes. Thus, Nepal has abolished capital punishment for all ordinary crimes, and no executions have taken place. In recent years, Costa Rica has been totally abolitionist and Peru is abolitionist for ordinary crimes. In Ireland, capital punishment has fallen into desuetude for decades, and Switzerland likewise has abolished capital punishment for all ordinary crimes and has not executed anybody for decades.

The remaining half of the subject countries do retain capital punishment for ordinary crimes, but in four out of five, executions are relatively rarely resorted to, i.e., in recent years one in Bulgaria (1977), one in Algeria and possibly five (between 1973 and 1976) in the German Democratic Republic. Figures for Saudi Arabia are not available. Among the ten subject countries, only Japan is reported to have made regular use of capital executions. The Report of the Secretariat to the Economic and Social Council of 1980 reports forty-four executions in Japan (1974-1978).[2] From these data, it is impossible to conclude that recourse to capital punishment, as an indicator of the punitiveness of a system, plays any significant role in the preservation of low crime rates. Nor can it be ruled out that, in some societies, the criminal justice system, as one of the social control systems, derives a certain strength and credibility from the existence of capital punishment on the books. But even that surmise

1. *Working Paper* prepared by the Secretariat on Capital Punishment, A/CONF. 87/9, United Nations, 1980.
2. *Capital Punishment,* Report of the Secretary-General, E/1980/9. Estimated figures are also contained in *The Death Penalty,* Amnesty International Report (London: Amnesty International Publications, 1979). See also, Antoinette D. Viccica, *Political Recourse to Capital Punishment,* (Ph.D Dissertation, Rutgers—The State University of New Jersey, 1982). According to this study, none of the ten low crime countries falls into the category of those having used the death penalty for political purposes.

has to be regarded with great caution. In sum, seven of the nine countries for which data are available make little or no use of capital punishment, one uses it modestly and one regularly. Here, too, diversity is the rule.

Certain conclusions could conceivably be drawn by studying the human rights approach to criminal justice in the various countries by reference to the basic international human rights instruments to which given countries adhere. In this regard, the following table is indicative of the fact that only two of the top low crime rate countries have not yet signed or ratified any of the major instruments, while the other eight have signed or ratified some or all of the basic human rights instruments, in one form or another, and have, thus, committed themselves to bring their criminal justice systems in line with the basic criminal justice tenets of these instruments. That ratification of a human rights instrument does not necessarily mean practical implementation, goes without saying.

TABLE*

Algeria	C1S	C2S		
Saudi Arabia	—			
Costa Rica	C1R	C2R	OPR	AR
Peru	C1R	C2R	OPR	AR
Bulgaria	C1R	C2R	H	
Germ. Dem. Rep.	C1R	C2R	H	
Ireland	C1S	C2S	ER	H
Switzerland	ER	H		
Nepal	—			
Japan	C1R	C2R		

Source: Willems, (ed.), *The International Bill of Human Rights,* Glen Ellen: Entwhistle Books, (1981), pp. 101-102.

Key:
C1S = signed Covenant on Economic, Social and Cultural Rights
C2S = signed Covenant on Civil and Political Rights
C1R = ratified Covenant on Economic, Social and Cultural Rights
C2R = ratified Covenant on Civil and Political Rights
ER = ratified European Covention on Human Rights
AR = ratified American Convention on Human Rights
H = party to Helsinki Accord

There is, thus, diversity not only in the extent to which our ten countries have pledged their adherence to the great human rights principles which affect the criminal process, but undoubtedly also in the extent to which they have been able to practically implement such principles.

Thus far we have found little in the way of similarities in criminal justice among our countries which might account for their low crime status. It is necessary, then, to take a final country-by-country look at the ten criminal justice systems under review, in search of any commonalities.

Peru is vested with a system which is the outgrowth of a colonial structure, perpetuated and cultivated in an alien setting with little outreach to the indigenous population. But since Peru's crime problem is largely to be found in the cities, where indigenous social control is relatively weak, and not in the countryside, where indigenous social control is relatively strong—and the formal criminal justice system rarely gets involved, it might be surmised that the "popular," yet informal crime control system of the village is more successful than the "unpopular" formal control system of the cities. Conceivably the same could hold true for largely rural Nepal, where the agents of the formal criminal justice system are valiantly trying to reach out into the countryside, as yet with little success.

Costa Rica, located in the same cultural region as Peru and basing its system on the same juridical culture, appears to have succeeded in combining the traditional Spanish-American juridical culture with popular demands and a more pro-active approach to crime control, under involvement of the community.

In Saudi Arabia, the criminal justice system is completely derived from the indigenous culture, and it required only the introduction of modern methodology and technology to make this crime control system consonant with the demands of the twentieth century. Thanks to Saudi Arabia's wealth, this task could be accomplished with ease.

In a separate category are the countries which have experienced a significant shift in status. Ireland, Algeria, Bulgaria, and the German Democratic Republic all had to revamp their criminal justice systems following the acquisition of a new status, yet all retained the basic outline of the legal systems in existence prior to their new status. All four managed to retain what was laudable and useful about those systems, yet three of the four (Algeria, Bulgaria and the German Democratic Republic) adopted far greater popular participation than had been in vogue before. Ireland exchanged the interests of the British Crown, virtually an occupation power, for the interests of the Republic and its people. It is noteworthy that in Ireland's case, popular participation in the administration of justice did not increase significantly, but that an alien system of criminal justice became the people's own upon establishment of independence. Algeria's case was somewhat more difficult. Not only did it have to do what Ireland did, but it also had to train a new cadre of specialists, to remove a considerable amount of discriminatory legislation and to introduce principles consistent with the goals of ancient national heritage, Islam, and newly acquired Socialism. The latter demanded a far greater degree than theretofore of popular participation in the creation and implementation of crime prevention programs.

We noted an extraordinarily high degree of popular participation for the two capitalist countries of Switzerland and Japan, and the two Socialist countries of Bulgaria and the German Democratic Republic. For Switzerland, popular participation is in its eighth century. It is deeply ingrained and the only challenge to it is that imposed by the sophistication and specialization which legal scholarship on the one hand and the technocracy of the criminal justice process impose in the computer age, on the other. We were able to note that Switzerland is handling this challenge well.

Japan has had some tradition of popular participation but managed to introduce a far greater degree of community involvement in crime control during the last generation, to some extent on foreign stimulation, but to a far greater degree on her own initiative. The result has been an unprecedented and harmonious integration of three diverse elements: a highly developed juridical culture, a technically superior approach to prevention, and a large degree of popular participation.

The two popular democratic republics, Bulgaria and the German Democratic Republic, share with the previously colonial countries, the predicament of having had to start from scratch in the establishment of a popularly acceptable crime control apparatus. As noted, both retained their previous juridical culture, yet both created a new cadre of criminal justice administrators and reoriented their systems in accordance with the demands of socialist legality which, *inter alia,* demanded an unprecedented involvement of the masses in the creation of new legislation, in the establishment and maintenance of the criminal justice system, and in the day to day administrations of crime control mechanisms including, and particularly, crime prevention efforts reaching the very young.

The reader may perceive in the analysis of the criminal justice systems of the ten countries under study that one relatively common element seems to emerge. That is the element of popular involvement in the criminal justice system, or of the popularity of that system. Thus, six of our ten countries are marked by an extraordinarily high degree of popular participation in crime countrol. Four of these are highly industrialized nations: Japan, Switzerland, Bulgaria, and the German Democratic Republic. For two countries located at the other end of the development scale, namely, Nepal and Peru, indigenous crime control still appears to be effective. In both of these countries, where crime control is located at the local-rural level, and rests in the hands of clans and local organizations, it is popular, while the official and urban criminal justice systems simply have not (yet) had any popular outreach. Saudi Arabia, at the moment where it is being thrust from the caravan age into the jet age, has managed to keep its indigenous and popularly grounded social control system intact. Rural Costa Rica has managed to involve the community in crime prevention to a certain extent, but, above all, its Swiss-style emphasis on local self-government, has resulted in the popularity of administration, including that of criminal justice. A certain degree of popular participation could also be reported for Algeria. But, more importantly, Algeria and Ireland both, by replacing the interests of their people for those of an alien occupying power, rendered their adopted criminal justice systems popularly acceptable.

It would be premature to proclaim that it is the degree of popularity of a criminal justice system, whether it is the official one or a surrogate system, which makes for low crime rates. Rather, it now becomes important to take a close look at surrogate or supplementary social control systems which may be operative in our ten countries. This must be done within the overall context of political and social forces extant in our countries, for all of these—including criminal justice forces—are inextricably interwoven. We should also guard ourselves from concluding that it is any or all of these forces which are *directly* associated with low crime rates. Rather, it may be necessary to search for whatever it is that these forces stand for or produce, and then to examine whether, indirectly or secondarily, low crime rates may result therefrom.

We shall begin our examination of non-criminal justice social controls—composed of political and social forces—by noting that certain of these appear to have little to do with low crime rates. Thus, our countries represent a gamut of different types of government, including people's republic, military government, parliamentary democracy, popular democracy, absolute monarchy and constitutional monarchy. The varieties of economies range from subsistence agriculture (Peru and Nepal) to highly industrialized economies (German Democratic Republic, Switzlerland, Japan).

Some have urbanized slowly (Ireland, Switzerland), while others have undergone rapid transitions (Saudi Arabia, Japan). There are both high unemployment rates (Peru) and low unemployment rates (German Democratic Republic, Bulgaria, Japan, Switzerland). Homogeneous cultures (Saudi Arabia, Japan, Costa Rica) seem as resistant to crime as heterogeneous countries (Switzerland, Peru, Nepal). Some of the ten low crime-rate countries have strong social welfare programs (German Democratic Republic, Bulgaria, Algeria, Saudi Arabia) while to others such programs are unacceptable (Switzerland), and still a third group has economies which have not yet developed such a system (Peru, Nepal). Indeed, there are many more differences among these countries than can be dealt with here. Suffice it to say that these countries represent a broad spectrum of socio-economic and politico-cultural systems. Is there nevertheless some thread that weaves its way through the various social fabrics?

The major findings of the qualitative part of the study suggest that all ten countries appear to have developed some form of strong social control, outside and apart from the criminal justice system. The social control systems of which I speak do not aim to control by formal restraint. Rather, they transmit and maintain values by providing for a sharing of norms and by ensuring cohesiveness.

Among those social control systems, there is, above all, the family. Most of the countries under study have seen little disruption of their strong family system. For Nepal, where no rural-to-urban flight has yet occurred, the clans, as extended families, remain as a formidably effective system serving the preservation of harmony and the transmission of values. Extended families form the basis of the social structure by serving as the social, economic, and, often, the political unit. Thus, Peruvian kinship groups provide the mainstay of stability among both Indians (where tribal values are more important than individual needs) and Hispanics (with their overriding commitment to family loyalty). Costa Rican families are characterized as tightly-knit units with defined membership roles and rigid discipline, and that is true for Swiss families. Saudi Arabian and Algerian societies expect family loyalties to supersede all others, as dictated by the Moslem tradition. In Bulgaria, young people stay home and close to the family where they receive a solid grounding in social and moral duties. The Japanese system is patriarchal in structure, highly indulgent and highly restrictive. Any disgrace which befalls the individual shames the entire family.

It is noteworthy that among our sample of ten countries, family controls have been maintained even in the wake of modernization, i.e., mechanization of agriculture and dwindling agricultural employment opportunities and industrialization with new employment opportunities at distant industrial sites, usually urban areas. Bulgaria, the German Democratic Republic, Japan, Saudi Arabia and Switzerland are among the countries which were faced with that challenge. Each has responded with imagination and within the context of its own cultural traditions and ideological commitments. Each has made a deliberate and costly governmental effort to keep the family intact as a strong social control organ. Just as one can plan for and work toward crime control, one can plan for and work toward preservation of the viability of the family—and, secondarily, thereby to plan for crime control.

But the efforts of the successful countries did not end there. In highly industrialized societies, with their relative labor mobility, the family remains vulnerable, yet the clan is no longer there to offer its protective shield, to create and maintain a "sense of community." Thus, all of the successful countries felt challenged to provide communal surrogates for the vanishing clan. In Switzerland, there is the *Gemeinde,* a socio-political unit which remains intact largely because a superb transportation system makes it possible for Swiss workers to retain their homes in the Gemeinde, yet to easily reach their places of employment on a daily basis. Deliberate efforts have been made to maintain employment opportunities in small towns all over the country, rather than in a few metropolitan areas. Similarly, in Bulgaria, the emphasis is on the provision of employment opportunities within contiguous, non-metropolitan areas which have their own social, administrative, political and cultural services and organizations, whether productive units or politico-cultural groups, which serve as social control agencies, and thus ensure an effective transmission and preservation of communal values and control. And what has been said of Bulgaria is largely true for the German Democratic Republic.

The German Democratic Republic and Bulgaria both have developed kindergartens and various other specialized children's establishments to act as functional equivalents of the family for the day-time hours. As the industrialized home closes down between eight and five, another institution assumes total responsibility for the physical, emotional and academic development of the young.

Leisure time is planned, citizens, young and old, are encouraged to play active roles in various after-school clubs and sports activities, with an overall commitment to the advancement of their society.

Japan, perhaps, has been most fortunate in the discovery of a "surrogate family" to supplement the dwindling natural family. There emerged, in Japanese society, the concept of the industrial community, which young workers enter pretty much as they would have entered the clan of an in-law in times past. Just as the production unit of Socialist countries serves as a surrogate or additional family, the industrial community of a capitalist Japanese enterprise provides many of the protections, services and controls which the clan once had available, ranging virtually from birth to death, and including child rearing services, leisure time activities, vacations, pensions and burial. While the Japanese industiral community was probably organized as a means of ensuring efficient industrial productivity, it nevertheless turned out to be a culturally harmonious agency of social service and control.

From the Japanese factory, to the Bulgarian commune to the Nepalese village Panchayat to the Swiss *Gemeinde* and Canton to the Algerian assemblies, there appears to be a steady effort on the part of most of the ten countries to maintain the involvement of the citizens in the affairs which concern their own destiny. The sharing of activities "for the common good" accounts for an apparently strong social solidarity.

The sharing of values is of course also achieved through religion which, thus, operates as another forceful control system. Although the patterns of spiritual activity may differ, from the Five Pillars of Islam to the Nepalese adoration of their own village deities, to the ancestor worship of the Japanese, to the strong communal churches of Switzerland or Costa Rica, they are all a manifestation of group solidarity. In the Islamic countries, in particular, the strength of the Koran is felt in all aspects of daily living, including business and politics. It is, undoubtedly, the all-pervading influence of Islam, not just as a religion but as a way of life, practiced in the family, the mosque and in the community, which exerts a powerful influence on society. Prayer five times a day is a constant reminder of the presence of God, and pilgrimages to Mecca are the realization of a universal brotherhood. These religious gatherings solidify the moral obligations of the community to reaffirm in common their common sentiments. The moral precepts, based on religion, of some of the countries under study, conceivably have their counterparts in the secular ethical precepts of some other countries.

We may conclude, then, that all ten low crime rate countries appear to have in common a certain success in maintaining or creating effective social control agencies which, in all cases, include the family plus one or several other control mechanisms which assist in maintaining, preserving and transmitting shared values.

These surrogate or supplementary control agencies are not identical. Nor does any of our ten low crime rate countries have all of the social controls. Moreover, priorities vary among countries. Above all, it is not imaginable that a transfer of social control systems could be designed without risking grave havoc. Saudi Arabia's Islamic control system can work as little in Switzerland as Switzerland's *Gemeinde* system in Saudi Arabia. It is, thus, not the one or the other social control system which is associated with low crime rates. Rather, the point is that all ten countries with low crime rates have developed social control agencies which, in their proper cultural setting, are popularly accepted and then serve as successful agents in maintaining social solidarity. To reiterate: successful crime control appears to go hand in hand with the existence of effective systems of popularly accepted and culturally harmonious social controls, of which the criminal justice system is one, capable of maintaining, generating and transmitting shared values.

The implications of this finding, however tentative, are somewhat frustrating if it be considered that all societies have tolerance limits which, politically, they are unwilling to exceed. Any one of the social controls—including those of criminal justice—developed by our ten low crime countries may be too rigid or too demanding for any high crime rate country to accept or to emulate. The predicament, thus, consists of having to accommodate the right to be free from depradation by criminality, on the one hand, and to be free from restraint or regimentation, on the other. Each society determines its own upper and lower tolerance levels in crime control. The upper tolerance level is the maximum amount of crime which a given society is willing to accept, the lower is the maximum amount of restraint which it is willing to impose upon itself for purposes of crime control. Just as any society has to decide how much in the nature of sickness or infant mortality it is willing to tolerate, a society has to decide how much crime it is willing to tolerate. Crime control can never be the principal and utmost end of any society. For that matter, nor could the preservation of health, for, if it were, society might have to live in a sterile environment; nor could industrial growth be the principal and utmost end, for, if it were, the products of industrial production would clutter the earth, together with blighted soil and pestilential air. If crime control were to be made the utmost aim of a society, the streets might be safe and the accountants' books might be immaculate, yet the population might be stifled in an atmosphere of complete control and rigidity.

No society, of course, makes a deliberate, planned decision to limit its homicides to a range from W to X and its robberies from Y to Z. Rather, the choice is determined in the process of long-range, intuitive communal decision-making, occasionally speeded up by indignation or dissatisfaction in the case of particularly heinous occurrences, or the rhetoric of the political process. Our ten low crime countries have revealed to us their social and political choices which resulted in the emergence of control systems that proved successful in keeping their crime rates low. They have thus found their accommodation between the two tolerance levels, that of crime rates and that of social restraints.

13

From Anomie to Synnomie

Up to this point we have been concerned with the examination, in criminological, legal, and sociological terms, of ten different societies of which we have a reasonable assurance that they share the advantage of low crime rates. We have been able to identify—however tentatively—certain fairly common characteristics, both in their criminal justice systems and their social control structure, which we have called social control systems. As yet we have not addressed ourselves to the theoretical implications of our findings. We must, then, consult sociological and criminological theory in an effort to ascertain whether our surmise—that effective and popularly acceptable social control systems create conditions in which crime is infrequent—is supportable by principles which transcend and encompass cultural variations or indeed, whether a distinct theory emerges which might explain the theoretical implications of our findings.

Darwin's theory of evolution is one of profound optimism: from ape to man. Those who wrote under the impact of early Darwinism reflected this optimism. Their writings took many forms. To Marx it meant that with the perfection of industrialism, only socialism with equal sharing in the ownership of the means and in the output of production, would create universal well-being.[1] To Sir Henry Sumner Maine the evidence of history proved an unerring path of progress from man's enslavement by his social

---

1. Karl Marx, *Das Kapital*, 1867.

status to the freedom which would come with the recognition of his contractual right to create relations with others and thereby to condition his well-being.

> The movement of the progressive societies has been uniform in one respect. Through all its course it has been distinguished by the gradual dissolving of family dependency and the growth of individual obligation in its place. The individual is steadily substituted for the Family, as the unit of which civil laws take account. The advance has been accomplished at varying rates of celerity. . . . Nor is it difficult to see what is the tie between man and man which replaces by degrees those forms of reciprocity in rights and duties which have their origin in the Family. It is Contract. Starting, as from one terminus of history, from a condition of society in which all the relations of Persons are summed up in the relations of Family, we seem to have steadily moved towards a phase of social order in which all these relations arise from the free agreement of individuals. In Western Europe the progress achieved in this direction has been considerable. Thus, the status of the Slave has disappeared—it has been superseded by the contractual relation of the servant to his master. The status of the Female under tutelage, if the tutelage be understood of persons other than her husband has also ceased to exist; from her coming of age to her marriage all the relations she may form are relations of contract.
>
> The word Status may be usefully employed to construct a formula expressing the law of progress thus indicated, which, whatever be its value, seems to me to be sufficiently ascertained.[2]

To Maine the movement of the progressive societies has been a movement from status to contract.

On the European continent, Ferdinand Tönnies studied the evolution of social units and perceived this evolution in terms of a development which led from small, self-contained units, marked by a sharing of values—which he called *Gemeinschaft*—to a larger and more political organization in which divergent values had to be subordinated—called *Gesellschaft,* or Society. The distinguishing characteristics of these two types of societal organizations are outlined as follows.[3]

2. Henry Sumner Maine, *Ancient Law,* (London, 1861) 163-165.
3. Don Martindale. *The Nature and Types of Sociological Theory.* (Boston: Houghton Mifflin Co., 1960) p. 84.

Social Characteristics	Societal Type	
	Gemeinschaft	Gesellschaft
Dominant Social Relationship	Fellowship, Kinship Neighborliness	Exchange Rational calculations
Central Institutions	Family law; Extended kinship	State Capitalistic economy
The Individual in the Social Order	Self	Person
Characteristic Form of Wealth	Land	Money
Type of Law	Family law	Law of contracts
Ordering of Institutions	Family life Rural village life Town life	City life Rational life Cosmopolitan life
Type of Social Control	Concord Folkways and mores Religion	Convention Legislation Public opinion

Tönnies saw the greater value of *Gemeinschaft,* which he viewed as a natural accommodation of the interest or will of the component members; but he was not oblivious to the emergence of the *Gesellschaft,* which he viewed as the somewhat compulsory subordination of the interest, or will, of the component members. Society, to Tönnies, is a mechanical social construct based almost on arbitrary will. Whereas *Gemeinschaft* is an harmonious social organ based on a commonality of interests, the relationships of *Gesellschaft* are built on the rational will, or on calculated means to ends. There is inherent in Tönnies' evolutionary theory the possibility that *Gesellschaft* bears within it the germ of disharmony and conflict, a possibility which, by definition, is excluded for *Gemeinschaft.* But he did not develop that thought.[4]

Both Maine and Tönnies viewed evolution in terms of social control mechanisms. To Maine, the social control mechanism shifted from family accommodation to enforceable political relations. But in essence both realized the significance of social control in terms of the unit that exercises it.

Others who wrote under the impact of social Darwinism viewed social control systems as being functional rather than hierarchical. Thus, Spencer dichotomized religious-militaristic versus modern

4. Ferdinand Tönnies, *Gemeinschaft und Gesellschaft,* (Leipzig, 1887.).

industrial–peaceable systems,[5] and Comte posited a tripartite division of social controls, namely, the theological, the metaphysical and the positivistic.[6] Subsequent scholars were to be more specific in terms of the type of social control exercised.

In terms of social control by the criminal justice system, an evolutionary theory was suggested by Mueller and Besharov:

> As we trace mankind through recorded history, we note with fascination that the jurisdictional units are becoming larger and larger, not only in terms of sheer numbers of component members but also in terms of hierarchical order. The family as a basic jurisdictional unit is replaced by the clan, the clan by the tribe or city, which, in turn loses out to the kingdom or empire, until today, when nations are yielding some slices of their criminal law sovereignty to yet higher units, such as regional international groupings . . . or world bodies.[7]

Mueller and Besharov posit that "Criminal law always seeks and ultimately finds that jurisdictional unit which can handle its definitions and administration with the optimal ease and efficiency."[8] They leave unexplained what happens if in this evolutionary process a given jurisdictional issue is passed on to the next higher level, and that level is not yet ready to assume effective social control, i.o.w., what happens if there is a conflict in the capacity to effectively deal with the question of control.

While there are many explanations of the conflicts which inevitably arise as one social control unit—or one jurisdictional control unit, in terms of Mueller and Besharov—is replaced by another, a particularly intriguing explanation is offered by Redfield. His studies, based on Mexico, show that the conflict is primarily one of conflict between city people and country people. One wonders whether this is not tantamount to the conflict between jurisdictionally diverse units, e.g., the clan versus the political unit of the "polis," or city-state, or between the status society and the contract

5. Herbert Spencer, *The Study of Sociology*, (New York: Appleton, 1929.); Idem, *First Principles of a New System of Philosophy*, (New York: DeWitt Revolving Fund, 1958); Idem, *Social Statistics*, (New York, D. Appleton, 1904.)

6. Auguste Comte, *Positive Philosophy*, Transl. by Harriet Martineau. 3 vols. (London: George Bell and Sons, 1896).

7. G.O.W. Mueller and D. Besharov, "The Existence of International Criminal Law and Its Evolution to the Point of Its Enforcement Crisis," in *A Treatise on International Criminal Law*, (eds.) M. Cherif Bassiouni and Ved Nanda (Springfield, Ill.: Charles C. Thomas, 1973): pp. 5-22.

8. *Ibid.*, p. 9.

society, or between the *Gemeinschaft* and the *Gesellschaft*. According to Redfield, cultural differences existed not between regions, but rather between city people *(los correctos)* and country folk *(los tontos)*. The characteristics of the isolated communities included cultural homogeneity, interpersonal social relationships, importance of family and kinship groups, accent on sacred sanctions, and dominance of local groups. In contrast, disorganization, secularization, heterogeneity and individualization were found to be related to city life. In his comparison of four communities, the tribal village (Tusik), the peasant village (Chan Kom), the town (Dzitas), and the city (Merida), he found that it was the city where the distribution of productive responsibilities became more complex, the family controls weakened, the strength of custom disappeared, and religion became secularized (with holy days transformed to holidays.)[9] Redfield's thoughts ultimately were presented in a general theory of civilization which traces the problems of humankind after the emergence of the city. The main thrust of the argument is that the transition from a rural-preliterate to an urban-literate society was responsible for the replacement of the moral order with a technical one, of custom with formal law.[10]

The scholars who studied the evolution of social institutions, whether on the basis of law, of anthropology, or of pure history, basically confined themselves to historical and non-evaluative descriptions of the facts as they saw them. Indeed, if one were to attribute any axiological motives to them, beyond the normative, one would have to characterize these as positive, if not optimistic. Critical analysis of evolution theories in terms of impact on society started with Durkheim, who detected the phenomenon of evolution gone wrong, i.e., disharmony, which he called anomie. His discussion of anomie is profound, yet it constituted only a small part of his work. Nevertheless, the American students of disharmony, viz., particularly the criminologists, seized upon his discussion of an abnormal form of social evolution, namely anomie, as a possible explanation of criminality. From that point on, the criminologists' emphasis, within the confines of Durkheim's sociological theory, was entirely on disharmony—anomie—to the neglect of Durk-

9. Robert Redfield, *Tepoztlan: A Mexican Village.* (Chicago: University of Chicago Press, 1930); Idem, *The Folk Culture of Yucatan,* (Chicago: University of Chicago Press, 1941.)

10. Robert Redfield, *The Primitive World and Its Transformations,* (Ithaca, N.Y.: Cornell University Press, 1953); Idem, *The Little Community,* (Chicago: University of Chicago Press, 1955); Idem, *Peasant, Society and Culture,* (Chicago: University of Chicago Press, 1956.)

heim's far greater interest in social solidarity. Thus, for almost a century the opportunity of studying social harmony as an explanation of the absence (or low incidence) or criminality was lost.

Durkheim's concept of "social solidarity" refers to the cohesion of groups within social units.[11] He looked for varying types of solidarity at different levels of social evolution and found that society had progressed from a stage of mechanical solidarity, based on standardization of behavior, to organic solidarity, based on individual differences. Unity in modern society was achieved not by similarity and like parts, but by the interdependence of differentiated parts. As civilization progressed, so, too, did individual rights and the growth of autonomous groups.

> It is the division of labor which, more and more, fills the role that was formerly filled by the common conscience. It is the principal bond of social aggregates of higher types.[12]

It was in his work on suicide that Durkheim developed his discussion of social disharmony. He used statistical data to demonstrate that the rates of suicide were associated with business cycles, for economic depression and sudden prosperity alike. Both of these crises appeared to be associated with a breakdown of the normative system. Old rules no longer applied. Suicide, according to Durkheim, is related to the amount of regulation and control in a given society.

> . . . this aggravation springs not from the intrinsic nature of progress but from the special conditions under which it occurs in our day, and nothing assures us that these conditions are normal. For we must not be dazzled by the brilliant development of sciences, the arts and industry of which we are the witnesses; this development is altogether certainly taking place in the midst of a morbid effervescence, the grievous repercussions of which each one of us feels. It is then very possible and even probable that the rising tide of suicide originates in a pathological state just now accompanying the *march* of civilization *without being its necessary condition* [emphasis added].[13] . . . In the case of economic disasters,

11. Emile Durkheim, *The Division of Labor*, (New York: The Free Press, 1964.) (First published in 1893.)
12. *Ibid.*, p. 173.
13. Emile Durkheim. *Suicide*. (Glencoe, Ill.: The Free Press, 1951) p. 368.

indeed, something like a declassification occurs which sud-
denly casts certain individuals into a lower state than their
previous one. . . . But society cannot adjust them spontane-
ously to this new life and teach them to practice the increased
self-repression to which they are unaccustomed. . . . It is the
same if the source of the crisis is an abrupt growth of power
and wealth. Then, truly, as the conditions of life are changed,
the standard according to which needs were regulated can no
longer remain the same. . . . The scale is upset. . . . Time is
required for the public conscience to reclassify men and
things. So long as the social forces thus freed have not
regained equilibrium, their respective values are unknown
and so all regulation is lacking for a time. . . . The state of
de-regulation or anomie is thus further heightened by persons being less disciplined, precisely when they need more
disciplining.[14]

It was only too easy for social scientists to explain that the same
state of anomie, or extended anomie, which causes an increase in
suicide—aggression against oneself—also causes an increase in
criminality—aggression against others. Future studies, even
remotely referring to Durkheim, would explain criminality in these
terms; few would endeavor to explain the opposite, namely, low
crime rates in conditions signifying the opposite of anomie, which
Durkheim had tentatively called social solidarity.

Thus, Merton adopted the concept of anomie to explain how
social disorganization is responsible for pushing individuals into
illegitimate adaptations. Strain ensues in societies which urge all
people to strive for like success goals while at the same time blocking
many from attaining such goals because they lack the necessary
means. Some who lack such legitimate means use innovative
methods to reach their ends, i.e., criminal acts. Merton looked at
both the culturally defined goals and the social structure's ability to
provide acceptable modes of pursuing them. Thus, according to
Merton,

it is only when a system of cultural values extols, virtually
above all else, certain common success-goals for the population at large while the social structure rigorously restricts or
completely closes access to approved modes of reaching these

14. *Ibid.*, p. 253-254.

goals for a considerable part of the same population, that
deviant behavior ensues on a large scale.[15]

It is the social structure, then, that

exerts a definite pressure upon certain persons in the society
to engage in non-conforming rather than conforming
conduct.[16]

Merton's theory has been expanded and enlarged in a number of
scholarly works. While all of them are important contributions,
most are not central to the present study, e.g., those of Talcott
Parsons who encompasses Merton's work in a more general theory
of deviant behavior,[17] or of Robert Dubin, who develops fourteen
categories of deviant behavior in his related typology.[18] Anomie
theory has also been used in recent years in a variety of applications,
ranging from the all-encompassing social disorder concept of
DeGrazia,[19] to specific applications explanatory of gang behavior,
drug addiction, alcoholism, and mental disorder, among others.
Marshall B. Clinard presented a critique of these approaches,
together with a discussion of their theoretical explanations, in the
volume *Anomie and Deviant Behavior.*[20]
    We previously noted that scholars concentrated on Durkheim's
anomie, under neglect of his "social solidarity." It is noteworthy
that this emphasis on pathology, sometimes to the neglect of its
opposite, namely salubrity, is not confined to anomie theory. The
emphasis on pathology can similarly be found in another major
criminological school, the school of cultural transmission, known
as the Chicago School. The scholars of this school have successfully
demonstrated that the urban decay which occurs around the core of

15. Robert K. Merton, *Social Theory and Social Structure*, (New York: The Free Press of
Glencoe, 1957) p. 146.
    16. *Ibid.*, p. 132.
    17. Talcott Parsons, *The Social System*, (New York: The Free Press of Glencoe, 1951).
    18. Robert Dubin, "Deviant Behavior and Social Structure," *American Sociological
Review*, 24 (1959): pp. 147-164.
    19. Sebastian DeGrazia, *The Political Community: A Study of Anomie*, (Chicago: The
University of Chicago Press, 1948) XII-IX. "The Study of anomie is the study of ideological
factors that weaken or destroy the bonds of allegiance which make the political community."
    20. Marshall B. Clinard, (ed.), *Anomie and Deviant Behavior*, (New York: The Free
Press, 1964) pp. 1-66.

cities is conducive to criminality in a variety of ways. Shaw and McKay, for example, studying the high delinquency areas of Chicago during the periods 1900-1906 and 1917-1923, found that high delinquency occurred in neighborhoods characterized by poor housing, poverty, rapid population growth and adult crime. Proceeding from these core areas toward the outer city, there was a gradual decline associated with increasing distance. The fact that ethnic group composition changed over time did not alter these patterns. Additionally, delinquency occurred in small groups and the "traditions of delinquency [were] transmitted through personal and group contacts."[21]

Shaw and McKay came close to focussing on areas of social salubrity, as contrasted with social pathology, when they recognized that "in the areas of low rates of delinquency there is more or less uniformity, consistency, and universality of conventional values and related matters."[22] Their empirical work, however, was restricted entirely to high delinquent areas where they found that

> . . . competing and conflicting moral values have developed. Even though in [this] situation conventional traditions and institutions are dominant, delinquency has developed as a powerful competing way of life. It derives its impelling force in the boy's life from the fact that it provides a means of securing economic gain, prestige, and other human satisfactions and is embodied in delinquent groups and criminal organizations, many of which have great influence, power, and prestige.[23]

The inclination to accent the negative has remained the hallmark of subsequent criminological studies as well. Perhaps that was to be expected during an era when criminologists saw it as their prime function to study the causes of crime and delinquency. (Does it follow that an accent on the positive would not occur until criminologists would discover a duty to be concerned with crime prevention? The analogy to the transfer from reactive medicine to preventive medicine is obvious.)

21. Clifford R. Shaw and Henry D. McKay, *Social Factors in Juvenile Delinquency*, Vol. II, National Committee on Law Observance and Law Enforcement, Report of the Causes of Crime. (Washington, D.C.: U.S. Government Printing Office, 1931).

22. Clifford R. Shaw and Henry D. McKay, *Juvenile Delinquency in Urban Areas*, (Chicago: University of Chicago Press, 1942).

23. *Ibid.*

In keeping with the traditions of the cultural transmission theory of the Chicago School, Sutherland posited that

> a person becomes delinquent because of an excess of defini-
> tions favorable to violation of law over definitions unfavor-
> able to violation of law. This is the principle of differential
> association. It refers to both criminal and anti-criminal asso-
> ciations and has to do with counteracting forces. When per-
> sons become criminal, they do so because of contacts with
> criminal patterns and also because of isolation from anti-
> criminal patterns.[24]

Frequency, duration, priority and intensity of the associations are key factors in the learning process. Sutherland and his students were to pursue the task of explaining criminal behavior through differential association, although Sutherland himself had been aware that differential association can work in the opposite direction as well.

The implications of this recognition for criminological theory and practice are not inconsiderable. Thus, conceivably, in correctional settings, if the number of definitions unfavorable to violations of law could be so vastly increased as to render the impact of definitions favorable to law violations tangential, then the correction of convicts could be assured over a given period of time. The trouble with this is that the code of American prisoners does not permit associations with persons holding conventional values. In community settings, Sutherland's theory, likewise, is relevant. If community leaders, planners, and organizers were to succeed in mobilizing forces holding definitions unfavorable to law violations in one of those areas identified by Shaw and McKay, conceivably such neighborhoods could be turned around with a resulting decrease in criminality. But the stage of that preventive thinking had not been reached; the accent remained on the negative.[25]

At about the same time, Thorsten Sellin was encouraging criminological researchers to pay close attention to conduct norms and to the criminal behavior which might be caused by the clashing of

24. Edwin H. Sutherland, *Principles of Criminology*, 4th ed. (New York: Harper & Row, 1947). Although the major thrust of differential association accounts for the process by which one becomes delinquent, reference is also made to social changes, including increasing individualism, materialism and mobility with their attendant cultural conflicts. This state was termed "differential social organization."

25. In all fairness it should be mentioned that during the era when the Chicago School was active, there were numerous attempts to impact criminogenic neighborhoods and other settings, e.g., prison, with more or less reference to the theories expanded by that school.

these norms in a society continually growing more complex. According to him:

> . . . culture conflicts are the natural outgrowth of processes of social differentiation, which produce an infinity of social groupings, each with its own definitions of life situations, its own interpretations of social relationships, its own ignorance or misunderstanding of the social values of other groups. The transformation of a culture from a homogeneous and well-integrated type to a heterogeneous and disintegrated type is therefore accompanied by an increase of conflict situations. Conversely, the operation of integrating processes will reduce the number of conflict situations.[26]

Just as culture conflicts may occur when two separate cultures meet and clash, conflict may also occur when, within the same culture, several subcultures have been formed holding different values and when these come into friction with each other. The question then arises how these subcultures are being formed within a given culture. Both anomie theory and cultural transmission theory had a considerable impact on the conceptualization of these subcultural theories of delinquency which were to become popular during the 1950's. In *Delinquent Boys,* for example, Cohen criticizes cultural transmission theory because of its failure to answer the question of why, in fact, there is a delinquent subculture to be transmitted.[27] In other words, how do these subcultures come into existence in the first place? To answer this question he initially looked at the social structure and suggested, (as did Merton), that it is this structure which created the problems by equipping some people with insufficient means for achieving their aspirations. When this happens, it is likely that those unattainable aspirations are rejected, and new ones that fall within reach are set up. In the case of personal worth and self-respect, when conventional criteria of measurement are rejected, the new criteria may require or justify delinquent behavior.

Up to this point Cohen acknowledged that he had not gone much beyond Merton's work on anomie.[28] He then added another

---

26. Thorsten Sellin, *Culture, Conflict and Crime,* Bulletin No. 41 (New York: Social Science Research Council, 1938).

27. Albert K. Cohen, *Delinquent Boys,* (The Free Press, 1955).

28. Albert K. Cohen, *Deviance and Control,* (Englewood Cliffs, N.J.: Prentice-Hall, 1966).

dimension, i.e., the importance of the reference group, a key dimension in cultural transmission theories. Without reference group support from people who share the same problem, there could be no solutions. To Cohen, then,

> the crucial condition for the emergence of new cultural forms is the existence, in effective interaction with one another, of a number of actors with similar problems of adjustment.[29]

Delinquency, then, is viewed as a solution to a shared problem. These problems have their origin in the low status position that lower class boys have in the social order. They begin to realize these

> status problems in the schools where they are evaluated by middle class teachers who use a middle class measuring rod or set of expectations. These expectations cover a gamut of social characteristics encompassing such traits as rationality, courtesy and ambition. Having grown up in a different milieu, these boys withdraw from the hurtful environment (e.g. school) and make their way to a gang subculture which "deals with these problems by providng criteria of status which these children can meet."[30]

These delinquent subcultures have become

> a way of life that has somehow become traditional among certain groups in American society. These groups are the boys' gangs that flourish most conspicuously in the 'delinquent neighborhoods' of our larger American cities.[31]

It should be added that subcultures are not necessarily a manifestation of lower-class belonging. Thus, subcultures similarly arise among the non-achievers within middle-class high schools. Supporting Cohen's line of reasoning, the formation of these peer group subcultures with values different from those of the predominant cultures would also not be a question of class alone but rather one of status.

The question of the creation of subcultures is independent of their identification. Identifiers may classify a subculture in terms of

29. *Op. cit., supra*, n. 27, p. 57.
30. *Ibid.*, p. 121.
31. *Ibid.*, p. 13.

the predominant beliefs or practices of a given subculture as contrasted with those of the culture itself. Such identification may be in
terms of a sexual preference or in their means of responding to
conflict and stress. Thus, Wolfgang and Ferracuti identified the
subculture of violence, marked by the facile resort on the part of its
members to violence in conflict situations.[32] It is, of course, that
subculture which accounts for a large part of violent criminality in
the United States, influenced by what some see as an American
tradition of violence and which, in turn, powerfully conditions
attitudes toward violence on the part of the dominant culture.

In their explanation of the formulation of delinquent subcultures, two other scholars attempted to unite the anomie and cultural
transmission paradigms. While Cohen's "delinquent boys" were
concerned with the quest for status, to Cloward and Ohlin, delinquent boys have economic concerns.[33] Similar to Merton, and
within anomie tradition, they begin with the problem of limited
access to conventional means to reach such goals. Pressure is created
to lessen the goals-means disparity through deviant channels. However, expanding on Merton, Cloward and Ohlin suggest that not
only are legitimate opportunities blocked but so also are illegitimate
ones. Thus, the type of deviant subculture that is found is dependent
on the illegitimate opportunity structure in various lower-class
areas. In neighborhoods characterized by an integration of criminal
and conformist patterns, gang subcultural activities serve as training grounds for careers in criminal behavior. Disorganized neighborhoods foster delinquency which takes the form of conflict
behavior where status is measured by toughness. Lastly, for boys
who fail in both of these subcultures, there are the retreatist subcultures which provide an escape through addiction. This idea of
differential opportunities, then, allowed the authors

> to unite the theory of anomie, which recognizes the concept
> of differentials in access to legitimate means, and the 'Chi-
> cago tradition,' in which the concept of differentials in access
> to illegitimate means is implicit.[34]

While the subcultural theorists discussed thus far relate the
formation of deviant cultures to societal strain, Walter Miller does

32. Marvin Wolfgang and Franco Ferracuti, *The Subculture of Violence*, (London:
Tavistock, 1967).
33. Richard Cloward and Lloyd Ohlin, *Delinquency and Opportunity*, (The Free Press,
1960).
34. *Ibid.*, p. 151.

not. He finds that the lower class value system has an integrity all its own even though it may be at odds with that of the dominant culture.[35] To him, delinquent behavior is inherently tied to the focal concerns or values of lower-class life. *Trouble* means avoiding confrontations with officials (e.g., police), *toughness* refers to daring and bravery, *smartness* is demonstrated by one's ability to outfox or 'hustle,' and *excitement* is sought to break with the monotony of routine life. *Fate* allows luck to change life's chances and *autonomy* means avoiding control by others. Simply living according to these focal concerns puts one outside the framework of lawful behavior.

It does not take much to go from this characterization of lower-class, deviant, law violative behavior to the Marxist explanation of criminality which views criminal behavior of the exploited classes in capitalist society as not only necessary for individual survival but as consistent with the class struggle, indeed as requisite in order to overthrow that upper class which is responsible for oppressive norm creation. With the rise of the proletariat, the cultural norms of the theretofore law-violative class would thus become the cultural norms of the new law-determinative class.[36]

While the major schools which attempted to explain the causes of crime and delinquency were making their mark on criminological thinking, several scholars branched off from the mainstream, intent more on determining what it is that, individually or socially, keeps persons from committing crime, especially under circumstances favoring a delinquent life style according to any of the theories of the major paradigms. I am referring to scholars who derive their orientation from the sociology of social control. The term "social control" had emerged around the turn of the century in a series of papers presented by one of the founders of American sociology, E.A. Ross, subsequently published in a volume entitled "Social Control."[37] According to Ross it is beliefs, rather than specific "laws" of social control, which guide what men do, and these belief systems, although found in different forms, universally serve the same control function. In like fashion, Ross' contemporary William Graham Sumner described the mechanism by which

35. Walter Miller, "Lower Class Culture as a Generating Milieu of Gang Delinquency," *Journal of Social Issues*, 14, No. 3 (1958): pp. 5-19.

36. Ian Taylor, Paul Walton and Jock Young, *The New Criminology*, (New York: Harper and Row, 1973); Richard Quinney, *Crime and Justice in Society*, (Boston: Little, Brown and Co., 1969).

37. E.A. Ross, *Social Control*, (New York: MacMillan, 1922).

society controls individuals. To him it is the habits and customs of "folkways . . . that become regulative for succeeding generations."[38]

Other scholars took different approaches to the role that social control plays in determining behavior. According to La Pierre it is an individual's quest for social status which makes a person amenable to social control. It is, therefore, not the social control factors themselves that are

> the sole cause of human conduct. Rather, they frequently, but not invariably, enter to some degree or another into the complex interaction with personality and situational factors out of which individual conduct emerges.[39]

In addition to writings concerned with what people believe in and why, there is a body of literature which falls under the rubric of the sociology of influence and power. To Wood, for instance, social control is "the use of power with the intention of influencing the behavior of others,"[40] to Martindale it involves the "forming, maintenance, and carrying through of decisions binding on the community as a whole,"[41] to Lumbey it involves "getting others to do, believe, think, feel, . . . as we wish them to,"[42] and to Cave it is "the process by which subgroups and persons are influenced to conduct themselves in conformity with group expectations."[43] Although Parsons also refers to institutional means of securing social control, his major thrust deals with social psychological aspects, rather than considerations of influence and power in society. Thus, "a mechanism of social control . . . is a motivational process in one or more individual actors which tends to counteract a tendency to deviate."[44]

More specific orientations zero in on social control as a means of managing deviant behavior. According to Berger, the concept refers to "the various means used by a society to bring its recalcitrant

38. William Graham Sumner, *Folkways*, (Boston: Ginn, 1906) iii-iv.

39. Richard T. LaPiere, *A Theory of Social Control*, (New York: McGraw Hill Company, 1954).

40. Arthur Lewis Wood, *Deviant Behavior and Control Strategies*, (Lexington, Mass.: D.C. Heath Company, 1974) p. 53.

41. Don Martindale, *Institutions, Organizations and Mass Society*, (Boston: Houghton Mifflin Company, 1966) p. 292.

42. F.E. Lumbey, *Means of Social Control*, (New York: Appleton-Century-Crofts, 1924) p.3.

43. Floyd A. Cave, "State, Law and Government," in *Social Control*, (ed.) Joseph S. Roucek (Princeton, N.J.: D. VanNostrand, 1947) p. 40.

44. Talcott Parsons, *The Social System*, (Glencoe, Ill: The Free Press, 1951) 206.

members back into line.''[45] Others add yet another dimension to the definition—one that suggests the close relationship between law and social control. As Schwartz notes, social control is a process

> involving interaction, i.e., behavior on the part of one actor which affects the behavior of another. Control is distinguished from the other forms of interaction in that it includes sanctions, i.e., the administration of gain or loss to an actor.[46]

The emphasis of the social control theories, thus, is heavy on the utilization of social institutions for purposes of exercising social control. Roscoe Pound considered law to be one of those social institutions.

> I am content to think of law as a social institution to satisfy social wants—the claims and demands involved in the existence of civilized society—by giving effect to as much as we may with the least sacrifice, so far as such wants may be satisfied or such claims given effect by an ordering of human conduct through politically organized society. For present purposes I am content to see in legal history the record of a continually wider recognizing and satisfying of human wants or claims or desires through social control; a more embracing and more effective securing of social interests; a continually more complete and effective elimination of waste and precluding of friction in human enjoyment of the goods of existence—in short, a continually more efficacious social engineering.[47]

To Roscoe Pound, the lawyer, the apparatus called law is a social institution which is effective as a control agency. To Malinowski, the anthropologist, the social control agency, i.e., the clan, enforces social constraint and thus performs a legal function.

> . . . The unity of the clan is neither a mere fairy tale, invented by Anthropology, nor yet the one and only real principle of savage law, the key to all its riddles and difficulties. The

45. Peter L. Berger, *Invitation to Sociology: A Humanistic Perspective*, (New York: Doubleday and Co., 1963) p. 68.

46. Richard Schwartz, "Social Factors in the Development of Legal Control: A Case Study of Two Israeli Settlements," *Yale Law Journal*, 63 (1964): p. 475.

47. Roscoe Pound, *An Introduction to the Philosophy of Law*, (New Haven: Yale University Press, 1922) p. 99.

actual state of affairs, fully seen and thoroughly understood, is very complex, full of apparent as well as of real contradictions and of conflicts due to the play of the Ideal and its actualization, to the imperfect adjustment between the spontaneous human tendencies and rigid law—in all native doctrine, that is in all their professions, and statements, sayings, overt rules and patterns of conduct—an absolute subordination of all other interests and ties to the claims of clan solidarity, while, in fact, this solidarity is almost instantly sinned against and practically non-existent in the daily run of ordinary life.[48]

Whatever the specific orientation of the various social control theories expounded in this overview might be, most of them suggest that the maintenance of social control depends on the interdependence of both informal and formal mechanisms in any given society, although these mechanisms may have different weights depending on the particular culture or on the approach of an individual scholar. As early as 1902, Cooley stressed the important role played by the primary group as the "nursery of human nature." Primary groups are described as those face-to-face associations which are responsible for the formation of the social nature of the individual. Members of these groups share intimacy and common interests. These have a greater impact than other groups, because they play a major role in the developmental years of the child, providing the earliest notions of a social unity and teaching conformity to group standards of conduct.[49] According to Cooley modern societies differ little from ancient societies in this regard. Thus, no matter how developed a particular culture might be, it is the immediate surroundings , e.g., parents, siblings, peers, that supply the crucial support or control system. May's studies of modern industrial workers,[50] and the masses of data gathered in World War II studies of soldier moral,[51] lend support to the idea that even the behavior of modern man is influenced more by small-group forms of social life, a *Gemeinschaft* type of organization, a homogeneous network, than by the formal legal

48. Bronislaw Malinowski, *Crime and Crustom in Savage Society*, (Paterson, N.J.: Littlefield, 1959) p. 119; see also, H. Ian Hogbin, *Law and Order in Polynesia*, (Hamden, Conn.: The Shoestring Press, Inc. 1961).

49. C.H. Cooley, *Social Organization*, (New York: Scribner, 1909).

50. E. May, *Human Problems of Industrial Civilization*, (New York: Macmillan, 1933).

51. S.A. Stouffer, et al., *Studies in Social Psychology in World War II*, 2 vols. (Princeton, N.J.: Princeton University Press, 1949)

system. Parson sums up this view by calling informal controls the "fundamental foundation of 'social control' in all societies."[52]

These insights into social control mechanisms found their way into criminology. In an early paper, Albert J. Reiss, Jr., spoke of both personal and social controls which act to keep a person from engaging in, or repeating, delinquent behavior.[53] He succeeded in isolating a set of personal and social controls which are associated with delinquent recidivism and he evaluted these as prognostic of recidivism. "Personal and social controls" were to be concepts that would prove to be very useful in subsequent criminological developments.

Walter Reckless, who, like Shaw, McKay, Sutherland, and Reiss, came out of the "Chicago School," pursued the same thought: when all the switches on the track point in the direction of delinquency, why do some youngsters succeed in deviating from the appointed course by adopting legitimate careers?[54] In 1955, he and his associates gained access to sixth graders in predominantly white elementary schools in high delinquency areas of Chicago. Teachers were asked to indicate from among the boys in their classes those who, they believed, would not get into trouble. One hundred ninety-two boys were nominated. In 1956, his researchers returned to the teachers for nomination of those who would get into trouble with the police or juvenile court in the future. Researchers interviewed the boys and their mothers, and administered a battery of psychological tests to the boys. Four years later the follow-up assessed how many of these "good" and "bad" boys were, in fact, known to the

52. *Op. cit., supra,* n. 44, p. 134.

53. Albert J. Reiss, *"Delinquency as the Failure of Personal and Social Controls,"* Paper read at the annual meeting of the American Sociological Society, Denver, September 7-9, 1950.

54. Walter C. Reckless, Simon Dinitz, and Ellen Murray, "Self-Concept as an Insulator against Delinquency," *American Sociological Review.* 21 (1956): pp. 744-56; Idem. "The 'Good Boy' in a High Delinquency Area," *Journal of Criminal Law, Criminology and Police Science,* 48 (1957): pp. 18-25; Walter Reckless, Simon Dinitz, and Barbara Kay, "The Self-Component in Potential Delinquency and Potential Non-delinquency," *American Sociological Review,* 22 (1957): pp. 566-70; Simon Dinitz, Barbara Kay, and Walter Reckless, "Group Gradients in Delinquency Potential and Achievement Scores of Sixth Graders," *American Journal of Orthopsychiatry,* 28 (1958): pp. 598-605; Jon Simpson, Simon Dinitz, Barbara Kay, and Walter Reckless, "Delinquency Potential of Pre-Adolescents in a High Delinquency Area," *British Journal of Delinquency,* 10 (1960): pp. 211-15; Frank R. Scarpitti, Ellen Murray, Simon Dinitz, and Walter Reckless, "The 'Good Boy' in a High Delinquency Area: Four Years Later," *American Sociological Review,* 25 (1960): pp. 555-58; Simon Dinitz, Frank Scarpitti, and Walter Reckless, "Delinquency Vulnerability: A Cross Group and Longitudinal Analysis," *American Sociological Review,* 27 (1962): pp. 515-17; Walter Reckless, and Simon Dinitz, "Pioneering with Self-Concept as a Vulnerability Factor in Delinquency," *Journal of Criminal Law, Criminology and Police Science,* 58 (1967): pp. 515-23.

juvenile court. Their data permitted them to conclude that a good self concept insulates slum boys from delinquency while a poor self concept provides no resistance to the delinquent subculture. Here, then, is the distinct identification of the role of individual, or internal, control. The relationship to Freud's superego is implicit.[55] But Reckless and his associates provided an explanation for the creation of these inner controls by the operation of outer controls which, according to the theory, could also have an independent control function even where they did not succeed in establishing inner controls.

> Outer containment represents the structural buffer in the person's immediate social world which is able to hold him within bounds. It consists of such items as a presentation of a consistent moral front to the person, institutional reinforcement of his norms, goals, and expectations, the existence of a reasonable set of social expectations, effective supervision and discipline (social controls), provision for reasonable scope of activity (including limits of responsibility), as well as for alternatives and safety-valves, opportunities for acceptance, identity and belongingness. . . .[56]

The theory which emerged from this research became known as Containment Theory.[57]

The sophistication of criminological research witnessed a constant progress, beginning at a time of uncritical acceptance of research, through a period when research methodology could be tested and critiqued by alternative or replicative criminological investigations, to the period of today when evaluative research has reached a high state of perfection. By these standards, the research of Travis Hirschi on the role of controls has reached a high mark.[58] He studied a group of some 1300 white males, distributed in grades seven through twelve in an urban California county. He postulated that the probability of delinquent behavior rises as an individual's

55. Sigmund Freud, *The Ego and the Id,* translated by J. Riviere, Hogarth Press, 1922; Idem, *A General Introduction to Psychoanalysis,* translated by J. Riviere. (New York: Garden City Publishing Co., Inc., 1938)

56. Walter C. Reckless, *The Crime Problem,* 5th ed. (Englewood Cliffs, N.J.: Prentice-Hall, 1973) pp. 55-56.

57. The same type of research was continued on a larger scale in Columbus in 1957, in Brooklyn and in Akron.

58. Travis Hirschi, *Causes of Delinquency,* (Berkeley: University of California Press, 1969).

bond to society weakens. The components of this *bond* are: attachment (to others), commitment (of time to conventional behavior), involvement (in conventional activities), and belief (in the moral validity of conventional norms). The thrust of the argument is that as these bonds weaken, delinquency becomes possible, but not certain.

Hirschi's main dependent variable is a "recency index," arrived at on the basis of a self report questionnaire measuring involvement in delinquency activity. His basic propositions are:

1. Strong parental attachment is a major deterrent to delinquent behavior. More precisely, parental values are more acceptable when the parent-child relationship is strong. The data show that the hypothesis is supported. The stronger the attachment, the stronger the bond to their expectations, the stronger the bond to conformity.[59] Attachment to the school is related to delinquency. This hypothesis was likewise supported, especially on the variable concerning the bond with the teacher. He posits a causal chain which runs from academic incompetence to poor performance to dislike of school, to rejection of its authority to involvement in delinquency. Furthermore, he found that favorable attitudes toward school act as a deterrent to delinquency regardless of the closeness of the boys' ties with their father.[60] Attachment to peers and attachment to parents are directly related to each other, and both variables are inversely related to self-reported delinquency. (Hirschi has been criticized for not specifying whether peer groups were deviant or conventioal.)

2. Commitment to conventional action is a deterrent to delinquency behavior. Hirschi argues that frustrated aspirations do not act as a motivating force to delinquent behavior, rather, aspirations to achieve conventional success goals help to constrain delinquency. In addition, the dropping out of school by many adolescents with low aspirations means that there is a hiatus between school and occupational career. This situation may well be conducive to the premature adoption of behavior appropriate to adults but not to youngsters. On the other hand, those who maintain a stake in student activities (measured by efforts expended on homework and the importance of grades) are less involved in delinquency.[61]

3. Involvement in conventional activities is a deterrent to delinquent behavior. The relationship was particularly strong on the

59. *Ibid.*, p. 94.
60. *Ibid.*, p. 132.
61. *Ibid.*, p. 166.

variable dealing with concern for, and time spent working on, homework.[62]

4. Delinquency is made possible by an absence of beliefs that prohibit delinquency.[63] Hirschi postulated the causal chain to be that of attachment to parents, concern for the approval of people in positions of authority, and ultimately, belief in the moral validity of societal norms. He suggests that respect for the police taps the same dimension as "attachment to conventional others," a variable also related to respect for the law. He found a strong inverse relationship between both "respect for the police" and "respect for the law" and involvement in delinquent behavior.[64]

Hirschi's emphasis on bonds to society as control factors prompted several scholars to apply this approach to somewhat more narrowly defined situations. Thus, Hindelang replicated the research on a sample of male and female adolescents in a rural setting, coming to very similar conclusions, except that he did not find a positive relationship between attachment to parents and attachment to friends.[65] Higgins and Albrecht demonstrated a negative relationship between frequency of church attendance and delinquency, suggesting that the causal pattern which links the two is respect for the juvenile court.[66] Hepburn presented alternative explanations of the causal structure of the family and peer group variables,[67] Wiatrowski, et al., challenged some of Hirschi's components of bond,[68] and Meadow et al. looked at the family component of societal attachment among one hundred and thirty-five Mexican families.[69]

A discussion of control theory would be incomplete without reference to Daivd Matza who posited that:

> Those who have been granted the potentiality for freedom through the loosening of social controls but who lack the

62. *Ibid.*, p. 191.

63. *Ibid.*, p. 198..

64. *Ibid.*, p. 204.

65. Michael J. Hindelang, "Causes of Delinquency: A Partial Replication and Extension," *Social Problems*, 21 (1973): pp. 471-487.

66. Paul C. Higgins and Gary L. Albrecht, "Hellfire and Delinquency Revisted," *Social Forces*, 55 (June 1977): pp. 952-958.

67. John R. Hepburn, "Testing Alternative Models of Delinquency Causation," *The Journal of Criminal Law and Criminology*, 67, No. 4 (December, 1976): pp. 450-460.

68. Michael D. Wiatrowski, David B. Griswold and Mary K. Roberts, "Social Control Theory and Delinquency," *American Sociological Review*, 46, No. 5 (October, 1981): pp. 525-541.

69. Arnold Meadow, Stephen I. Abramowitz, Arnold De La Cruz, and German Otalura

> position, capacity, or inclination to become agents in their
> own behalf, I call drifters, and it is in this category that I place
> the juvenile delinquent.[70]

Matza suggests that some youths exist in a state of drift, a kind of
limbo between a conventional lifestyle and a criminal lifestyle. Drift
into delinquency is unpredictable, involving neither compulsion
nor complete freedom of choice. Drifters avoid moral blame by
using "techniques of neutralization" to justify their behavior. These
include denying responsibility, i.e., claiming the act was accidental
or caused by factors beyond their control.

Matza's drift theory is crucial to an understanding of social
control theories which, among others, are exemplified by the theoretical approach of the Socialist countries. Thus, one of the foremost
Soviet pedagogues, I.A. Pechernikova, posited

> We cannot risk our children's future by allowing their
> upbringing to be determined by *spontaneous drift* [emphasis
> supplied]. The school and the parents must hold the reigns of
> upbringing in their own hands and take all necessary mea-
> sures to insure that children obey their elders.[71]

The point bears stressing since it marks the convergence of an effort
to explain the causation of crime with an almost immediate reference to means for its prevention, although it should be made clear
that Matza's theory does not necessarily have any ideological
implications.

We have now completed our survey of contemporary criminological theories. The explanations of crime can be grouped in three
categories: (1) explanations of crime couched in terms of the strain
caused by the disequilibrium between the basic elements of the
social structure, (2) causal statements focusing on the clash of
opposing value systems, and (3) paradigms which measure an individual's bond to society and its conventional norms and behaviors.
It probably would not go too far to say that all of these schools are
basically related to, or derived from, anomie theory in the sense that
all could be deemed to attribute, or at least relate, crime and delin-

Bay, "Self-Concept, Negative Family Affects, and Delinquency," *Criminology*, 19, No. 3
(November 1981): pp. 434-448.

70. David Matza, *Delinquency and Drift*, (New York: John Wiley and Sons, 1964) p. 29.

71. I.A. Perchernikova, *The Development of Obedience and Diligence Among Children
in the Family*, (Moscow: Prosveshchenie, 1965) p. 7.

quency to the absence of effective social controls which would offer
and impose conventional norms to such an extent that the development of an alternative set of standards would be precluded. The line
of reasoning is as follows: Societies proceed from a state of social
solidarity. As they move on the development ladder, traditional
norms frequently no longer retain relevance and new ones take root
in their place. Different societal goals emerge, but not all members
of the society have like access to these goals. Strain ensues. No longer
able to achieve "acceptable" goals, those who share the same frustra-
tions develop a new set of standards, albeit different from that of the
dominant culture, to which they are capable of adhering and, in fact,
which provides the sought-after status.[72] These groupings give to
their members a like stock of ideas, values and behavioral forms,
many of them standing in opposition to the conventional system. As
these deviant cultures grow, they erode, little by little, the extant
social control organs, i.e. family, religion, schools, by offering a
substitute, indeed competing, value system. As the strength of the
traditional institutions diminishes, the control that they exercise
over individuals becomes less and less and there is an increasing
likelihood that the individual's bond to society is weakened. At its
extreme, a complete state of norm chaos, or anomie, would exist.

What we have described, then, is a progression whereby societal
goals are unattainable by a segment of the population, alternative
values emerge, conventional systems are eroded, and individuals
begin to lose personal and social controls, thereby being drawn into
deviant life styles. Thus, all of the theoretical schools do, in fact,
relate to anomie.

If this interpretation is useful for exploring increasing crime
rates, then it must be possible to describe a society with an optimum
of norm cohesion and conformity resulting in low crime rates. It is
proposed that this opposite of anomie be called synnomie. This
term, like its opposite anomie, is derived from the Greek: *syn,*
meaning congruence or togetherness, and *nomos,* meaning norms
and values. This concept is meant to describe the state of sharing of
norms or customs and, beyond that, a system of intact social controls
capable of assuring such a sharing. It is posited that in order to
achieve a state of culture worthy to be designated synnomic, there
must be a sharing of values with an optimum of tolerance for
diverging values, whether emanating from adjoining cultures, or

72. On this topic, see the discussions of Albert K. Cohen and Richard Cloward and Lloyd
Ohlin, *op. cit., supra,* at notes 27, 28, 29, 30, 31, 33, 34.

whether derived from a convergence of subcultures within that culture, or whether attributed to individual beliefs. Achievement of a state of synnomie would require an accommodation by all parts toward all parts, i.e., tolerance levels of the culture may have to be raised and stretched, norm-conflicting values of subcultures, or of individuals, may have to be altered, accommodated, or even, occasionally, abandoned. In short, a common denominator must be found. Synnomie, then, is a convergence of norms to the point of harmonious accommodation.

It may be that the historical segmenting of theoretical thinking into unitary concepts has resulted in a profusion of partial explanations reminiscent of Aesop's fable of the blind men and the elephant. Each of the theories is correct as far as it goes, but none goes far enough to encompass the others. Each has something valuable to contribute to our understanding of crime causation, but alas, no single one has been able to see it steady and see it whole. It is suggested that the phenomenon of crime can be understood better within the juxtaposition of anomie and synnomie as the extreme ends on a continuum within which the other theoretical schools can be found.

Appendix I

Crime/Socio-Economic Variables

	Correlation Coefficient
Population growth/annum (%)	−.27
Crude birth rate/1000	−.37
Crude death rate/1000	−.25
Male life expectancy	.34
Female life expectancy	.35
Proportion urban 1975 (%)	.16
Proportion urban 1960 (%)	.17
Total average persons/household	−.36
Urban average persons/household	−.40
Rural average persons/household	−.44
Population under 20 years old (%)	−.15
Total population of major cities	−.13
World rank of major city	.25
Total population as of 1975	−.22
Population economically active (%)	.21
Population in agriculture 1960 (%)	−.24
Population in agriculture 1975 (%)	−.26
Population unemployed in 1975 (%)	−.16
Growth gross domestic product 1970-76 %/annum	−.27
National income/person/annum 1976	.27
No. of radio receivers/1000	.38
No. of TV receivers/1000	.48

No. of telephones/1000   .40
Newspaper circulation world ranking   −.24
Population/physician 1976   −.15
Illiterate males under 15 yrs. 1966 (%)   −.11
Illiterate females under 15 yrs. 1966 (%)   −.16
Population with no schooling 15-24 yrs.
  1966 (%)   −.37
Population with no schooling over 25 yrs.
  1966 (%)   −.31
Population with no schooling 15-24 yrs.
  1971 (%)   −.18
Population with post-secondary education (%)   .25
Expenditures on education/pupil 1965   .40
Expenditures on education/pupil 1974   .42
Urban growth = V14 (proportion urban 1975)
  minus V15 (Proportion urban 1960)   .40
Population with no schooling = V64 (% of
  population with no schooling 1966/15-24
  minus V67 (% of population with
  no schooling 1971/15-24)   −.48

                                                    Correlation
                                                    Coefficient
                                                    Below 0.10

Population density per square km
Divorce rate
% of alien population
% of city population in slums
Gross domestic product
Newspaper circulation/1000
Population/hospital bed 1976
% of illiterate males under 15 yrs. 1971
% of illiterate females under 15 yrs. 1971
% of population with no schooling over 25 yrs.
  1971
% of expenditures on education as % of total
  public budget
(Education expenditure change) = V77
  (expenditures on education/pupil 1974)
  minus V75 (expenditures on education/
  pupil 1966)

Appendix II

*Socio-Economic Variables by
Regions and Countries*

MEAN FOR INDIVIDUAL VARIABLES BY UN AREA

UN Area	Arrest Rate per 100,000 V3*	Pop. Growth/ annum % V6	Crude Birth Rate/ 1000 V8	Crude Death Rate/ 1000 V9	Male Life Exp. V10	Female Life Exp. V11	Pop. Density/ sq. Km. V12	Percent Urban 75 V14	Percent Urban 60 V15
1. North Africa Middle East	790.8	3.1	42.4	13.4	54.5	57.6	69.1	48.2	36
2. Africa South of Sahara		2.6	45.8	19.9	43.4	46.6	50.4	17.1	12.9
3. Asia and the Pacific	1069.3	2.6	35.1	11.3	57.4	60.5	179.3	39.9	31.9
4. Eastern Europe	324.56	0.533	15.7	10.3	68.5	73.7	115.0	62.6	52.3
5. Latin America and Caribbean	892.3	2.3	33.9	8.9	61.4	65.5	95.6	47.6	40.1
6. West. Europe North America Australia New Zealand Israel	1848.0	0.753	16.6	9.8	69.4	75.3	94.1	69.1	60.7

*Comment on Column V3 (Arrest Rates per 100,000:
(1) while the regional aggregate figures of the world crime survey (A/32/199, p. 26) are given for the period 1970-1975, for purposes of selecting ten low crime rate countries, only the figures for the latest year submitted were used. In addition to the figures reported to the United Nations, other available data were consulted for purposes of identifying the ten low crime rate countries, the aggregate of Column V3 includes such additional information. (See footnotes 8-10 of the Introduction). An apparent discrepancy is notable in the case of Bulgaria whose arrest rate per 100,000 appears to be higher than the regional aggregate (mean). This is explainable by the fact that among the few countries from which statistics were available, one country had such low rates that the mean for the region tipped below the rates of the other countries. It is also to be noted that, in case of doubt, selections of countries ultimately depended on a consensus of international and national experts. (2) Arrest rates in the world crime survey were calculated by the respondents on the basis of the following crimes: intentional homicide, assault, sex crimes, kidnapping, robbery, theft, fraud, illegal drug traffic, drug abuse, alcohol abuse.

COUNTRY STATISTICS

Low Crime Rate Countries									
1. Algeria	L 78.4	H 3.2	H 48.7	H 15.4	L 51.7	L 54.8	L 7	H 49.7	L 31.1
2. Saudi Arabia	0	L 2.9	H 49.5	H 20.2	L 44.2	L 46.5	L 4	L 20.7	L 12.2
3. Japan	L 326.4	L 1.3	L 19.2	L 6.6	H 70.6	H 76.2	H 294	H 75.1	H 62.5
4. Nepal	0	L 2.3	H 42.9	H 20.3	L 42.2	L 45.0	L 89	L 4.8	L 3.4
5. Bulgaria	H 367	H 0.7	H 16.2	L 9.1	H 69.8	H 74.0	L 79	L 57.7	L 37.7
6. German Democratic Republic	L 67.7	L 0.1	L 14.0	H 13.2	S 68.5	H 73.9	H 158	H 74.86	H 12.0
7. Costa Rica	L 114.7	H 2.8	H 33.4	L 5.9	H 66.5	H 69.9	L 39	L 39.7	L 33.8
8. Peru	L 408.7	H 2.9	H 41.0	H 11.9	L 53.9	L 57.5	L 12	H 58.4	H 47.0
9. Ireland	L 438.9	H 1.2	H 22.1	H 10.4	H 69.5	L 74.2	L 45	L 55.1	L 45.5
10. Switzerland	L 306.7	H 0.8	L 14.7	H 10.0	H 69.8	L 75.1	H 158	L 57.2	L 51.5
Seven of Ten Countries Above Area Mean	7L			7H					
Seven of Ten Countries Below Area Mean	7L								7L

H = Higher than area mean, L = Lower than area mean, S = Same as area mean, 0 = No data

MEAN FOR INDIVIDUAL VARIABLES BY UN AREA

	Total Avg. Person/ Household V16	Urban Avg. Persons/ Household V17	Rural Avg. Persons/ Household V18	Divorce Rate V20	% Pop. < 20 yrs. V21	% of Alien Pop. V24	Pop. of Major City V28	Rank of Major City V29	% of Pop. in Slums V31	Total Pop. '75 (1000) V33
1. North Africa Middle East	5.6	5.1	5.4	.81	52.4	18.5	2339.8	87.3	45.5	11363
2. Africa South of Sahara	4.7	4.3	4.7	.40	44.1	6.4	939.4	117.0	60.0	15456.6
3. Asia and the Pacific	5.2	5.2	5.1	7.2	47.7	2.9	4093.3	30.5	30.0	43140
4. Eastern Europe	3.0	3.0	3.9	1.8	32.0	6.7	1178.3	143.0	0	19872
5. Latin America and Caribbean	4.8	4.8	5.2	.30	51.5	4.1	3669.6	55.4	27.7	13645.4
6. West. Europe North America Australia New Zealand Israel	3.2	3.0	3.4	1.6	31.3	5.7	2597.0	81.9	0	18063

COUNTRY STATISTICS

Low Crime Rate Countries																			
1. Algeria	H	5.9	H	5.6	H	6.1	L	0.5	0		0		L	1504	H	97	0	H	16792
2. Saudi Arabia	0		L	3.5	0		0		0		0		0		0		0	L	8966
3. Japan	L	3.7	H	5.4	L	4.1	L	1.1	L	31	L	.57	H	11282	L	2	0	H	111570
4. Nepal	0		0		0		0		0		L	1.2	L	123	L	0	L	22	H	125727
5. Bulgaria	L	2.9	0		0		L	1.5	0		0		L	966	H	178	0	L	8741
6. German Democratic Republic	L	2.6	0		0		H	2.6	0		0		L	1106	H	150	0	L	17034
7. Costa Rica	H	5.8	H	5.4	H	6.0	L	0.2	H	53	L	1.9	0		0		0	L	1994
8. Peru	H	4.9	S	4.8	L	4.9	L	0.1	H	54	L	0.50	L	3303	L	32	H	40	H	15326
9. Ireland	H	3.9	H	4.0	H	3.9	0		0		L	4.6	0		0		0	L	3131
10. Switzerland	L	2.9	L	2.7	L	3.3	L	1.5	0		H	17.2	0		0		0	L	6535
Seven of Ten Countries Above Area Mean																			
Seven of Ten Countries Below Area Mean																			

H = Higher than area mean, L = Lower than area mean, S = Same as area mean, 0 = No data

MEAN FOR INDIVIDUAL VARIABLES BY UN AREA

	% Pop. Econom. Active V35	% Pop. in Agr. '60 V36	% Pop. in Agr. '75 V37	% Pop. Unempl. '75 V38	Gross Dom. Prd $m V40	Growth Gross Dom. Prd 1970-76 Annum/% V42	National inc./ Person '76 V44	No. of Radio Rec./ 1000 V46	No. of TV Rec./ 1000 V48	No. of Phones 1000 V50
1. North Africa Middle East	29.9	54.2	44.2	6.1	10184.4	7.6	1997.1	220	60.6	49.3
2. Africa South of Sahara	41.7	76.8	72.7	0	8454.4	4.2	426.3	90.3	3.0	20.4
3. Asia and the Pacific	32.8	61.4	53.8	3.4	71472.4	5.7	1104.9	162.1	73.0	76.7
4. Eastern Europe	50.0	41.0	25.7	0	61666.7	7.3	2866.7	306.7	227.7	113.7
5. Latin America and Caribbean	31.6	46.2	38.2	9.5	16245.4	5.0	1088.0	267.5	63.0	62.1
6. West. Europe North America Australia New Zealand Israel	41.3	22.9	13.6	4.4	103578.7	3.4	5355.0	436.5	280.5	398.7

COUNTRY STATISTICS

Low Crime Rate Countries										
1. Algeria	L 23	H 67	L 51	0	H 15600	0	L 840	L 173	L 30	L 15
2. Saudi Arabia	L 26	H 71	L 54	0	H 49300	H 12.3	H 4990	L 28	L 14	L 17
3. Japan	L 23	L 44	L 36	L 1.9	H 555157	L 5.5	H 4465	H 530	H 239	H 427
4. Nepal	H 46	H 94	H 89	0	L 1600	L 2.3	L 120	L 12	L 0	L 1
5. Bulgaria	H 53	H 57	H 34	0	L 20000	H 7.8	L 2100	H 314	L 176	L 97
6. German Democratic Republic	L 46	L 18	L 10	0	H 70000	L 5.1	H 4000	H 367	H 309	H 164
7. Costa Rica	L 28	H 52	H 41	L 4.4	L 2345	H 6.3	L 1064	L 74	H 77	L 62
8. Peru	L 30	H 52	H 42	L 4.9	L 12000	H 5.5	L 700	L 129	L 37	L 18
9. Ireland	L 38	H 36	H 23	H 12.2	L 7975	L 3.1	L 2367	L 300	L 207	L 151
10. Switzerland	H 44	L 11	L 6	0	L 56284	L 0.3	H 8246	L 332	H 285	H 638
Seven of Ten Countries Above Area Mean	7H									7L
Seven of Ten Countries Below Area Mean	7L									7L

H = Higher than area mean, L = Lower than area mean, S = Same as area mean, 0 = No data

MEAN FOR INDIVIDUAL VARIABLES BY UN AREA

	Newspaper Circ./ 1000 V52	Newspaper Circ. World Rank V53	Pop./ Hosp. bed V54	Pop./ Physician V56	% Illit. Males <15 '66 V58	% Illit. Females <15 '66 V59	% Illit. Males <15 '71 V61	% Illit. Females <15 '71 V62	% Pop. no Sch. 15-24 '66 V64	% Pop. no Sch. 25+ '66 V65
1. North Africa Middle East	1127.9	95.6	772.8	3028.3	63.4	86.0	42.2	69.9	41.9	74.3
2. Africa South of Sahara	15.0	105.2	847.9	13501.6	73.2	75.7	44.4	40.2	28.1	45.3
3. Asia and the Pacific	144.5	64.7	1697.1	9677.6	43.8	57.0	33.4	53.4	48.4	53.3
4. Eastern Europe	305.3	18.3	112.3	530.3	3.7	10.2	1.5	2.8	0	8.6
5. Latin America and Caribbean	92.0	55.6	306.4	2209.5	22.8	28.2	21.0	27.6	24.6	34.1
6. West. Europe North America Australia New Zealand Israel	309.7	19.3	97.8	613.7	6.3	10.9	5.5	14.5	0	3.7

COUNTRY STATISTICS

Low Crime Rate Countries										
1. Algeria	L 17	H 99	L 387	H 4942	H 70.1	H 92.0	H 58.2	H 87.4	H 67.3	H 88.8
2. Saudi Arabia	L 11	H 106	H 840	L 2200	H 95.0	H 100.0	0	0	0	0
3. Japan	H 526	L 2	L 95	L 845	L 1.0	L 3.3	0	0	0	L 2.9
4. Nepal	L 8	H 113	H 6626	H 36450	H 88.3	H 98.5	H 77.6	H 97.4	H 96.5	H 99.0
5. Bulgaria	L 227	H 28	H 115	L 453	H 4.5	H 14.1	0	0	0	0
6. German Democratic Republic	H 452	L 3	L 93	L 523	0	0	H 1.6	L 2.4	0	0
7. Costa Rica	H 97	L 47	L 261	L 1524	L 15.3	L 16.0	L 11.4	L 11.8	L 10.4	L 20.6
8. Peru	H 95	L 49	H 463	L 1556	L 25.6	H 51.7	L 16.8	H 38.2	H 26.6	H 42.8
9. Ireland	L 236	H 25	L 94	H 831	0	0	0	0	0	0
10. Switzerland	H 391	L 9	L 87	L 524	0	0	0	0	0	L 0.2
Seven of Ten Countries Above Area Mean										
Seven of Ten Countries Below Area Mean				7L						

H = Higher than area mean, L = Lower than area mean, S = Same as area mean, 0 = No data

MEAN FOR INDIVIDUAL VARIABLES BY UN AREA

	% Pop. no Sch. 15-24 V67	% Pop. no Sch. 25+ V68	% Pop. w. post sec. Ed V70	% Exp. on Ed. of Public Budget V72	Exp. on Ed/ Pupil '65 V75	Exp. on Ed/ Pupil '74 V77	% Change in Urban Growth 1960-75 V80	Change in Ed. Expdr./ pupil 1966-74 V81	Change in % Pop. w. no Sch. (15-24) 1966-74 V82*
1. North Africa Middle East	40.6	70.2	1.8	16.2	107.2	204.5	12.8	92.36	
2. Africa South of Sahara	34.1	52.1	1.1	19.0	21.4	35.8	5.43	19.66	
3. Asia and the Pacific	40.6	44.0	3.0	13.1	51.4	199.3	6.91	55.5	
4. Eastern Europe	0	5.2	5.1	8.4	307.2	624.5	9.65	297.34	
5. Latin America and Caribbean	12.1	25.8	2.6	20.5	49.0	74.5	8.52	24.12	
6. West. Europe North America Australia New Zealand Israel	3.0	6.5	4.6	15.7	271.2	647.2	8.01	380.40	

*No analysis due to insufficient data from all regions.

COUNTRY STATISTICS

Low Crime Rate Countries								
1. Algeria	H 52.8	H 84.4	L 0.3	L 11.0	L 39.1	L 60.3	H 13.6	L 21.2
2. Saudi Arabia	0	0	0	L 11.7	0	0	L 8.5	0
3. Japan	L 0	L 0.9	H 5.5	H 21.4	H 113.9	H 647.9	H 12.6	H 534
4. Nepal	H 91.1	H 99.6	L 0.1	L 11.4	0	0	L 1.4	0
5. Bulgaria	0	0	L 1.3	H 8.6	L 78.0	L 244.2	H 20	L 166.2
6. German Democratic Republic	0	0	H 8.5	L 7.6	H 533.3	H 741.3	L 2.8	L 208
7. Costa Rica	L 4.3	L 16.1	H 5.8	H 31.3	H 51.7	L 68.9	L 5.9	L 17.2
8. Peru	H 14.1	H 35.0	H 4.5	H 21.7	L 44.0	L 63.0	H 11.4	L 19
9. Ireland	0	0	L 4.5	L 12.0	L 106.5	L 162.1	H 9.6	L 55.6
10. Switzerland	H 4.8	L 5.1	L 2.9	H 19.4	H 419.7	H 930.2	L 5.7	H 510.5
Seven of Ten Countries Above Area Mean								
Seven of Ten Countries Below Area Mean								

H = Higher than area mean, L = Lower than area mean, S = Same as area mean, 0 = No data

Bibliography

Abadjieva, Nevena. *Tradition and Modernity in Bulgarian Village Life.* Sofia: Sofia Press, 1980.

The Address. By Commissioner Patrick McLaughlin to Members of the Honourable Society of the Kings Inns. *Garda Review*, 10, No. 1 (6 Jan. 1982).

Ad Hoc Meeting of Experts on World Crime Trends and Crime Prevention Strategies, with experts representing all Continents and all United Nations Institutes for the Prevention of Crime and the Treatment of Offenders. Rutgers, the State University, School of Criminal Justice, Newark, New Jersey, 5-9 October 1981.

Adler, Freda. *The Incidence of Female Criminality in the Contemporary World.* New York: New York University Press, 1981.

Al-Athl, Abdullah Mohamed. "Saudi Arabia." *Justice and Troubled Children Around the World,* Vol. III. Edited by V. Lorne Stewart. New York: New York Univeristy Press, 1981.

Al-Shawi, Tawfug. See Saudi Arabia, Kingdom of, Ministry of Interior.

al-Thakeb, Fahed and Scott, J. "Islamic Law: an Examination of its Revitalism." In *British Journal of Criminology,* (January 1981).

Ancel, Marc. "Observations on the International Comparisons of Criminal Statistics." *International Journal of Criminal Policy,* 1, (1952).

Ancel, Marc and Marx, Yvonne, (eds). "Code Penal Bulgare," In *Les Codes Penaux Europeens,* Vol. 1, Paris (n.d.).

Angell, Robert Cooley, *Free Society and Moral Crisis.* Ann Arbor: University of Michigan Press, 1965. (Chapter Four: The Transmission of Values and Norms, pp. 61-84; Chapter Eleven: Incompatibility in the Moral Order, pp. 192-219)

Angelov, M. "Sur la criminalité an république populaire de Bulgarie et les perspectives de son deperissement." *Soc. Pravo,* 15, No. 1 (1966): 52.

Apaza Ramos, J.L. "La Reincidencia en el Codigo Penal Peruano." *Rev. Policia Tecn.,* 36 (1969-1970): 382.

Archer, Dane and Gartner, Rosemary. "Homicide in 110 Nations: the Development of the Comparative Crime Data File." *International Annals of Criminology,* 16, Nos. 1-2 (1977).

Atilio, Vincenzi. *Codigo Penal y Codigo de Policia.* San José: Imprenta Trejos Hermanos, 1965.

Baghle, Sid-Ahmed. *Aspects of Algerian Cultural Policy.* Studies and Documents on Cultural Policies, UNESCO, 1978.

Bailis, Lawrence Neil. *Bread of Justice: Grassroots Organizing the Welfare Rights Movement.* Lexington, Massachusetts: D.C. Heath & Co., 1974 (Chapter Nine: Accomplishments of the Welfare Rights Movement.)

Banks. *Political Handbook of the World.* New York: McGraw-Hill, 1979.

Bantawa, B.K. "On Juvenile Delinquency in Nepal." UNAFEI, *Resource Material Series,* No. 10, 1975.

Bassiouni, M. Cherif, (ed.). *The Islamic Criminal Justice System.* New York: Oceana Publications, Inc., 1982.

Bartholomew, Paul C. *The Irish Judiciary.* Notre Dame: University of Notre Dame Press, 1971.

Bayley, David. *Forces of Order: Police Behavior in Japan and the United States.* Berkeley: University of California Press, 1976.

Becker, Harold. *Police Systems of Europe.* Springfield, Illinois: Charles C. Thomas, 1973.

Bedford, Sybille. *The Faces of Justice.* New York: Simon and Schuster, 1961.

Berger, Peter L. *Invitation to Sociology: A Humanistic Perspective.* New York: Doubleday and Company, 1963.

Berger, R. "L'office de la jeunesse de Genéva Comme instrument de prévention." *Rev. Int. de Crim. et de Police Technique,* 26, No. 1 (1973): 71.

Bernal Comez, J. "La policia y los problemas que causan los menores inadaptados." In *Rev. Policia Tecn.*, 38, (1971).

Bey, Mohammed-Cherif, M. Salah. "La detention preventive dans la pratique judiciare." *Rev. Alger Des Sc. Juridiques, Econ. et Pol.*, XIV, No. 1 (1977): 15.

Bey, Mohammed-Cherif, M. Salah. *La Justice en Algerie.* 1969.

Bianchi, Herman; Simondi, Mario; and Taylor, Ian. *Deviance and Control in Europe: Papers from the European Group for the Study of Deviance and Social Control.* London: John Wiley and Sons, 1975.

Birzea, Cesar. "Recherche Pedagogique Dans Cinq Pays Socialistes Europeens." In *Une Enquête 1972.* Hambourg: Institut de l'unesco pour l'education, 1973.

Bizot, Judithe. *Educational Reform in Peru.* UNESCO, 1975.

Blanc, Emile, and Egger, Eugéne. *Educational Innovations in Switzerland: Traits and Trends,* UNESCO, 1978.

Bloembergen, H.R.; Hauber, A.R.; Jasperse, C.W.G.; Toornuliet, L.G.; and Willemse, H.M. "Criminality and Social Characteristics: a Report of Trial and Error." *Criminology: Between the Rule of Law and the Outlaws* (Volume in honour of Willem H. Nagel, Kluwer-Deventer, The Netherlands, 1976.)

Blüthner, H., and Dahn, U. "Actual Problems and Results in the Battle Against and Prevention of Criminality in the GDR." In Samarbetsradet, Nordiska, *First Seminar for Criminologists from Socialist and Scandinavian Countries.* Helsinki, Finland, 26-29 August 1974.

Bonilla, F. *Codigo de procedimientos penales con todas sus modificaciones (anotado).* Lima: Editorial Mercurio, 1968.

Brady, Conor. *Guardians of the Peace.* Dublin: Gill and Macmillan, Ltd., 1974.

Breathnach, Seamus. *The Irish Police from Early Times to the Present Day.* Dublin: Anvil Books, Ltd., 1974.

Bruckner, C. *Der Gewohnheitsverbrecher und die Verwahrung in der Schweiz gemäss Artikel 42 St. G.B..* Basel: Helbing und Lichtenhahn, 1971.

Buchholz, Erich; Hartmann, Richard; Lekschas, John; and Skiller, Gerhard. *Socialist Criminology.* Westmead: Saxon House, D.C. Heath, Ltd. 1974.

Buchholz, Erich. "The Role of Penal Law in Combatting Crime in the German Democratic Republic." *Int. Rev. Crim. Policy,* 35 (1979): 49.

Buchholz, Erich. "The Social Courts in the German Democratic Republic—Bodies of Criminal Justice." *Int'l J. Comp. and Appl. Crim. J.* 4, No. 1 (1980): 38.

Buchholz, Irmgard. "Problems of Juvenile Delinquency and Juvenile Justice in the G.D.D." *Int'l J. Comp. and Appl. Crim. J.*, 5, No. 1 (1981): 29.

Burckhardt, L.; Müller, E.; Peter H.; und Bang R. *Verstehen, Helfen. Wege zum Verständniss des schwierigen Jugendlichen.* Basel, 1965.

Cable of the People's Republic of Bulgaria to the Sixth United Nations Congress on the Prevention of Crime and the Treatment of Offenders. Caracas, Venezuela, 1981.

Campion, H. "International Statistics." *Journal of the Royal Statistical Society*, Series A, Part II, Vol. 112, 1949.

Capital Punishment. Report of the Secretary-General, E/1980/9.

Cavan, Ruth Shonle and Cavan, Jordan T. *Delinquency and Crime: Cross-Cultural Perspectives.* Philadelphia, Pennsylvania: J.B. Lippincott Company, 1968.

Cave, Floyd A. "State, Law and Government." *Social Control.* Edited by Joseph S. Roucek. Princeton, New Jersey: D. Van Nostrand, 1974.

Cawley, Mary. "Rural Industrialization and Social Change in Western Ireland." *Sociologica Ruralis*, 19, No. 1 S, (1979).

Ceppi, T. "Jugendkriminalität." In *Kriminalistik*, 22 (1968): 378.

Ceppi, T. "Ursachen der Jugendkriminalität und Möglichkeiten zu ihrer Verminderung." *Kriminalistik*, 23 (1969): 481.

Christian Science Monitor, 13 April 1981.

Churchill, Stacy. *The Peruvian Model of Innovation: The Reform of Basic Education.* UNESCO, 1976.

Clagett, Helen L. *The Administration of Justice in Latin America.* New York: Oceana Publications, 1952.

Clerc. "Les récentes transformations du Code Pénal Suisse." *Rev. de Sci. Crim. et de Droit pen. comp.* (1972) 301.

Clifford, William. *Crime Control in Japan.* Boston, Massachusetts: Lexington Books, 1976.

Clifford, William. "Criminal Justice Adaptations and Innovations in Japan." *Innovations in Criminal Justice in Asia and the Pacific.* Edited by William Clifford. Canberra: Australian Institute of Criminology, 1979.

Clinard, Marshall B. *Anomie and Deviant Behavior.* New York: The Free Press, 1964.

Clinard, Marshall B. *Cities with Little Crime: The Case of Switzerland.* London: Cambridge University Press, 1978.

Clinard, Marshall B. *Sociology of Deviant Behavior,* fourth edition. New York: Holt, Rinehart and Winston, Inc., 1963.

Cloward, Richard and Ohlin, Lloyd. *Delinquency and Opportunity.* New York. The Free Press, 1960.

"Code Algerien, de l'organisation penitentiare et de la reeducation." *Journal Officiel,* 22 February and 3 March 1972.

Codes of 18 June 1966, published in the *Journal Officielle de la Republique Algerienne,* Les 10 et 11 Juine 1966.

Codigo Penal, Codigo de Policia. San Jose: Imprenta Nacional, 1950.

Cohen, Albert K. *Delinquent Boys.* New York: The Free Press, 1955.

Cohen, Albert K. *Deviance and Control.* Englewood Cliffs, New Jersey: Prentice-Hall, 1966.

Committee on Human Rights. 31st Session, E/CN.4/1155/Add. 8, 21 May 1974.

Communication from the Ministry of Justice. Sofia, 3 March 1982.

Community Service Orders, laid by the Minister of Justice before each House of the Oireachtas, June 1981.

Comte, Auguste. *Positive Philosophy.* (translated by Harriet Martineau, 3 vols.), London: George Bell and Sons, 1896.

Conger, Rand D. "Social Control and Social Learning Models of Delinquent Behavior—a Synthesis." *Criminology: An Interdisciplinary Journal,* 14, No. 1 (May, 1976).

Conza, Anne-Marie and Siminet, Danielle. "La delinquance juvenile: Enquete faite sur 100 Dossiers de garcons ayant passe devant la Chambre Penale de L'Enfance a Geneva, 1965-1966." *Etudes Sociales,* Geneve (mimeo), 1971.

Cooley, C.H. *Social Organization.* New York: Scribner, 1909.

Cooper, H.H.A. "A Short History of Peruvian Criminal Procedure and Institutions." *Revista de Derecho y Ciencias Politicas,* Vol. 132.

Cooper, H.H.A. *Commentarios sobre la nuova legislacion penitenciario en el Peru.* Lima, 1972.

Cooper, H.H.A. "Crime, Criminals and Prisons in Peru." *International Journal of Offender Therapy and Comparative Criminology,* 15, No. 2 (1971): 135.

Cooper, H.H.A. "Law and Medicine in Peru." *Chitty's Law Journal,* 24, No. 1, 1976.

Cooper, H.H.A. "Medico-Legal Problems in Peru." *International*

Journal of Offender Therapy and Comparative Criminology, 19 (1975): 191.

Cooper, H.H.A. "New Look Judiciary." *Judicature,* 53, No. 8 (April, 1972): 334-337.

Cooper, H.H.A. "Peru's Island Prison of El Fronton." In *International Journal of Offender Therapy and Comparative Criminology,* 13 (1969): 183.

Cooper, H.H.A. "Prison Problems in the U.S.A. and Peru." *International Journal of Offender Therapy and Comparative Criminology,* 16, No. 1 (1972): 25.

Cooper, H.H.A. "The Administration of Justice in Peru." *Judicature,* 53, No. 8 (March 1973): 338-340.

"Costa Rica." *People,* 7, No. 2, London, 1980.

Cottrell, Jr., Leonard S.; Hunter, Albert; and Short, Jr., James F. *On Community, Family and Delinquency.* Chicago: University of Chicago Press, 1973. (Economic, Cultural and Social Factors in Family Breakdown, pp. 152-163).

"Crime Pays: Says Garda (police) Body Chief." *Irish Echo,* New York, 20 March, 1982.

Crime Prevention and Control, the Challenge of the Last Quarter of the Century, National Statement by Japan prepared for the Fifth United Nations Congress on the Prevention of Crime and the Treatment of Offenders, 1-12 September 1975.

Criminal Justice in Japan. Ministry of Justice, Japan, 1970.

Criminal Statistics: Standard Classification of Offenses, Report by the Secretariat, E/CN,5/377, 2 March 1959.

Dähn, Ulrich. "The General Tendencies of the Struggle Against Crime and the Socialist Penal Legislation in the G.D.R." *Law and Legislation in the German Democratic Republic,* 1, No. 2 (1979): 15.

Dähn, U. and Weber, H. "Probleme der differenzierten Anwendung des Socialistischen Strafrechts," *Staat und Recht,* 25, No. 8 (1976): 836.

Dando, Shigemitsu. "The Conscience of the Judge: His Role in the Administration of Criminal Justice." *Studies in Comparative Criminal Law.* Edited by Edward M. Wise and G.O.W. Mueller. Springfield, Illinois: Charles C. Thomas, publisher. (Publications of the Criminal Law Education and Research Center, Vol. 11), 1975.

Dando, Shigemitsu. *Japanese Criminal Procedure.* (B.J. George, transl.) South Hackensack, New Jersey: Fred B. Rothman & Co.

(Publications of the Comparative Criminal Law Project, Vol. 4), 1965.

Dando, Shigemitsu. "Japanese Criminal Procedure." *Essays in Criminal Science.* Edited by G.O.W. Mueller. South Hackensack, New Jersey: Fred B. Rothman & Co., London: Sweet and Maxwell, Ltd. (Publications of the Comparative Criminal Law Project, Vol. 1), 1965.

Das Bulgarische Strafgesetzbuch, Vol. 16, 1968, Berlin: Walter de Gruyter and Co., 1973.

Death Penalty. Amnesty International Report, London: Amnesty International Publications, 1979.

Decree Law No. 18978.

DeGrazia, Sebastian. *The Political Community: A Study of Anomie.* Chicago: The University of Chicago Press, 1948.

Delaney, V.T.H. *The Administration of Justice in Ireland.* (C. Lysaght, ed.), 4th rev. ed., 1975.

Delegation of the German Democratic Republic to the Fifth United Nations Congress on the Prevention of Crime and the Treatment of Offenders, *The Importance Offered by the Socialist Society for the Activities of the People's Police of the German Democratic Republic which are Aimed at Preventing and Combatting Crime.* Geneva, 1975.

"Democratic and Popular Algerian Republic." *Documents on Self-Mangement.* Ministry of Information, 1964.

Demographic Yearbook 1977, Department of International Economic and Social Affairs, Statistical Office, United Nations, New York, 1978.

Department of Justice, *Annual Report on Prisons,* Dublin, 1981.

Department of Justice, *Report on the Probation and Welfare Service with Statistics for the year 1980,* Dublin, 1981.

Der strafrechtliche Schutz des Kindes. Protokoll des 2. Internationalen Symposiums junger Rechtswissenschafter der A.I.D.P., 1980.

Devlin, Patrick. *The Enforcement of Morals.* London: Oxford University Press, 1977.

"Die durchgehende Sozialhilfe bei Straffälligen." *Bewährungshilfe,* 20, No. 2 (1973): 126.

Dinitz, Simon. *Preventing Juvenile Crime and Delinquency.* International Union of Local Authorities (Preconference Draft), n.d.

Dinitz, Simon; Kay, Barbara; and Reckless, Walter. "Group Gradients in Delinquency Potential and Achievement Scores of

Sixth Graders." *American Journal of Orthopsychiatry,* 28 (1958): 598-605.

Dinitz, Simon; Scarpitti, Frank; and Reckless, Walter. "Delinquency Vulnerability: A Cross Group and Longitudinal Analysis." *American Sociological Review.* 27 (August, 1962).

Directives Issued by the 10th Congress of the SED for Five-Year Plan for the GDR's National Economic Development 1981-1985.

Dubin, Robert. "Deviant Behavior and Social Structure." *American Sociological Review,* 24 (1959).

Duhteva, Penka. *Working Women.* Sofia: Sofia Press, 1980.

Durkheim, Emile. *Suicide.* Glencoe, Illinois: The Free Press, 1951 edition.

Durkheim, Emile. *The Division of Labor.* New York: The Free Press, 1964 edition.

Durkheim, Emile. *The Elementary Forms of Religious Life.* London: George Allen and Unwin Ltd., 1954 edition.

"East Germany's Crime Rate is Up: Government Orders More Publicity." *Special to the New York Times,* East Berlin, 5 May 1980.

Economic Report, Peru. London: Lloyds Bank, Ltd., March 1980.

Education in Asia and Oceania: a Challenge for the 1980's. Educational Studies and Documents, No. 38, UNESCO, 1980.

Education in Africa in the Light of the Lagos Conference (1976). Educational Studies and Documents, UNESCO, 1977.

El-Ghannom, Mohammed A. *Education in the Arab Region Viewed from the 1970 Marrakesh Conference.* Educational Studies and Documents, UNESCO, 1971.

Encyclopedia Britannica—Macropedia. Encyclopedia Britannica, Inc. Helen H. Benton, publisher, 1977.

Espino Perez, Julia D. *Codigo penal, concordancias.* Lima: Editorial Juridica, 4th ed., 1968.

Europa Yearbook, 1981—A World Survey. Europa Publications Ltd., 1981.

Fachbl. "Die Minderjährigen im Strafrecht." *Schweiz. Heim. u. Anstalts W.,* 42, No. 1 (1971): 20.

Facultad de Derecho y Ciencias Politicas. *Facultad de Derecho, Universidad Mayor de San Marcos.* Lima, 1968.

Fantini, Mario; Gittell, Marilyn; and Magat, Richard. *Community Control and the Urban School.* New York: Praeger Publishers, 1970.

Ferdinand, Theodore N. "The Offense Patterns and Family Structures of Urban, Village, and Rural Delinquents." *The Journal of Criminal Law, Criminology and Police Science*, 55, No. 1 (March, 1964).

First Interim Report of the Interdepartmental Committee on Mentally Ill and Maladjusted Persons: Assessment Services for the Courts in Respects of Juvenile Offenders. Dublin, 1974.

Freud, Sigmund. *The Ego and the Id*, translated by J. Riviere, Hogarth Press, 1922; idem. *A General Introduction to Psychoanalysis*, translated by J. Riviere, New York: Garden City Publishing Company, Inc., 1938.

Furness, Norman and Tilton, Timothy. *The Case for the Welfare State.* Bloomington: Indiana Unversity Press, 1977. (Chapter Two: Justifying the Social Welfare State.)

Garcia Delaunde, Domingo. *El Habeas Corpus Interpretado.* Lima: Industrial Grafica, 1971.

Garcia Roda, Domingo. "Proteccion de los Derechos Humanos en el proceso penal Peruano." *Rev. Int. de Droit Penal*, 49 (1978): 233.

George, B.J., Jr. (guest editor). *A Preparatory Draft for the Revised Penal Code of Japan 1961.* South Hackensack, New Jersey: Fred B. Rothman & Co., London: Sweet and Maxwell, Ltd. (American Series of Foreign Penal Codes, Vol. 8) 1964.

Germann, O.A. "Bestimmungen des Schwerzerischen Strafgesetzbuches aufgrund der Revision von 1971." *Schw. Z. Str.*, 91 (1975): 225.

Germann, O.A. *Schweizerisches Strafgesetzbuch.* Zurich: Schulthess, 1972.

Germann, O.A. "Zum bedingten Strafvollzug nach Schweizerischem Recht." *Etudes en l'honneur de Jean Graven.* Geneve: Libraire de l'Universite, 1969.

Glock, Charles Y. *Religion and Society in Tension.* Chicago, Illinois: Rand McNally Co., 1965.

Gottfredson, Michael R. and Gottfredson, Don M. *Decision-making in Criminal Justice.* Cambridge, Massachusetts: Ballinger Publishing Company, 1980.

Gove, Walter R; Hughes, Michael; and Galle, Omer R. "Overcrowding in the Home, an Empirical Investigation of its Pathological Consequences." *American Sociological Review*, 44, no. 1, (February, 1979).

Graven, Jean. "La repression de l'homicide en droit Suisse." *Rev. Sci. Crim. et de Droit Penal Compare*, 21, No. 2 (1966): 233.

Guether, Anthony L. *Criminal Behavior and Social Systems: Con-*

tributions of American Sociology. Chicago, Illinois: Rand McNally and Co., 1970. (Legal Institutions and Social Controls, pp. 476-486.)

Gurr, Ted. R. "Crime Trends in Modern Democracies since 1945." *International Annals of Criminology,* 16, nos. 1-2 (1977).

Gusti, G. quoted in Jiri Musil, *Urbanization in Socialist Countries.* White Plains, New York: M.E. Sharpe, Inc., 1977.

Hagama, Hiroshi, "Changes in Life Styles of Industrial Workers." *Japanese Industrialization and Its Social Consequences.* Edited by Hugh Patrick. Berkeley, California: University of California Press, 1976.

Hall, D. "Sociale Devianz und Drogenkonsum." *Schweiz. Arch. Neurol., Neurochir. Psychiat.* 120, no. 2 (1977): 217.

Hannan, Damian F. *Displacement and Development, Class, Kinship and Social Change in Irish Rural Communities.* Dublin: The Economic and Social Research Council, 1979.

Hannan, Damian F. "Ireland's New Social and Moral Dilemmas." *New Society,* (18 Nov. 1982): 291-293.

Harris, L. *Area Handbook for Nepal, Bhutan and Sikhim.* Washington, D.C.: Government Printing Office, 1973.

Harrland, Harry. "Trends and Control of Crime in the G.D.R." *Int. Rev. Crim. Policy,* 35 (1970): 49.

Harrland, Harri. "Zwanzig Jahre Kampf für die Zurückdrängung der Kriminalität in der DDR." *Neue Justiz, Zeitschrift für Recht und Rechtswissenschaft,* (Juliheft, 1960): 13.

Hauser, Robert. "Die Behandlung der Bagatellkriminalität." *Schweiz. Z. ges Str. wsch.* 30 (1980): 295.

Hauser, Robert. *Kurzlehrbuch des Schweizerischen Strafprozessrechts.* 1978.

Hauser, Robert. "Problems and Tendenzen im Strafprozess." *Schweiz Z. f. Str.,* 88 (1972): 113.

Hawkes, Roland K. "Norms, Deviance and Social Control: a Mathematical Elaboration of Concepts." *American Journal of Sociology,* 80, No. 4 (January, 1975).

Hellman, Daryl. *The Economics of Crime.* New York: St. Martin's Press, 1980.

Hepburn, John R. "Testing Alternative Models of Delinquency Causation." *The Journal of Criminal Law and Criminology,* 67, No. 4 (December, 1976).

Higgins, Paul C. and Albrecht, Gary L. "Hellfire and Delinquency Revisited." *Social Forces,* 55 (June, 1977).

High Level Conference on the Employment of Women, 16-17 April 1980, National Report, Organization for Economic Co-operation and Development, EF (8) 4/10.

Hindelang, Michael J. "Causes of Delinquency, a Partial Republication and Extension." *Social Forces,* 21, 1973.

Hirschi, Travis. *Causes of Delinquency.* Berkeley, California: University of California Press, 1969.

Hirst, D. "Saudi Arabia—A Sense of Fraternity." *The Guardian,* 10 July 1977.

Hogbin, H. Ian. *Law and Order in Polynesia.* Hamden, Conn: The Shoestring Press, 1961.

Hubatka, W. *"Probleme der Prostitution." Kriminalistik,* 20 (1966): 503.

Huber, Peter. "Die Stellung des Beschuldigten." In *Zücher Beiträge zur Rechtswissenschaft,* No. 433, 1974.

Hutchinson, Bertram. *Social Status and Intergenerational Scoial Mobility in Dublin.* Dublin: The Economic and Social Research Institute, Paper No. 48, 1969.

ILANUD (United Nations Lat$_{ay}$ American Institute for the Prevention of Crime and the Treatment of Offenders), *United Nations Training Course on Human Rights in the Administration of Criminal Justice.* San Jose: Imprenta Nacional, 1975.

Incorporation of Crime Prevention Policies in Educational and Vocational Training Programs. Report of the Secretary-General, E/A.C. 57/ - 1978.

Institute of Public Administration. *Administration Yearbook.* Dublin, 1974.

Internationales Symposium junger Rechtswissenschaftler der AIDP, 1980:51-55.

International Herald Tribune, 24 July 1981.

Jaffe, Lester D. "Delinquency Proneness and Family Anomie." *The Journal of Criminal Law, Criminology and Police Science,* 54, No. 2 (June, 1963).

Janowitz, Morris. *Social Control of the Welfare State.* New York: Elsevier, 1978.

Japan: Its Land, People and Culture. Compiled by the Japanese Commission for UNESCO, Tokyo: Printing Bureau, Ministry of Finance, 1958.

Japan, Ministry of Justice. *Criminal Justice in Japan,* 1970.

Jenny, Rolf. "Drogenkonsum und Drogenhandel im Blickpunkt des Kriminologen." *Zürcher Beitrage zur Rechtswissenschaft,* no. 425, 1973.

Jost, Andreas. "Die neuste Entwicklung des Polizeibegriffs im Schweizerischen Recht," *Abhundlungen zum Schweizerischen Recht,* vol. 438.

Jubier, Muhammad Ibn Ibrahim Ibn. "Definition of Crime According to Islamic Law and Islamic Legislative Sources." See Saudia Arabia, Kingdom of, Ministry of Justice.

Karakasher, Vesselin *Certain Problems of Crime and its Structure.* (Bulgarian), Sofia, 1977.

Katz, Fred E. *Autonomy and Organization, The Limits of Social Control.* New York: Random House, 1968.

Kephart, William M. *The Family, Society and the Individuals.* Boston: Houghton Mifflin and Co., 1966. (Family Breakdown: Causes and Effects, pp. 602-617.)

Kharas, P. *Profile of Women in Rural Development—Nepal.* Home Economics and Social Programmes Service, Human Resources Institution and Agragarian Reform Division, FAO, Rome, March 1978.

Kishartri, Ved V. "Criminal Justice System in Nepal." *Resource Material* Series, No. 2, UNAFEI, November 1971.

Klare, Hugh J. *Delinquency, Social Support and Control.* The London School of Economics and Political Science, G. Bell and Sons, Ltd., 1966.

Knauerhouse, R. "Saudi Arabia's Foreign and Domestic Policy." *Current History,* January 1981.

Knudten, Richard D. *Crime, Criminology and Contemporary Society.* Pacific Palisades, California: Goodyear Publishing Company, 1974. (Social Control and Social Change, pp. 385-428.)

Koch, Hans. *Cultural Policy in the German Democratic Republic.* UNESCO, 1975.

Krohn, Marvin and Wellford, Charles F. "A Static and Dynamic Analysis of Crime and the Primary Dimensions of Nations." *International Journal of Criminology and Penology,* 5 (1977).

Ladewig, D. "Entstehung und Auswirkung der Medikamentenabhängigkeit." *Med. Lab.* 22 (1969): 71.

Laggoune, Walid. "La Justice dans la Constitution Algerienne, 22 Novembre 1976." *Rev. Alger. des sc. juridiques, econ. et polit.* XVIII, No. 2 (1981): 73.

La Piere, Richard T. *A Theory of Social Control.* New York: McGraw Hill Company, 1954.

"Land, Man and Development in Algeria." Part II: *Population, Employment and Emigration, Field Staff Report.* North African Series, XVII, No. 2, 1973.

Lapassat, Etienne-Jean. *La Justice en Algerie, 1962-1968.* Paris: Armand Colin, 1969.

Laudendale, Pat. "Deviance and Moral Boundries." *American Sociological Review,* 41 (August, 1976).

"Law and Legislation in the German Democratic Republic." I, n. 2 (1979): 37.

"Law and Medicine in Peru." *Chitty's L.J.,* 24, No. 1 (1976).

Lehmann, Günter. *Zum Entwicklungsstand der marxistisch-leninistischen Theorie der Vorbeugung der Tat im Sozialismus.* Potsdam: Babelsberg Akademie für Staats—und Rechtswissenschaft der GDR, 1978.

Lekschas, John and Hennig, Walter. "On the Historic Conditionality and the Social Character of Crime in the Advanced Socialist Society of the G.D.R. *Law and Legislation in the German Democratic Republic,* 1, no. 2 (1979): 5.

"Les realisations et les projects de l'Institut Suisse de Police de Neuchâtel." *Rev. Int. de Crim. et de Police Techn.,* 24 (1970): 59.

Levene, Ricardo (h) and Zeffaroni, Eugene. *Los Codigos Penales Latino-americanos,* Vol. 3, 1978.

Ley de Defense Social, with an introduction by Victor M.L. Obando Segura, Director de Defensa Social, 1953.

Lippman, T. "Census Confirms Saudi Fears." *The Guardian,* 12 June 1977.

Litwak, Eugene. "Divorce Law as Social Control." *A Modern Introduction to the Family.* Edited by Norman W. Bell and Ezra F. Vogel. Illinois: Free Press, 1970.

Ljutow K. "Zur Effektivität der kurzfristigen Freiheitsstrafe und der Strafen ohne Freiheitsentzug im Kampf gegen die Rückfallkriminalität." *Staat und Recht,* 17, No. 5 (1968): 794.

Lloyds Bank Limited. *Economic Report, Algeria,* February 1980.

Loertscher, W. "Ideas on Crime Investigation." *International Crim. Police Review,* 21 (1966): 201.

Lofland, John. *Deviance and Identity.* Englewood Cliffs, New Jersey: Prentice Hall, 1969. (Disorienting Social Control Practices, pp. 253-260)

Lopez-Rey, Manuel. "The Correction of the Criminal Offender in Latin America." Edited by Robert J. Wicks and H.H.A. Cooper.

International Corrections. Lexington: D.C. Heath and Company, 1979.

Lourdjane, Ahmed. "La reforme penitentiaire en Algerie." *Rev. Alger. des sc. juridiques, econ. et pol,* XV, No. 1 (1978): 75.

Lumbey, F.E. *Means of Social Control.* New York: Appleton-Century-Crofts, 1924.

Madkour, Mohammad Salam. "Defining Crime Responsibility According to Islamic Legislation." See Saudi Arabia, Kingdom of, Ministry of Interior.

Maine, Henry Sumner. *Ancient Law.* London, 1861.

Malinoski, Bronislaw. *Crime and Custom in Savage Society.* Paterson, New Jersey: Littlefield, 1959.

Malla, Balram Singh. "How to Change Negative Public Attitudes toward Criminals." UNAFEI, *Resource Material Series,* vol. 1, 1970.

Mancev, N. *Offenses and Antisocial Manifestations* (Bulgarian), Sofia: BAN, 1967.

Martin, John M. and Fitzpatrick, Joseph P. *Delinquent Behavior: A Redefinition of the Problem.* New York: Random House, Inc., 1965. (Chapter Two: Theories of Delinquency Causation: Society's Defects; Chapter Three: Defects in the Operating Milieu.)

Martindale, Don. *Institutions, Organizations and Mass Society.* Boston, Massachusetts: Houghton Mifflin Company, 1966.

Martindale, Don. *The Nature and Types of Sociological Theory.* Boston, Massachusetts: Houghton Mifflin Company, 1960.

Maruo, Naomi. "The Levels and Welfare in Japan Re-Examined." *Japanese Economic Studies,* 8 (Fall, 1979).

Marx, Karl. *Das Kapital.* 1867.

Material submitted by the Delegation of the German Democratic Republic to the Fifth United Nations Congress on the Prevention of Crime and the Treatment of Offenders.

Matza, David. *Delinquency and Drift.* New York: John Wiley and Sons, 1964.

Maunier, Rene. *Independence, Convergence, and Borrowing in Institutions, Thought and Art.* Cambridge, Massachusetts: Harvard University Press, 1937.

May, E. *Human Problems of Industrial Civilization.* New York: Macmillan, 1933.

Mays, John Barron. *Crime and Its Treatment.* London: Longman

Group Ltd. 1970. (Chapter Five: The Socialization Process and Crime.)

McCabe, James and Padhye, N.R. *Planning the Location of Schools: The District of Kaski, Nepal.* International Institute for Educational Planning, UNESCO, 1975.

McHale, T. "A Prospect of Saudi Arabia." *International Affairs.* Oxford University Press, Autumn 1980.

Meadow, Arnold; Abramowitz, Stephen I.; DeLa Cruz, Arnold; and Otalura Bay, German. "Self-Concept, Negative Family Affects, and Delinquency." *Criminology,* 19, No. 3 (November, 1981).

"Medico Legal Problems in Peru." *Int. J. Off. Therapy and Comp. Crim. 19 (1975): 191.*

Memorandum 99-00-7 of the Ministry of Justice, People's Republic of Bulgaria, 1982.

Mendoza, Jose Rafael. "Les legislations de l'Amerique Latine relative a la delinquance juvenile: Systéme de Costa Rica." *Societe Internationale de Defense Sociale.* Actes du Cinquieme Congres International de Defense Sociale, Stockholm, 1958.

Merton, Robert K. *Social Theory and Social Structure.* New York: The Free Press of Glencoe, 1957.

Miller, Walter. "Lower Class Culture as a Generating Milieu of Gang Delinquency." *Journal of Social Issues,* 14, No. 3 (1958).

Milner, Alan. *African Penal Systems.* London: Routledge and Keegan, Paul, 1969.

"Moslem Justice—Islam's Revival Spreads Use of the Sharia Law, a Flexible Legal Set-up." *Wall Street Journal,* 11 May 1979.

Mostafa, Mahmoud J. *Principes de Droit Pénal des Pays Abrabes,* Paris, 1973.

Mourad, Farouk Abdul Rahman. *See* Saudi Arabia, Kingdom of, Ministry of Interior.

Mourad, Farouk Abdul Rahman. "Effect of the Implementation of Islamic Legislation on Crime Prevention in the Kingdom of Saudi Arabia—A Field Research." *See* Saudi Arabia, Kingdom of, Ministry of the Interior.

Moynahan, J.M. *Prison Officer Training.* An unpublished paper presented to the Annual Meeting of the Academy of Criminal Justice Sciences, Philadelphia, Pennsylvania, 11-14 March 1981.

Müeller, G.O.W. *Layman as Judges in Germany and Austria.* University of Chicago, 1954.

Mueller, G.O.W. "Preface" to Dando, Shigemitsu, *Japanese Criminal Procedure. See* Dando, Shigemitsu.

Mueller, G.O.W. "Resocialization of the Young Adult Offender in Switzerland." *Journal of Criminal Law, Criminology and Police Science,* 43 (1953): 578.

Mueller, G.O.W. and Besharov, D. "The Existence of International Criminal Law and Its Evolution to the Point of Its Enforcement Crisis." *A Treatise on International Criminal Law.* Edited by M. Cherif Bassiouni and Ved Nanda. Vol. 1. Springfield, Illinois: Charles C. Thomas Pub., 1973.

Mueller, G.O.W. (with Lenore R. Kupperstein and Michael Gage). *The Legal Norms of Delinquency: A Comparative Study.* New York University, Criminal Law Education and Research (CLEAR) Center Monograph Series, No. 1, 1969.

Müller, Edgar Jacques. *Die heutige Bedeutung der Schwurgerichte in der Schweiz.* 1957.

Müller, Martin. "Die Entwicklung der Bundespolizei und ihre heutige Organisation." *Zürcher Beiträge zur Rechtswissenschaft,* 1949.

Murop, R. *Area Handbook for Saudi Arabia, 1977.* Foreign Area Studies, American University.

Musil, Jiri. *Urbanization in Socialist Countries.* White Plains, New York: M.E. Sharpe, Inc., 1980.

Naegeli, Eduard. *Die Gesellschaft und die Kriminellen.* Zürich: Flamberg Verlag, 1972.

National Committee on Law Observance and Law Enforcement. *Report on the Causes of Crime.* Washington, D.C.: U.S. Government Printing Office, 1931.

National Institute of Culture. *Cultural Policy in Peru.* UNESCO, 1977.

National Paper for the United Nations Conference on Science and Technology for Development. Japan, August 1978.

National Union of Algerian Women. *Report of the Role of the Algerian Women in the Economic Development of Their Country.* Submitted by the Algerian Delegation to International Women's Year Regional Seminar for Africa, April 1975.

Nelson, Harold D., ed. *Algeria—A Country Study.* Washington, D.C.: American University, 1976.

Nenov, I. "Le Droit Penal Bulgare et l'humanisme socialiste." *Etudes en l'honneur de Jean Graven.* Geneve: Libraire de L'Universite, 117, 1969.

Nenov, I. "Le nouveau Code Pénal de la R.P. de Bulgarie." *Rev. Sci. Crim. et de Droit Pen. comparee*, 25, No. 1 (1970): 13.

Nenov, Liliana. "Le nouveau code Bulgare de la famille." *Union des Juristes de Bulgarie*, Droit Bulgare, No. 2-3, Sofia Presse, 1971.

"New Detective Squad to Take On Dublin Crime." *Irish Echo*, New York, 17 April, 1982.

Newmeyer, Martin H. *Juvenile Delinquency in Modern Society*. London: D. van Nostrand Company, Inc., 1949.

Noll, Peter. "Die Arbeitserziehung." *Schw. Z. f. Str.*, 89 (1973): 149.

Pan American Union, *Constitution of the Republic of Costa Rica*, 1949.

Pandy, Indra Rai, quoted in "Public Role in Crime Prevention, Police, Prosecution and Court." UNAFEI, *Resource Material Series*, vol. 13, 1972.

Panev, Baitcho; Stankoucher, Todor; Ketchkova, Alexandrina; and Miteva, Joulia. "Abus et trafic de drogues—Rapport de la Bulgarie." *Rev. Int. de Droit Penal*, 44, Nos. 2-3 (1974).

Parsons, Talcott. "Family and Church as 'Boundary' Structures." *Sociology of Religion*, Edited by Norman Birnbaum and Gertrude Lenzer. Englewood Cliffs, New Jersey: Prentice-Hall, Inc., 1969.

Parsons, Talcott. *The Social System*. Glencoe, Illinois: The Free Press, 1951.

Pechernikova, I.A. *The Development of Obedience and Diligence among Children in the Family*. Moscow: Prosveshchenie, 1965.

"Peripheral Capitalism and Rural-Urban Migration: a Study of Population Movements in Costa Rica." *Latin American Perspectives*, 7 (Spring/Summer, 1980).

Petras, James and Havens, A. Eugene. "Peru: Economic Crises and Class Confrontation." *Monthly Review—New York*, vol. 30, February 1979.

Petrova, Elka; Sheitanova, Tsonka; and Slavova, Radka. *Pre-School Education in Bulgaria*. Sofia: Sofia Press, 1979.

Pfenninger, Hans Felix. "Das schweizerische Strafrecht." Edited by Mezger-Schönke-Jescheck *Das ausländische Strafrecht der Gegenwart*, Vol. II. Berlin: Duncker and Humblot, 1957.

Phillipson, Michael. *Sociological Aspects of Crime and Delinquency*. London: Routledge and Kegan Paul, 1971. (Sociological Interpretations of Juvenile Delinquency, pp. 116-153).

Popov, Kistadine. *Cultural Policy in Bulgaria*. UNESCO, 1972.

Population and Population Policy. Ministry of Information and Communication. Research Institute on Statistics, People's Republic of Bulgaria, Sofia, 1974.

Pound, Roscoe. *An Introduction to the Philosophy of Law.* New Haven: Yale University Press, 1922.

Pravna misal, 13, 5, 51, 1969.

Prison Study Group, an Examination of the Irish Penal System, The. Dublin, 1973.

Profils demographiques. New York: Le Population Council, Juillet 1974.

"Protection of children in the Bulgarian Criminal Code." *The Criminal Legal Protection of Children.* Proceedings of the Second International Symposium of Young Jurists, Vol. I.

Provisional Report of the Sixth Congress A/CONF.87/14, 1980.

Public Reprimand, (Bulgarian). *Soc. Pravo,* 21, No. 1 (1972): 42.

Purgand, Winifried. "The Experience of the GDR in the Situation of Women in Technical and Vocational Education." *A Report to the United Nations Educational, Scientific and Cultural Organization,* International Congress on the Situation of Women in Technical and Vocational Education, Bonn, Federal Republic of Germany, 9-12 June 1980.

Quinney, Richard. *Crime and Justice in Society.* Boston: Little, Brown and Co., 1969.

Radeva, Radka. "Protection des droits de l'homme dans la procedure penale de la republique populaire de Bulgarie." *Rev. Int. de Droit Penal,* 49, Nol 3 (1978).

Rajcev, P. "Irresponsibility in Minors." (Bulgarian), *Pravna Misal,* 9, No. 4 (1965): 56.

Rana, Dhenu Shisjere. "Drug Abuse and Other Problems." UNAFEI, *Resource Material Series,* No. 9, 1975.

Rasheed, Mohammed Sa'ad, see Saudi Arabia, Kingdom of, Ministry of Interior.

Reckless, Walter and Dinitz, Simon. "Pioneering with Self Concept as a Vulnerability Factor in Delinquency." *Journal of Criminal Law, Criminology and Police Science,* 58 (1967): 515-23.

Reckless, Walter. *The Crime Problem.* Fifth edition. Englewood Cliffs, New Jersey: Prentice-Hall, 1973.

Reckless, Walter; Dinitz, Simon; and Murray, Ellen. "Self Concept as an Insulation against Delinquency." *American Sociological Review,* 21 (1956): 744-56.

Reckless, Walter; Dinitz, Simon; and Murray, Ellen. "The 'Good Boy' and High Delinquency Area." *Journal of Criminal Law, Criminology and Police Science,* 98 (1957): 18-25.

Reckless, Walter; Dinitz, Simon and Kay, Barbara. "The Self-Component in Potential Delinquency and Potential Non-delinquency." *American Sociological Review,* 22 (1957): 566-70.

Redfield, Robert. *Peasant, Society and Culture.* Chicago: University of Chicago Press, 1956.

Redfield, Robert. *Tepoztlan: A Mexican Village.* Chicago: University of Chicago Press, 1930.

Redfield, Robert. *The Folk Culture of Yucatan.* Chicago: University of Chicago Press, 1941.

Redfield, Robert. *The Little Community.* Chicago: University of Chicago Press, 1955.

Redfield, Robert. *The Primitive World and Its Transformations.* Ithaca, New York: Cornell University Press, 1953.

Rehberg, J. "Zum Verhältnis von Strafe und Massnahme im Schweizerischen Jugendstrafrecht." *Schw. Z. f. Str.,* 87 (1971).

Reiss, Albert J. *Delinquency as the Failure of Personal and Social Controls.* Paper read at the annual meeting of the American Sociological Society, Denver, 7-9 September 1950.

Rescher, Henry M. *Welfare: The Social Issue in Philosophical Perspective.* London: Henry M. Anuder and Co., Inc., 1972.

Roberts, Roland and Taylor, Lauri. "Problems in Comparative Analysis of Deviance." *Deviance and Social Control,* Edited by Paul Rock and M. McIntosh. London: Tavistock Publication, 1974.

Rose, L. *Nepal, Profile of a Himalayan Kingdom.* Boulder, Colorado: Westview Press, 1980.

Ross, E.A. *Social Control.* New York: Macmillan, 1922.

Ross, E.A. *Social Control: A Survey of the Foundations of Order.* Cleveland: The Press of Case Western Reserve University, 1969. (Part 2: The Means of Control; Part 3: The System of Control.)

Rottman, David R. *Crime in the Republic of Ireland: Statistical Trends and Their Interpretation.* Dublin: The Economic and Social Research Institue, 1980.

Rottman, David B. *Journal of Statistical Inquiry.* Society of Ireland, vol. 23, 1977-1978.

Rottman, David B; Hannan, Damian F.; Hardiman, Niamh; and

Wiley, Miriam M. *The Distribution of Income in the Republic of Ireland: A Study in Social Class and Family Cycle Inequalities.* Dublin: *The Economic and Social Research Council, 1982.*

Rovinski, Samuel. *Cultural Policy in Costa Rica.* Studies and Documents on Cultural Policies, UNESCO, 1977.

Russell, M. "The Irish Delinquent in England." *Studies 53,* Summer 1964.

Russell, M. "The Preliminary Hearing in the Criminal Process of Ireland." In J.A. Coutts (ed.), *The Accused—A Comparative Study.* London: Stevens and Sons, 1966.

Saito, Kinsaku. "Das Japanische Strafrecht." *Das ausländische Strafrecht der Gegenwart,* vol. 1. Edited by Mezger-Schönke-Jescheck. Buncker und Humblot, 1955.

Sandes, Robert L. *Criminal Law and Procedure in the Republic of Ireland,* 3rd ed., 1951.

Saudi Arabia, Kingdom of, The Ministry of Planning, Second Development Plan, 1975-1980.

Saudi Arabia, Kingdom of, Ministry of the Interior. "The Effect of Islamic Legislation on Crime Prevention in Saudi Arabia; Proceedings of the Symposium held in Ryadh, 10-21 Shawal 1396, A.H. (9-13 October 1976), translated, edited and printed in collaboration with the United Nations Social Defense Research Institute (UNSDRI), Rome, 1980.

Scarpitti, Frank R.; Dinitz, Simon and Reckless, Walter. "The 'Good Boy' in a High Delinquency Area: Four Years Later." *American Sociological Review,* 25 (1960): 555-558.

Schmid, N. "Der Wirtschaftsstraftäter." *Schweiz. Z. f. Str.,* 92 (1976): 52.

Schroeder, Friedrich Christian. *Das Strafrecht des realen Sozialismus.* Opladen: Westdeutscher Verlag, 1983.

Schultz, Hans. "Der bedinge Strafvollzug nach dem Bundesgesetz vom 18. März 1977." *Schw. Z. f. Str.,* 89 (1977): 53.

Schultz, Hans. "Dreissig Jahre Schweizerisches Strafgesetzbuch." *Schw. Z. Str.,* 88 (1972): 1.

Schultz, Hans. *Einführung in den Allgemeinen Teil das Strafrechts.* Bern: Stämpfli, 1977.

Schultz, Hans. "Schweizer Strafrecht." *Z. ges. Strwsch.,* 84 (1971): 1045.

Schwartz, Richard. "Social Factors in the Development of Legal Control: A Case Study of Two Israeli Settlements." *Yale Law Journal,* 63 (1964).

Second Development Plan 1975-1980, The Ministry of Planning, Kingdom of Saudi Arabia.

Sellin, Thorsten. *Culture Conflict and Crime.* Bulletin No. 41. New York: Social Science Research Council, 1938.

Shanley, Peter. "The Formal Cautioning of Juvenile Offenders." V. (n.s.) Part 2, *The Irish Jurist*, 262, 1970.

Sharma, B.P. "Cannabis and Its Users in Nepal." *British Journal of Psychiatry*, 227 (1975).

Shaw, Clifford R. and McKay, Henry D. *Juvenile Delinquency in Urban Areas.* Chicago: University of Chicago Press, 1942.

Shaw, Clifford R. and McKay, Henry D. *Social Factors in Juvenile Delinquency.* Vol. II. National Commission on Law Observance and Enforcement, Report on the Causes of Crime, Washington, D.C.: U.S. Govt. Printing Office, 1931.

Simpson, Jon; Dinitz, Simon; Kay, Barbara; and Reckless, Walter. "Delinquency Potential of Pre-Adolescents in a High Delinquency Area." *British Journal of Delinquency,*10:211-15.

Silberman, Charles E. *Criminal Violence, Criminal Justice.* New York: Random House, 1978. (Social Control, pp. 575-606).

Siochana, Garda. *Report on Crime 1979.* Dublin, 1980.

Sites, Paul. *Control: The Basis of Social Order.* London: Dunnellen Publishing Company, 1973.

Social and Labour Bulletin. International Labour Organization, Geneva, No. 1, January 1980.

Sokolov, D.K.; Asvall, J.E. and Zollner, H. *The Gabrova Health Services Model in the People's Republic of Bulgaria.* Regional Office for Europe. World Health Organization, Copenhagen, 1980.

"Special Rules for Investigation of Juvenile Offenses: The Bulgarian Code of Criminal Procedure." *The Criminal Legal Protection of Children,* Proceedings of the Second International Symposium of Young Jurists, Vol. I.

Spencer, Herbert. *First Principles of a New System of Philosophy.* New York: DeWitt Revolving Fund, 1958.

Spencer, Herbert. *Social Statistics.* New York: D. Appleton, 1904.

Spencer, Herbert. *The Study of Sociology.* New York: D. Appleton, 1929.

Statistical Report on the State of Crime, 1937-1946. E/CN.5/204, 23 February 1950.

Statistisches Jahrbuch 1978, der Deutschen Demokratischen Republik. Berlin: Staatsverlag der Deutchen Demokratischen Republik, 1980.

Statistisches Jahrbuch 1980, der Deutschen Demokratischen Repub-

lik. Statliche Zentralverwaltung fur Statistik, Staatsverlag der Deutschen Demokratischen Republik. Berlin, 1980.

Stefanov, Ivan and Naumov, Nicola. "Bulgaria." *Population Policy in Developed Countries*, 1974.

Stern, Peter J.; Richman, Judith and Hannon, Natalie. *The Family, Functions, Conflicts and Symbols*. Massachusetts: Wesley Publishing Company, 1977. (Chapter Twelve: The Future of the Family).

Stoinov, A. "Politique penale et regles de stimulation dans le droit penal de la republique populaire de Bulgarie." *Quaderni-Rassegna di S Studi*, Anno. 1—Maggio, 1978.

Stouffer, S.A., et al. *Studies in Social Psychology in World War II*, 2 vols. Princeton, New Jersey: Princeton University Press, 1949.

Strafprozessordnung, Textausgabe. Berlin: VEB Deutscher Zentralverlag, 1966.

Strafrecht—Allgemeiner Teil, Lehrbuch. Berlin: Staatsverlag der Deutschen Demokratischen Republic, 1976.

Stratenwerth, Günther. *Schweizerisches Strafrecht-Besonderer Teil*, 2 vols. Bern: Stämpfli, 1973.

Stratgesetzbuch, Textausgabe. Berlin: VEB Deutscher Zentralverlag, 6th ed. 1966.

Studia Kryminologiczne, Kryminalistyczne i Penitencjarne. No. 1, 1974.

Suggestions for Development of Criminal Statistics. Statistical Commission. ECOSOC, E/CN.3/102, 17 April 1950.

Sumner, William G. *Folkways*. Boston: Ginn, 1906.

Sutherland, Edwin H. and Cressey, Donald R. *Principles of Criminology*. Philadelphia, Pennsylvania: J.B. Lippincott Company, 1966.

Suzuki, Yoshio. "Corrections in Japan." *International Corrections*. Edited by Robert J. Wicks and H.H.A. Cooper. Lexington: D.C. Heath and Company, 1979.

Suzuki, Yoshio. *Criminal Law Reform in Japan*. UNAFEI, Resource Material Series, no. 13, 1977.

Takahashi, Nabuko. "Women's Employment in Japan in a Period of Rapid Technological Change." *International Labor Review*, 98 (December, 1968).

Tanizawa, Tadahiro. "Sentencing Standards in Japan." UNAFEI, *Resource Material Series*, no. 16, 1979.

Taylor, Ian; Walton, Paul; and Young, Jock. *The New Criminology*. New York: Harper and Row, 1973.

Tha, Abhay Kant. "Speedy Trail," UNAFEI, *Resource Material Series*, no. 11, 1976.

Thakur, Bahuan. "Role of Environment on Juvenile Delinquency." UNAFEI, *Resource Material Series*, no. 17, 1980.

Thapa, Sudarshan S. "Special Problems Related to Criminal Justice Process." UNAFEI, *Resource Material Series*, no. 12, 1976.

Thorp, Rosemary and Bertram, Geoffrey. *Peru: 1890-1977, Growth and Policy in an Open Economy.* London: MacMillan Press, 1978.

Tillie, A.A. and Schevkov, G.V. *Stravnitelnyj Metod v Jurisditscheskich Kisceplinach.* (Comparative Method in Juridical Disciplines). Moskva, 1973, Vyschaia Schkola.

Tinnin, David. "The Strange Ordeal of the Swiss." *Fortune*, 18 December 1978.

Tönnies, Ferdinand. *Gemeinschaft and Gesellschaft.* Leipzig, 1887.

Traikov, Zdravko. "Privation de liberte de courte duree et son execution." In *Quaderni-Rassegna di Studi*, Anno 1- Maggio, 1978.

"Training Senior Police Officers and Police Laboratory Personnel." *Int. Crim. Police Rev.*, 24 (1969): 229.

Tunley, Roul. *Kids, Crime and Chaos: A World Report on Juvenile Delinquency.* New York: Harper and Brothers, 1962.

UNAFEI. "Crime Trends and Crime Prevention Strategies in Asian Countries." *Int. Rev. Crim. Policy*, 24 (1979): 35.

UNAFEI Series. Volumes 1 through 10. Published by the United Nations Asia and Far East Institute for Social Defence, Fuchu, Tokyo, Japan.

United Nations. *Compendium of Social Statistics 1977.* Department of International Economic and Social Affairs, Statistical Office, United Nations, 1980.

United Nations. *Criminal Statistics: Standard Classification of Offenses.* Report by the Secretariat, E/CN.5/337, 2 March 1959.

United Nations. *Report of the Secretary-General on Capital Punishment.* E/1980/9, United Nations, 1980.

United Nations. *Report of the Secretary-General on Crime Prevention and Control.* World Crime Survey, A/32/199, United Nations, 1977.

United Nations. *Report on the Sixth United Nations Congress on the Prevention of Crime and the Treatment of Offenders.* A/CONF.87/14 and Add. 1.

United Nations. *Statistical Yearbook, 1978.* Department of International Economic and Social Affairs, Statistical Office, United Nations, 1979.

United Nations. *Statistical Yearbook, 1980.* Department of International Economic and Social Affairs, Statistical Office, United Nations, 1981.

United Nations. *Treatment of Offenders in Custody or in the Community with Special Reference to the Implementation of the Standard Minimum Rules for the Treatment of Prisoners Adopted by the United Nations.* Working paper prepared for the Secretariat, A.C.56/6, 1975.

United Nations. *Working Paper Prepared by the Secretariat on Capital Punishment.* A/CONF.87/9. United Nations, 1980.

Valkov, I. "Some Data on Trials Involving Juvenile Delinquents and the Penalties Imposed on Them. (Bulgarian). *Soc. Pravo,* 17, No. 3 (1968).

Veillard-Cybulska, H. *L'application des mesures psychosociales et educatives aux delinquants mineurs.* Lyons: Etabliss. Ed. Charix and Filanosa, S.A., 1971.

Veillard-Cybulska, H. "Modern Juvenile Courts in Switzerland." *Int. J. of Off. Ther. and Comp. Crim.* 17, no. 2 (1979): 189.

Veillard-Cybulska, H. "Switzerland." *Justice and Troubled Children Around the World,* vol. 1. Edited by V. Lorne Stewart. New York: New York University Press, 1980.

Viccica, Antoinette. *Political Recourse to Capital Punishment.* Ph.D. Dissertation, Rutgers, the State University of New Jersey, 1982.

Vincenzi, Atilio. *Codigo Penal y Codigo Policia.* San Jose: Imprenta Trejos Hermanos, 1965.

Vincenzi, Atilio. *Ley Organica del poder judicial.* San Jose: Libreria las Americas, 1957.

Walsh. "Expectation, Information and Human Migration: Specifying an Econometric Model of Irish Migration to Britain." *Journal of Regional Science,* 14, No. 1 (1974).

Weil, Thomas E.; Black, Jan Knippers; Blutstein, Howard I.; McMorris, David S.; Munson, Frederick P.; and Townsend, Charles. *Area Handbook for Peru.* Washington, D.C.: U.S. Government Printing Office, 1972.

West, D.J. (in collaboration with Farrington, D.P.). *Who Becomes Delinquent? Second Report of the Cambridge Study in Delinquent Behavior.* London: Heinemann Educational Books, Ltd., 1973. (Chapter Four: More About Home Backgrounds.)

Wiatrowski, Michael D.; Groswold, Daivd B.; and Roberts, Mary K.

"Social Control Theory and Delinquency." *American Sociological Review*, 46, no. 5 (October, 1981).

Wiesendanger, W. "Aufgaben und Probleme der strafrechtlichen Schutzaufsicht." *Bewahrungshilfe*, 13, No. 1 (1966): 50.

Williams, (ed.). *The International Bill of Human Rights*. Glen Ellen: Entwhirtle Books, 1981.

Wolfgang, Marvin E. "International Comparative Statistics: A Proposal." *Journal of Criminal Law, Criminology and Police Science*, 58 (1967).

Wolfgang, Marvin E. and Ferracuti, Franco. *The Subculture of Violence*. London: Tavistock, 1967.

Women of Japan: Conditions and Policies. Report of the National Plan of Action, (2), Prime Minister's Office, 1980.

Women in the G.D.R. *Facts and Figures*. Verlag Zeit im Bild, Dresden, 1975.

Women in the People's Republic of Bulgaria, Demographic and Social Survey. Committee for the Unification System for Social Information at the Ministers and the Committee of the Movement of Bulgarian Women. Sofia: Sofia Press, 1980.

"Women of the Whole World." *Journal of the WJDI*, No. 3 (1973).

Wood, Arthur Lewis. *Deviant Behavior and Control Strategies*. Lexington, Massachusetts: D.C. Heath and Co., 1974.

Working Paper prepared by the Secretariat on Captial Punishment. A/CONF.87/9. United Nations, 1980.

World Conference on Agrarian Reform and Rural Development. *Country Review Paper of Ireland*. Rome: 72 (July 1979): 11-20.

World Conference of the United Nations Decade for Women. Copenhagen, Denmark, July 1980. National Paper submitted by Ireland.

World in Figures. The Economist Newspaper Limited, England, 1978.

World Statistics in Brief. United Nations, New York, 1979.

Yearbook of Labour Statistics, 1980. International Labour Office, Geneva.

Zdravkov, P. "Special Provisions in the New Bulgarian Penal Code Relating to Juveniles (Bulgarian)." *Soc. Pravo*, 16, no. 3 (1967): 74.

Zelditch, Jr., Morris. "Family, Marriage and Kinship." *Handbook of Modern Sociology*. Edited by Robert E.L. Faris. Chicago: Rand McNally and Co., 1964.

Ziegenhagen, Edward R. *Victims, Crime and Social Control*. New

York: Praeger Publishers, 1977.
Ziembinski, Stanislaw. "Miezynarodowa statystyka kryminalna."
    (International Crime Statistics), *Studia Kryminologiczne, Kry-
    minalistyczne i Penitencjarne,* No. 1 (1974).

Index

199

72155